❊ THE VAST DESIGN

Patterns in W. B. Yeats's Aesthetic

THE VAST DESIGN

Patterns in W. B. Yeats's Aesthetic

EDWARD ENGELBERG

UNIVERSITY OF TORONTO PRESS

Reprinted 1965

I think that in early Byzantium . . . religious, aesthetic and practical life were one, that architect and artificers—though not, it may be, poets, for language had been the instrument of controversy and must have grown abstract—spoke to the multitude and the few alike. The painter, the mosaic worker, the worker in gold and silver, the illuminator of sacred books, were almost impersonal, almost perhaps without the consciousness of individual design, absorbed in their subject-matter and that the vision of a whole people. They could copy out of old Gospel books those pictures that seemed as sacred as the text, and yet weave all into a vast design, the work of many that seemed the work of one, that made building, picture, pattern, metal-work of rail and lamp, seem but a single image. . . .

A VISION

FOR ELAINE

and to the Memory of
my Parents

PREFACE

IT WAS while reading Goethe that I was first attracted to Yeats, though I had, of course, for years admired the work I knew. The spectacle of Goethe's long and productive life was awe-inspiring, possessing and possessed as it was by the spirit of two centuries. As I shall have further occasion to remark, when I began reading Yeats in earnest, I was at once struck by the many similarities between the man from Weimar and the man from Dublin (though Yeats was at times severely critical of Goethe). Yeats, too, lived a long, creative life, during which intellect and imagination matured and became firmer with age. Like Goethe, Yeats survived and transcended a *fin de siècle*; like Goethe he was a youthful gatherer of *Volkspoesie* who, in time, turned to classical Greece, a romantic who would repudiate the weakness and the "vapour" of romanticism as "unhealthy." Goethe's insistence that all poetry should be "occasional" and, however ethereal, be rooted in some kind of "reality" seemed to me to have come to some form of perfection in many of Yeats's poems in which his personal responses to moments that held deep significance for him were elevated to the height of the momentous and made into a kind of "history." Though Synge was no Schiller (we do not know what he might have become had he lived), Yeats's relationship to some of his fellow-poets was that of master, a role which he played, on the whole, with dignity, assurance, and fierce loyalty. Both Goethe and Yeats were destined to be attracted to a number of extraordinary women, and to love with "passion"; and Goethe's poem to Charlotte von Stein seemed almost a model for some of Yeats's poems to, or about, Maud Gonne. Even the aim of reviving a national renaissance by creating a National Theatre was shared by both poets, as was their equally genuine effort to transcend provincialism. Indeed, it was finally that transvaluation of nationalism into something pre-eminently European which made Yeats seem so like Goethe. Both poets were also to turn at times to the East: Goethe in writing his *West-östlicher Divan*; Yeats in turning first to the Japanese Noh drama and later to the *Upanishads*. Yet both remained in the end European poets, though the word poet describes neither man adequately. Goethe and Yeats were "men of letters," a phrase that has sadly become pejorative: they were committed not only to the making of good art but to the making of good artists. Each was intent on shaping wholeness, unity, and coherence for both work and life, and on sustaining that work and life by a capacious, if at times eccentric, "philosophy." Each wished to embrace a "world" and to wed poetry to truth, art to culture. Both were "personalities": and if the arrogance, the stubbornness, and the snobbery which often accompanied the self-conscious effort of cultivating the image of the "sage" is today more easily forgivable in Goethe than it seems to be in Yeats, I am fairly confident that this is merely a matter of time.

In writing this book I have had the encouragement and aid of both individuals and institutions; to some of them I should now like to express my gratitude.

In 1955 I was awarded a Fulbright Scholarship to Cambridge where, at St. Catharine's College, I had the good fortune to study with Mr. T. R. Henn, whose pioneering study of Yeats, *The Lonely Tower*, had much to do with enticing me to pursue Yeats seriously. For more than a year I gathered, as best as I could, the wisdom which Mr. Henn so generously gave. To help an American through a chilly English winter, he always provided a fire, hot tea, and his own warmth of interest. I am indebted to him in more ways than I can set down here, though that debt is not intended to place any responsibility on him for the shortcomings that this book might have.

At Cambridge I also made the acquaintance of Dr. F. A. C. Wilson, who on several occasions rewarded me with conversations about his forthcoming important books on Yeats, and who was also kind enough to read some of my work and to offer valuable suggestions.

At the same time I also received the aid and comfort of Professor Paul L. Wiley of the University of Wisconsin, who guided me with patience, kindness, and an inestimable store of knowledge.

My gratitude to my colleagues at the University of Michigan is very great: to Professor Arthur J. Carr, who read the manuscript, some of it in different drafts, and whose vast and detailed knowledge of my subject and its wide context was generously and sympathetically made available to me at all times. Professor Carr charted maps to treasures I would not have found myself. My gratitude to Professor Charles O'Donnell is equally great, for reading the entire manuscript, for making innumerable suggestions of value both on matters of style and organization and on content, and for living through the experience of writing this book as a friend, a stimulating talker, and a faithful listener. I wish also to express my indebtedness to Professor Mark Spilka (now at Brown University) who read and criticized, to my benefit, two chapters in early draft; to Professor Austin Warren whose conversations on Yeats and literature were always a source of profit; to Professor Bruce M. Johnson (now at the University of Rochester) who was always eager to talk Yeats; to Professor John Arthos and Professor Arthur M. Eastman for some useful information and encouragement; and to Professor Warner G. Rice who supported applications for several grants which helped to make this book possible.

Although my specific debts to a number of Yeats scholars are acknowledged in the notes and my more general debts are cited in the Selective Bibliography, I want to express here an over-all indebtedness to the many fine critics who have travelled the road before me: indeed, without some of whom there might not have been any road to travel. Yeats scholarship is now far-flung and international: if I have inadvertently omitted debts I express regrets in advance.

Many books, I think, are also enriched by more indirect influences, and in this particular instance I must give my thanks to three men who had nothing directly to do with shaping this book but who had considerable contributions to make toward the shaping of its author by setting for him the high examples of their own teaching and scholarship: Professor Merritt Y. Hughes, Professor Jerome H. Buckley, and Professor Heinrich Henel.

I wish to thank Dr. Harriet C. Jameson and her staff at the Rare Book Room of the University of Michigan for the many kindnesses over the years in making available to me the Yeats collection under her effective guardianship.

Miss Mary Richards and Mrs. Dorothy Foster must be thanked for expertly typing successive drafts. Mrs. Reona Wilcox and Mrs. Margaret L. Neal served as very capable assistants in preparing the manuscripts. Mrs. Neal and Mrs. Elizabeth Barlow have laboured indefatigably to compile the index.

I wish to express my gratitude to the Horace H. Rackham School of Graduate Studies at the University of Michigan for their grants which provided me with some of the necessary time to complete this book, and to the Publications Fund of the University of Toronto Press.

To Professor Millar MacLure, editor of the *University of Toronto Quarterly*, I express a debt for his initial encouragement.

I should like to thank the readers of the University of Toronto Press for many suggestions; and I am grateful to Miss Francess G. Halpenny, Editor of the Press, for her steady encouragement; her editorial guidance always improved the manuscript.

Last, but hardly least, I must thank my wife, to whom this book is dedicated, not merely for the thankless chore of reading manuscripts and proofs, but just for being there over the years and for always having faith.

E. E.

July 23, 1963
Ann Arbor, Michigan

CONTENTS

ILLUSTRATIONS

(following page 96)

INTRODUCTION

> The Celtic nature . . . [possesses] an organisation quick to feel impressions, and feeling them very strongly; a lively personality therefore, keenly sensitive to joy and to sorrow; . . . this temperament, just because it is so quickly and nearly conscious of all impressions, may no doubt be seen shy and wounded; it may be seen in wistful regret, it may be seen in passionate, penetrating melancholy; but its essence is to aspire ardently after life, light, and emotion, to be expansive, adventurous, and gay. Matthew Arnold, *On the Study of Celtic Literature*

Between ten and eleven, one November evening in 1923, the *Irish Times* telephoned Yeats in Dublin to tell him that he had just been awarded the Nobel Prize for literature. A few minutes later the Swedish ambassador confirmed the award and by twelve-thirty, no doubt exhausted but elated, Yeats and his wife were alone. The journalists, who had lost no time in calling for interviews, had left. Yeats searched for a bottle of wine, but the cellar yielded nothing: so, "as a celebration is necessary we cook sausages."[1] The incident points a moral in a vein that used to be called "romantic irony": Yeats and his wife, who that very year were dividing their home between Dublin and the reconstructed tower at Thoor Ballylee where Yeats was simulating some of his "imaginings" of the past, are unable to summon up a single bottle of wine and must resort for their celebrating to the unaristocratic sausage. It is an image of Yeats we reluctantly concede to the image we still tend to hold, influenced as we must be by every photograph or portrait of the poet, every line of self-portraiture in the poetry—and the prose. Regardless of what biographers have told us about Yeats's many-sidedness, the dominant

[1]*The Autobiography of William Butler Yeats*, p. 325.

associations hold a stubborn dominion: a man aloof, aristocratic, and romantic; bizarre, sometimes irresponsible, eclectic; and above all flamboyant.

These associations have produced a Yeatsian mystique that, despite Yeats's high rank among contemporary poets, has not come into being without exacting its price. While the poetry has gained steadily, the prose has never recovered from the assaults of an age impatient with and intolerant of all nineteenth-century manners and mannerisms. Yet that prose holds more than Yeats's metaphysical ponderings, those speculations on magic and occultism and psychic research which dismay so many admirers of the poetry: the prose holds also Yeats's aesthetic, his conceptions of what art is and how it affects us.

The aesthetic is not of course always an explicit systematized scheme, organized and articulated with the precision of the professional critic or philosopher. When F. R. Leavis chides Yeats in *New Bearings in English Poetry* (1932) for using such "dangerous words" as "reverie" and "trance," and for writing in seriousness that "All art is dream," we should be sympathetic with his impatience. Even when Yeats writes about art—though perhaps less so than Leavis suggests—he can infuriate and confound us with his "half-philosophical" and "half-mythological" language. Unlike Goethe, whom he resembled in some important respects, Yeats did not succumb entirely to the habit of the maxim, though he was capable, especially in later life, of the sharpest aphorisms. The early rhythms of his prose, learnt in part from Shelley and Pater, Arnold and Wilde, led him unavoidably into the embellished sentence, the hyperbolic metaphor, the allusive word, though again in later essays he adapts himself with amazing success to a Baconian and Swiftian style: brittle, pithy, contrapuntal. In 1932, when Leavis was so unhappy with Yeats's "dangerous words," Eliot was in the ascendant, and critics had begun to expect from poets, especially from their prose, the kind of precision and urbanity with which Eliot's criticism was being credited. Yeats was fuzzy; he was clearly out of fashion with the *avant-garde*. In *New Bearings* Leavis praised Yeats's life and his poetic achievements for the sacrificial heroism of his nevertheless useless poses (a view still prevalent today); but he found life and work wanting, filled with inevitable "waste" and "disillusion," and a "Victorian romanticism" which "adult minds could no longer take . . . seriously."[2]

The sculptor Brancusi once said that we shall be dead when we

[2]F. R. Leavis, *New Bearings in English Poetry* (rev. ed., London, 1952), pp. 39; 49.

cease to be children; and Leavis's cult of adulthood is perhaps a striking indication of such deadness. I do not mean to disparage Leavis's contributions, but his peculiar stress on what he considers "adult"—and therefore "non-adult"—seems to me symptomatic of a particularly dangerous form of criticism of which Yeats, for one, has sometimes been a victim. This form of criticism rallies under the banner of reasonableness, sophistication, and a stoic urbanity (though it often approves of unreasonable and unsophisticated artists); it demands a high seriousness which assumes that for a view of life to be adult it must be not only tragic but profoundly pessimistic, in that it accedes to things as they really are, to "reality." In Nietzsche's phrase from *The Use and Abuse of History* (his attack on the acutely self-conscious historical spirit of modernity), these critics engage in an "idolatry of the actual." Such a view naturally denies the very essence of metaphor since all metaphor heightens reality and has something of the flamboyant; and in denying metaphor it denies poetry itself. Worse still, in imposing tasks on the poet which he is unable and unwilling to perform *because* he is a poet, this criticism encourages the astonishing notion that a poet who wishes to be acceptably "adult" must surrender his little game and play the man at last. Yeats could not surrender to such urbanity—he would have called it "cosmopolitanism." He wore the poet's mask unabashedly and it never occurred to him to be guilty of it. Despite his frequent remarks about the high value of poet and poetry, we find extraordinarily little fuss in Yeats's writings about his "role"—far less, I think, than in the work of other modern poets. He accepted himself as a poet, and with that acceptance came what was natural to it: a language wrought by a rich imagination speaking of art in its own terms.

Granted, in many poems—particularly in the occasional poems that make up *Meditations in Time of Civil War*—Yeats questions the ultimate value of contemplation, the usefulness of the isolated Platonist in his lonely tower when all about him, as it were, "Reel shadows of the indignant desert birds." The man of action and the man of imagination shape, it is quite true, one of Yeats's chief antinomies: yet he discovered always that the "cold snows of a dream" had their creative energy manifest once given to a poem, a thing well made. And for Yeats, there is no feeling of embarrassment in being a contemplative—only a feeling of helplessness at times, when he felt impinging upon him events that were so close to him they forced their urgency deep into his active mind. Yet, when all was said and done, always the poet asserts himself, and the urge to participate "In something that all others understand or share" is laid bare as the heart's ambitious pride. In the end,

> ... The abstract joy,
> The half-read wisdom of daemonic images,
> Suffice the ageing man as once the growing boy.

If, like Baudelaire, Yeats sometimes thought of the poet as the albatross shot by a malicious, unforgiving public, and weighed down by its giant wings, he always remembered, too, that the albatross, though it might fall victim to a capricious mariner, was a bird of good omen.

In Leavis's view adulthood and modernity sometimes become uncomfortably synonymous, and modernity is measured by an accommodating "realism," or by the curious yardstick of a certain timely verbal relevance (whether in prose or in poetry)—at best relative and transitory criteria, at worst the most dangerously superficial indicators of "novelty." We need only look to the past to see that Spenser and Shakespeare suffered in their time, and long after, from such a view of their "childish" art—an art, that is, whose so-called "crudities" and "barbarisms" offended sophisticated town taste. So Yeats too has been called "childish" (significantly he admired in Shakespeare what he found kin to his spirit—the ghosts and the two tents aside each other at the end of *Richard III*). Admittedly his occultist mask is easily vulnerable, but the hostile have too often used it as a pretext for a more total rejection. To deny Yeats the place he deserves among *modern* poets by re-routing him into a magnificent transitional failure has been, I think, a serious error in gauging the nature of genuine modernity. Yeats's modernity—as we shall see—is deeply rooted and firmly rendered through his aesthetic, if only we allow him, at best, to appeal to us through what Coleridge called the "pure imagination." Beyond this initial concession, we shall often find a much more tough-minded and shrewd critic than we might have been led to expect.

If, therefore, we accept Leavis's demand for "adult" attitudes and urbane clarity, we are likely to encounter great difficulties in Yeats's prose, but one suspects that there are still other barriers to approaching Yeats's critical writings: the assumptions that his theories are unreliable and that his aesthetic is hopelessly embedded in his metaphysic which, if we come to know enough of it, will give us all the aesthetic we require. There is some justification in both assumptions: Yeats's theories of art may very well be unreliable as prescriptions for other poets—it is the cost of individuality; and Yeats seldom wrote pure aesthetics or pure criticism. Yet a glance at Yeats's development makes it clear that the metaphysic, the "System," took shape considerably later than the aesthetic, a fact in itself worth pondering. For all his early interest in the occult and magic, and the stories and essays dealing with those subjects, Yeats before his marriage in 1917 wrote chiefly—quantitatively speaking—about the problems of his art. This preoccupation with art was quite natural: these were the years of struggle, the years in which style was shaped and tested, the years of trial and error. By the time Yeats published his first full-length philosophic work, *Per Amica Silentia Lunae*, in 1918, he had explored thoroughly the central questions of his art and had formulated a whole, self-consistent theory. The metaphysical speculations that followed and culminated in *A Vision* could not, it is clear, have preceded the aesthetic. During the twenties, when Yeats read most of his philosophy, his prose shows a marked decline of interest in purely aesthetic problems; only in the late thirties, when he plays the role of a teacher to a younger poet, is his aesthetic thinking rekindled, though most of what he says now indeed smacks of the maxim—echoes of earlier ideas pronounced in the accent of the sage, free of the smoke of battle.

Of course, as we shall see, it is not easy to disentangle Yeats's aesthetic from his metaphysic—nor is it always desirable. Yeats said that he could not, as Goethe could not, keep philosophy out of his art; nor could he keep it out of his theorizing about art. As for Goethe, *Kunst* and *Philosophie* were two of Yeats's three fates: *Kultur* was the third. Together they made up Yeats's life: "interest in a form of literature, in a form of philosophy, and a belief in nationality."[3] This book chooses the "form of literature" as its chief concern.

II

Yeats himself stimulates a close scrutiny of his aesthetic since few poets have handed down so exhaustive a testament of their art. From start to finish he insisted on forging for himself an elaborate aesthetic, in itself an act of metaphysical engagement. Casting himself as one of two protagonists in "Ego Dominus Tuus," Yeats might argue that he seeks an "image, not a book," that a great style is not "found by sedentary toil/And by the imitation of great masters." But the emphasis is exaggerated for the sake of the argument. While he certainly did not imitate the great masters, he consciously cultivated the qualities he thought made them great: passion, wisdom, vastness, intensity,

[3] *If I Were Four-and-Twenty*, p. 1.

self-dramatization. And toil he did at his poetry, often to the point of physical collapse, though he warned against visible toil:

> "A line will take us hours maybe;
> Yet if it does not seem a moment's thought,
> Our stitching and unstitching has been naught."

Since "there is no fine thing/...but needs much labouring," such labour needs direction and aim—an aesthetic that will shape the art as much as, in turn, the art shapes the aesthetic. It was precisely through his aesthetic formulations, with their ever widening dimensions that embraced matters far outside the formal aspects of the artifact, that Yeats strove to attain the "European pose" which was the aim of his life.

As early as 1900 Yeats pleaded the necessity of fashioning a theory of art. First he maintained that criticism was a necessary condition of significant art: "certainly [the poet]...cannot know too much... about his own work...and almost certainly no great art...has arisen without a great criticism, for its herald or its interpreter and protector . . . ." From the beginning Yeats reacted against the notion of the *furor poeticus* which had been vulgarized by the Philistines. In the belief that art is purely affective, the journalist (Yeats's chief Philistine symbol) "is certain that no one, who had a philosophy of his art or a theory of how he should write, has ever made a work of art, that people have no imagination who do not write without forethought and afterthought...." But Yeats insisted that philosophy and theory were not merely desirable for the artist but necessary: he must work conceptually as well as perceptually: "All writers, all artists of any kind, in so far as they had any philosophical or critical power, perhaps just in so far as they have been deliberate artists at all, have had some philosophy, some criticism of their art; and it has often been this philosophy...that has evoked their most startling inspiration...."[4] We know that Yeats thought this true of himself; his philosophic speculations were merely "metaphors" for his poetry: the aesthetic itself is, after all, philosophic (as distinct from the "philosophy" of *A Vision*). While it would be too much to claim that Yeats achieved an ordered "system" of aesthetics, his formulations about the nature of art accumulated to surprising dimensions, and in the end we are rewarded with one of those typically Yeatsian gifts: a unity delicately balanced between opposites. In view of Yeats's concern with antinomies and his relentless search for Unity of Being, an aesthetic of

[4] "The Symbolism of Poetry," *Collected Works*, VI, 186–187.

balanced opposites should come as no surprise. Yet it is interesting how often critics of Yeats have readily conceded his pluralism, his dichotomized mind, only to proceed to examine one mask—to use the fashionable word—at the expense of others.

Certainly this has been to some degree the case with Yeats's conception of art, and there is considerable uncertainty about the nature of that aesthetic. No single work has concerned itself exclusively with the subject. Three books, however, emerge as central, though each renders quite a distinct account of the Yeatsian aesthetic: Donald A. Stauffer's *The Golden Nightingale*, Thomas Parkinson's *W. B. Yeats, Self-Critic*, and Frank Kermode's *Romantic Image* (see Bibliography).

Stauffer (1949) saw Yeats primarily as the poet of "lyrical stasis"; he belittled Yeats's dramatic work, underscored the quality of "immobile ecstasy," focused on the "marmorean stillness" of certain poems, and made of Yeats something of a pure lyric poet. Such a summary is undoubtedly unfair to all the details of Stauffer's book, many of which are incisive (he was the first, I think, to divine something of the "expansion"-"compression" dialectic in the aesthetic), but it approximates, I think, the thesis of Stauffer's study. Repeatedly Stauffer calls attention to the "demand for compression, for marmorean stillness, for lyrical stasis": Yeats's own yearning for the "emotion of multitude," for "overflowing turbulent energy," is scarcely attended. Two years later, Parkinson righted matters by balancing the lyric poet with the dramatist. Parkinson was the first—and remains the best—critic of Yeats's work with the Abbey Theatre; he set out to take it seriously and to demonstrate the profound influence the dramatic experience was to have on the later changes of style and conception. Of Kermode's study (1957) it is difficult to say anything comprehensive here, for Yeats is the vehicle, not the subject, of his book.[5] It is tempting

[5]Kermode's book is brilliant and provocative and has already stirred up a lively controversy on both sides of the Atlantic. My own point of view differs rather fundamentally from Kermode's and I shall spell out this difference in a later chapter. However, I may say at this point that my major quarrel with Professor Kermode's view of Yeats is that it is very partial and too easily associated with certain modern movements toward which Yeats was more sceptical than Kermode would allow. Further I think it is demonstrable that Yeats *anticipated* many of those views which some critics—Professor Kermode among them—would suggest he *learned*, whether from Pound or others. With one exception, the essays in *The Irish Dramatic Movement* (collected in *Plays and Controversies*, 1923), in *The Cutting of an Agate* (first published in 1912) and in *Ideas of Good and Evil* (first published in 1903) range in date from 1897 to 1911 and show anticipations of and significant deviations from later doctrines popularized by Pound, Hulme, Eliot, Wyndham Lewis and others under more organized banners. The image of Yeats as a Johnny-come-lately who was converted from the Celtic Twilight to the sophisticated

to suggest that Kermode saw Yeats somewhere between the lyric poet and the dramatist, for he speaks of the Image in Yeats as being full of both motion and stillness. Yet ultimately Kermode uses the aesthetic as an objectification of the Romantic conception of Image, and that is at one and the same time a narrower and broader view than would be yielded by a more exclusive focus on Yeats. It is narrower because it limits Yeats to the very special image of the Romantic Image; and it is broader because it aligns him to a whole tradition—a tradition which I am not convinced Yeats followed with anything like the enthusiasm, consistency, or even the knowledgeability Kermode suggests.

These three works nevertheless remain useful and have brought us, in some respects, closer to the truth. To them should be added the fine work of Hazard Adams and F. A. C. Wilson, both of whom have at times concerned themselves with Yeats's aesthetic and have in places reached conclusions close to my own, though to follow the paths that led to them has not been their method or aim.

Yeats's comments on art and artists, then, demand an ampler explanation than has so far been offered. They demand that explanation because, in matters of art, what repelled him mystifies us less than what attracted him, partly because his prejudices, which were strong, are reducible to a common denominator, while what he favoured seems often contradictory. He opposed, vigorously, naturalistic and realistic art; social literature spoiled by an overdose of pity (Owen), an overdose of protest (the young poets of the thirties), or an overdose of

---

complexities of a modern aesthetic is not supported by the evidence. Nor, of course, was the case reversed—Yeats as an influence on Pound and his compatriots—for until about 1910, or later, the *avant-garde* scarcely paid any attention to Yeats; and, for years to come, he would still be considered the elder statesman—respected but not always taken seriously. The disentangling of Yeats's aesthetic from later contemporary movements is not one of my aims, but it will be useful to keep in mind the dates I have given, 1897–1911, for they confirm and support one of the basic assumptions behind this study: that Yeats was an exceptionally original aesthetic philosopher. He diagnosed the ills of poetry in his time long before his younger contemporaries incorporated certain of his practices into a theory proclaimed more sensationally and under different auspices. That this was a conscious act I doubt, for I repeat that, whatever inconvenience it may sometimes cause, Yeats was in truth a solitary, whose writings on poetry were little known and little read until after his death in 1939. It is worth noting that, since this book was written, interest in Yeats's prose has obviously been revived if reprintings of it are any criterion. Within the last few years Macmillan has offered two volumes of Yeats's prose, the first such collections since the *Essays* of 1924 (long out of print): *Essays and Introductions* and *Explorations*. The esoteric writings have also been collected under the title *Mythologies*, and the *Autobiography* and *A Vision* are now both available in America in paperback editions.

discursive ideas (Shaw). But, unlike some of his great contemporaries and the movements to which they were at some time allied, Yeats's inclination toward the past was to accept more of it than any other modern poet writing in English. I do not mean that he was indiscriminate in his enthusiasm, and certainly he could strike as hard against the great as Eliot or Pound. But he embraced a more ample and a more variegated tradition than is customary among modern poets, much to the embarrassment of those who would wish to claim Yeats for their side.

Part of the explanation for Yeats's capacious and generous literary tastes lies in his background: we must not forget that he was already a poet for better than a decade before Victoria died, and that the English classics had not yet been re-evaluated, the tradition had not yet been re-defined. His father's tastes were by no means conventional but, by present standards, still catholic and—perhaps this was even a greater influence—still committed to *Weltliteratur*. But such an explanation will not go far enough, since Yeats emerges as an independent and mature poet who develops, in time, a taste perfectly suited to his temperament and his aesthetic ideals.

Yeats took delight in the ancient, primitive art of Egypt and Assyria and in the mathematical "calculations" of Phidian sculpture; he regarded Shakespeare with the same veneration as Goethe had and he was enchanted with the ceremony and ritual of that most un-Shakespearian of dramatic forms, the Japanese Noh. He could speak approvingly of Cervantes and Racine in a single sentence, envy the Chinese and Japanese painters their intricate subtlety of design and praise the striving motion of Michelangelo's massive figures. With guarded enthusiasm he would side with some of the French symbolists against common enemies and he admired that most mystical-occultist of writers, Count Villiers de l'Isle-Adam. But the servants who, according to the Count, were to do our living for us were to become the beggars and journeymen of Yeats's late poetry, the Irish peasantry whom, in his epitaph poem, "Under Ben Bulben," he instructs Irish poets to celebrate in their art. And so the ethereal Shelley was as dear as the earthy Villon, the vagabond; and the "lilt" of the ballad—as he told Stephen Spender—must always rescue poems from too much imagistic stasis. Though Homer and his "unchristened heart" were never far from Yeats's mind, neither was Dante and his architectural mastery, his orthodox procession of symbols which Blake, too, offered in such abundance. Goethe, Chaucer, Swift, Balzac (but not Stendhal or Flaubert)—one might add to the names endlessly and with the same sense of difference always curiously emerging: the high and the low, the aristocratic and the peasant song, the passionately withheld and the lustily given.

Either Yeats was confused or he was haphazard in bestowing his approval, or there is a more flattering answer. I reject the first two possibilities. Yeats was sometimes confusing but seldom confused. Nor were his tastes a mere will o' the wisp; in fact, except for exaggerating the value in the work of certain poets in his youth—the poems of Morris, for instance—he rarely changed his mind. Clearly an explanation of Yeats's apparently contradictory affirmations of a vast artistic tradition is necessary, and this book is an attempt to offer a coherent account of first why Yeats required an aesthetic of opposing qualities and second how Yeats developed the means which enabled him to balance these qualities in the art and artists he admired—the means of his aesthetic.

Since aesthetics is an abstract subject and Yeats no easy writer, it is wise to set forth the plan of this book in some detail. Although the "vast design" of my title is a phrase well suited to Yeats's aesthetic, in both its capaciousness and its intricacy, the argument of this study holds that the "vast design" is balanced by the conception of the "single image" (as the opening epigraph makes clear), the design itself becoming that image and the image transcending, finally, the design itself. Between the conception of the "vast design" and the triumphant emergence of the "single image" lies the subtle and intricate development of Yeats's aesthetic. I have, therefore, enclosed my study, at either end, with chapters bearing titles taken from the epigraph. Chapter I sets forth the "vast design" with its "First Principles"; chapter VI is an analysis of how the "single image" at last manages to attain selfhood, liberation from the design itself.

The four intervening chapters are organized according to four sets of opposing terms (the main titles are in each instance Yeats's own words), whose opposition, working always toward synthesis, charts the history of Yeats's emergence as a theoretician of his craft: Market Cart and Sky; Picture and Gesture; Emotion of Multitude and Still Intensity; and Passion and Reverie. Although I have made no attempt to write a chronological account of Yeats's thought, I have moved from simple to complex problems, attempting to demonstrate in the process how one solution led to another query, one synthesis to a new opposition, creating an ever growing and more subtly structured theory. It would be useful to keep in mind that my sets of "contraries"—to use Yeats's word—are not rigidly separable in time and that they recur, like motifs in music, in Yeats's writings. This structural inconvenience has at times forced me to slide back and forth chronologically for the sake of clarity and continuity of argument. Yeats's thought seldom developed in straight lines but, as his manner of thinking would have it, in circles—wider as these may become as he passes into a steadier maturity.

In the opening chapter, I have brought together four distinct but not discrete problems. I have asked first why Yeats, chiefly a lyric poet, should so often have concerned himself with more ample modes and genres. Part of the answer I find inherent in Yeats's endowments, his personality, and special issues attendant on his life and times; but a good part of this curious self-division grows out of certain historical reassessments of Greece and the Renaissance, which Yeats found most obviously in Pater, though the whole nineteenth century was deeply involved in the new awakening of interest in both periods. This, then, is the second issue: in Greek and Renaissance art and history—and in his own time—Yeats discovered a striving between vast conceptions of the imagination and a form that would contain them, what Pater had described in *Greek Studies* as a "struggle, a *Streben*... between the palpable and limited human form, and the floating essence it is to contain."[6] This *Streben* of the past Yeats found parallel in himself, and its historical confirmations were to strengthen and re-define his own solutions. Third, I find that Yeats's cyclical notions of history and art parallel and support his conception of art as a wedding of contraries: cycles had those very motions—up and down, in and out, contracting and expanding—that became the defining metaphors of Yeats's theory of art. Finally I consider Yeats's own comments on his first major works: one a long narrative-dramatic poem, the other a play. They presage the future and indicate the need for resolution. I suggest that this resolution is essentially European, a marriage of the three great elements in European literature: epic, drama, and lyric.

The second chapter begins where Yeats had to begin—with a young poet's search for a subject, what Arnold had rightly considered the first and principal business of the poet. Choosing a subject was for Yeats a special problem, since he became involved immediately in the Celtic Revival, which made demands upon him that would ultimately wreck his hopes for a common Irish literature. Nevertheless, the attraction to folklore and mythology prompted Yeats to search with equal enthusiasm for the ethereal and the earthy, the

[6]Walter Pater, *Greek Studies* (London, 1895), p. 28.

life of king and peasant, "sky" and "market cart." Out of this struggle with a subject-matter fitted to his talents and his nationalism—*his* conception of it—Yeats forged finally an aesthetic that would combine these "two ways of art" in drama.

As a result of his practical commitments to the Abbey Theatre and to drama, Yeats became involved in the most subtle aesthetic questions, and these are the subject of the third chapter. Yeats's crisis as a lyric poet was at no time more acute than during his sojourn in the theatre, for drama taught him both the necessity of action and the benefit of a simple language, an idiom that would shake him free from what he himself had diagnosed as a "strained lyricism." Yet he must take care not to move too far in the direction of realism. "Picture," the descriptive and spatial element of poetry, needed, to guard against its paralyzing effects, the temporal motion of "gesture," drama set against its antithesis of stasis. Again Yeats must reconcile both elements: neither alone would suffice.

By 1910 he was returning to the writing of lyric poetry, reassured from the experience of drama; but it yet remained for him to make proper use of what he had learned from the stage in the refinement of what was to be, after all, his chief medium: the lyric poem. Again drama came to reinforce and synthesize the previous alternatives, though this time the Japanese Noh, a drama quite unlike what he had experienced at the Abbey. Picture might now be regarded as "still intensity"; "gesture" as "emotion of multitude." Or, to use a second set of terms, which Yeats himself combined in one of his famous statements on art, "marmorean stillness" and "overflowing turbulent energy." A fruitful tension between these opposites would produce both the expanding energy learnt from the earlier drama and the silence of the Noh. Yet that silence was not to be regarded as an end in itself, but rather as an echo of the "multitudinous" which Yeats had demanded as early as 1903 (it was still the urge for epic vastness). For this reason I have subtitled my fourth chapter "The Echo of Silence," to stress that the Noh plays were not, as has sometimes been supposed, quite the radical shift of ground they would appear to be; that they did not constitute an abandonment of commitments to passion and action. In this chapter I have also undertaken to trace Yeats's developing theory of symbolism and the provenance of those speculations in the visual and plastic arts.

Passion and action were, in fact, strongly in Yeats's mind between 1910 and 1917, the period when he at last worked through to a proper theory of tragedy (and comedy), the subject of the fifth chapter. As with every set of opposites, here too there was to be a contrast—even a contest—between tumult and repose. Although tragedy required passion—and Yeats took pains to define his term—it needed also the repose of "reverie," the "check" which caught passion at the proper moment and enforced the "pause" necessary to permit the hero's contemplative nature space enough to ruminate. Tragedy, then, was "passionate reverie," and at the end of it was the comic gusto that closed the circle out of which the hero leapt, first through "ecstasy," finally through "gaiety" and "joy." The "tragic correlative," as I call it, was Yeats's final great aesthetic achievement: its embracing principles seemed somehow to complete the aesthetic. By 1917, and from that date on, Yeats is an artist who creates with a fully developed theory of his craft which undergoes little change. It is deepened and paralleled by his studies of philosophy and by the writing of *A Vision*: but the fundamentals have been firmly set down.

In my final chapter, the "single image" was, I felt, best approached in part through a consideration of "The Statues," difficult as that poem is and despite the many differing interpretations of it that have been offered. I admit readily that I use the poem—and not all of it—to illuminate the aesthetic and, conversely, the aesthetic to illuminate aspects of the poem. As in the opening chapter, I have here attempted to place "vast design" and "single image" into larger contexts, both metaphysical and historical. By a deliberately expansive use of the concept of design and single image, I have sought to imply the extensive meanings which Yeats's aesthetic brings to bear on the poet's total conception of his art in relation to himself and his time. Once again, I stress the Europeanness of Yeats's thought, implicit in his desperate efforts to reconcile—for the sake of Europe—what has so long been divided.

My use of Pater raises a legitimate scholarly question, as all "influence" questions do. It is generally assumed that Yeats was well read in Pater, and I have no evidence to doubt this; on the other hand, I am unable to prove with what thoroughness Yeats had absorbed *Greek Studies* and *Plato and Platonism*. But my argument does not rest on establishing this point. Yeats parallels Pater but he does not parrot him; and if "The Statues" gains in meaning through an examination of Pater's conceptions of Greek art, history, and philosophy I feel sufficiently justified in making use of them.

As he read history, especially the history of art, Yeats came to see that his own aesthetic was one traditionally achieved, if not so self-consciously sought, in the great periods of art: in Phidian sculpture, in the half-anonymity of Byzantine mosaics, in certain Renaissance paintings. In each instance the vast design of a whole culture-image, fully partaking of "reality," merged into the triumphant single image of art, motion and repose adroitly balanced in works that "moved or seemed to move."

Since it is widely recognized that Yeats's later poetry becomes increasingly passionate, life and the real world becoming fit subject-matter for his great "occasional" poems (the word is used as Goethe used it), it is not astonishing that in "The Statues" (1938), Yeats should cast his lot with "passion" and the "one image"; though this only after their opposites have been thoroughly accounted for, the design carefully wrought, order properly established.

If my pairings of opposites are set down in a simple double column between the two chief phrases that open and close the argument of this book, several obvious conclusions seem inevitable:

Vast Design

Market Cart	Sky
Gesture	Picture
Emotion of Multitude	Still Intensity
Passion	Reverie

Single Image

These contraries divide roughly into the active and the contemplative, the expanding and the contracting, the surge of the experiential world swept back, like a tide, by the containment of form; or, say, Becoming, the Heraclitean flux, checked by Plato's corrective philosophy of Being, or order, which, as Pater makes clear in *Plato and Platonism*, was expressly directed against Heraclitus. Each pairing suggests the rough and moving world of men and actions set against the quiet, intense, ascetic world of discipline and containment. To find an equipoise between them was Yeats's great task—a marriage between the reckless moment of life and the formal moment of art.

Certain areas about Yeats are, of course, at once eliminated by the nature of the subject I have chosen: Yeats's life and poetry remain outside my scope. About his life we already know a great deal; about his poetry we do not yet know enough, and I could not have the temerity to fill the gap in a book of this kind. I have not entirely neglected either life or poetry but used them only as background, and only when I felt they were essential to my argument. In spite of my analysis of several well-known poems as achievements of Yeats's aesthetic, I should make clear that I have not undertaken to test the validity of the aesthetic against the performance of the poetry, for reasons that become clearer in the first chapter. Nor do I pretend to approach my subject primarily from the viewpoint of literary history, to trace Yeats's thought to "influences," or to attach him, in specific ways, to particular poets or traditions. Such attempts would have curtailed my emphasis on Yeats himself; and there already exist several excellent studies on Yeats's alliances with such poets as Blake and Shelley. But again I do not ignore the background against which Yeats's thought developed, and the names of Schiller, Pater, Arnold, Symons—to cite a few examples—make their appearance in the course of my argument. I have emphasized not what Yeats borrowed but what he created, not that which is recognizable elsewhere in different dress, but that which is unique, that which can be only one man's doing. Yeats adopted and adapted ideas, and this is not a mere play on words. He adopted in the sense that many principles that were to become his own were not self-begotten but became part of his imagination, though he always felt a little ill at ease with them; and he adapted these borrowings in such a way as to transform them into something recognizably Yeatsian.

There remain two aspects of Yeats which might possibly have been given more attention here: Yeats's reading of philosophy and the esoteric Yeats, whose earlier previews in such books as *Rosa Alchemica* culminate in *A Vision*. Yeats and philosophy remains an unwritten book. The Platonic and neo-Platonic background has been examined scrupulously in F. A. C. Wilson's two books and, more recently, by Morton Irving Seiden's *William Butler Yeats: The Poet As Mythmaker, 1865–1939;* and the esoteric roots in Swedenborg and Boehme and occultist orders of various stripes have been given some attention by Mr. Wilson, Virginia Moore, and others. But in the twenties and thirties Yeats read scores of philosophers, historians, scientists: Kant, Berkeley, Schopenhauer, Hume, Hegel, Croce, Spengler, Bergson, Russell, Whitehead, Dunne, McTaggart, Indian philosophy—the list is by no means exhausted here. A good deal of Yeats's discussions of philosophy is scattered rather inconspicuously, though his correspondence with the poet T. Sturge Moore has been collected, and there one may follow Yeats's education in philosophy as he argues metaphysics with his friend. Reading this volume is a somewhat uncomfortable experience: neither Yeats nor Moore, one feels, was really well suited for the subject at hand, and it would take a third party —well trained in philosophy—to arbitrate between them. (That third party does in fact at times make his appearance in the correspondence when T. Sturge Moore, in desperation, calls upon his brother, the philosopher G. E. Moore, to set straight his obstinate friend.) Still, Ruskin's famous vision of the cat—which occupies a sizable portion of the exchange between Yeats and Moore—is not the main issue at hand; to make it such is to reduce the whole business with too deprecatory a gesture. While Yeats seems at times hopelessly stubborn and naive and Moore terribly literal and obtuse, the real issue at stake—the nature of reality—was a central one for both poets. Yeats's solution remained, I think, tentative and uncertain; and he clearly never conquered the inherited scepticism of his father. Yet this very hesitation to adopt a single view of reality is parallel to his aesthetic.

The aesthetic was Yeats's first task and, as I have stressed, he completed it before he seriously undertook to study philosophy. But the relationships between the aesthetic and the subsequent philosophic speculations are often undeniably clear. In spite of this, it has not seemed proper to discuss this analogy with any thoroughness here because the philosophy seems a much more unstable and confusing subject than the aesthetic and therefore threatens to fling us once more upon "hodos chameliontos." I do, however, concede this much: Yeats's philosophic inquiries serve as a bridge into the final version of *A Vision*, a way out of chaos toward some form of unity. At certain points in my argument I have, therefore, made some tentative suggestions to demonstrate how the aesthetic eased its way into philosophy, and I have not ignored such works as *Per Amica Silentia Lunae*, or Yeats's rather intimate knowledge of Plotinus, Nietzsche, Schopenhauer, and Bergson.

A Vision—counting both the early and the revised versions—occupied Yeats for better than twenty years. A work which is part of a man's life for so long cannot be wished away. Besides, it has been justly pointed out that the earlier esoteric interests were mere preludes to *A Vision,* so that it is no exaggeration to claim that certain aspects of *A Vision* were lifelong interests. But just as there is a danger in ignoring *A Vision* altogether, so is there a certain disadvantage in overestimating its importance at the expense of other aspects of Yeats to which critics and scholars have been less attentive.

Yeats's poetry was his first concern, and he himself worried that young men would read *A Vision* instead of it. Aside from his art Yeats had, in words already quoted, three interests that shaped his life—a sense of national identity, philosophy, and a theory of literature.

My business here is the last of these and, to refine this even further, to chart the dominant patterns of the aesthetic, not to catalogue all of Yeats's utterances on art and artists (Yeats on Art and Society remains a fruitful subject about which much more needs to be said). For Yeats, as for any great artist, everything had "aesthetic implications"; hardly a word he wrote, whether on philosophy, or history, or on the occult fails to shade into the issue of art. Like Goethe, Yeats sought deliberately to shape a *Weltanschauung;* and, as with Goethe, everything radiated from the artistic centre, no matter how profuse and far-flung the ideas would become. I have tried to keep close to the centre. *A Vision* and the esoteric writings bear the same relationship to Yeats's aesthetic as Goethe's speculations on the *Urpflanze* or *Farbenlehre* bore to his, and the *Autobiography* is remarkably similar in spirit to *Dichtung ünd Wahrheit*. There is also some truth in H. W. Häusermann's contention that Yeats's conclusions about art and artists "are founded on the universal principles of art itself, not upon any occult messages dictated by his wise communicators"; though one would not perhaps wish to go so far as to say that "There is no need . . . to know anything about the System expounded in *A Vision,*" in order to come to terms with the aesthetic. Strictly speaking, the need to know is unnecessary since *A Vision* was clearly the later product; but certainly *A Vision* enables us to see the aesthetic reflected and refracted from different angles. Häusermann is quite right in saying that Yeats "avoided the terminology" of the "System" when he wrote about art (the terminology was not yet in existence); and he is also correct in protesting that readers have refused to take Yeats's critical ideas seriously because their immediate confusion of them with the "System" either discourages them or increases their hostility, provided they are hostile to esoteric Yeats to start with.[7] I hope I have clarified in the course of this book that the disentangling of the aesthetic from the "System" is not only possible but chronologically necessary. *A Vision* does not, of course, remain outside my pages—both in the opening and in the closing chapters I make use of its implications to my subject; but I should also add that many of the aesthetic ideas in *A Vision* (or the tracing of the history of art) are expressed elsewhere (in the *Autobiography* and letters and assorted essays) with greater clarity, free of the rigour that systematization unavoidably imposes. Of these parallel ideas to *A Vision* I have made ample use.

[7]H. W. Häusermann, "W. B. Yeats's Criticism of Ezra Pound," pp. 454, 437–438.

III

It is suitable to conclude these introductory remarks with three quotations from Yeats that lead us straightaway to the heart of the matter:

The imaginative writer differs from the saint in that he identifies himself—to the neglect of his own soul, alas!—with the soul of the world. . . . (*Discoveries*, 1906).

All art is the disengaging of a soul from place and history. . . . ("J. M. Synge and the Ireland of his Time," 1910).

. . . man everywhere is more of his time than of his nation. . . . (Introduction to *Fighting the Waves*, 1934).

"Time" and "world," "place" and "history"—are they all synonymous? The artist, Yeats says in the first quotation, neglects—must neglect, however regretfully, it seems—his own soul for the sake of the world's: not art for art's sake, nor art for my sake. Yet the *soul* of the world is not the world, not the same as "place" or "history"—those particularizing goal posts which the historical self-consciousness of the nineteenth century rather overconfidently staked down to define the limits of our field: *Zeitgeist*. "Place" and "history" were too fixed to suit a cyclical mind: from these the soul must be disengaged, and that is the business of art. But "time" was perhaps a more suitable word to describe the very real sense of proximity that Yeats always felt toward the impinging events that touched his life at every turn. "Time" was at least motion by definition, whereas "nation," like "place" and "history," was too fixed, too narrow a space for the artist to breathe in: the soul, though of the "world," must "disengage" itself from "place", "history" and "nation." The artist must have world enough and time—and yet, as Yeats would have admitted readily, he must ultimately have nation, place and history too: these were some of the components of his "vast design"; and the disengaging soul—this was the "one image" defining its individuality within the art it creates. The single, original poet, still creating within a vast design which reflected, like a single image, the whole of a nation's traditions, the "race" and the "reality": that was Yeats's great aim as an artist.

By 1907 Yeats was already referring to Villiers de l'Isle-Adam as "crying in the ecstasy of a supreme culture, of a supreme refusal, 'as for living, our servants will do that for us.'" A decade of labour in the drama was to alert Yeats toward the essential drama of life itself: "One of the means of loftiness, of marmorean stillness, has been the choice of strange and far-away places for the scenery of art, but this choice has grown bitter to me, and there arc moments when I cannot believe in the reality of imaginations that are not inset with the minute life of long familiar things and symbols and places." Even Shakespeare's imaginary journeys to Rome and Verona seem to him now symptomatic "of unrest, a dissatisfaction with natural interests, an unstable equilibrium of the whole European mind. . . ."[8] To help stabilize the equilibrium of the European mind was for Yeats the responsibility of the modern poet.[9]

[8]*Discoveries*, in *Essays*, p. 367. *Discoveries* was published separately in December, 1907. In later editions, in *The Cutting of an Agate* (1912 and 1919), in which *Discoveries* was included, as well as in *Essays* (1924) and in *Essays and Introductions* (1961), the date given at the end of *Discoveries* is 1906. (In the 1908 *Collected Works* no date is given.) However, in his *Bibliography of the Writings of W. B. Yeats*, Allan Wade notes in the entry for the 1907 edition of *Discoveries* (item 72): "Finished on 12th September, 1907." He also notes that all but the last four chapters of *Discoveries* had been published previously, in various places, in 1906. The last four chapters—"A Tower on the Apennines," "The Thinking of the Body," "Religious Belief Necessary to Symbolic Art," and "The Holy Places"—were published in the autumn of 1907, several months prior to the publication of *Discoveries* as a separate volume. It is apparent that Yeats wrote these last four chapters in 1907. The quotation above comes from "The Holy Places" and should therefore be considered as belonging to the year 1907.

[9]I have argued that Yeats's literary tastes were wide and sympathetic, but not that he was an unfailingly good judge of his contemporaries. Any such claims are embarrassed by the inclusions and omissions in *The Oxford Book of Modern Verse*, which Yeats edited in 1936. I am concerned primarily with Yeats's views of the past, where his judgment was firm and usually right. In making his choices for the Oxford anthology, he admittedly engaged in editorial prejudices and perhaps committed errors of judgment: some poets omitted or scantily represented have since risen in value; many whom he overpraised have not proven to be of enduring value. But history has not yet made any definitive judgments on many of the poets represented in this volume. What was important for Yeats was a poet's *quality*: in Turner a daring use of images; in Edith Sitwell a quality of puckish innocence; in Dorothy Wellesley an earthy treatment of love but metaphysically oriented. We cannot forget, of course, that Yeats must have chosen some poems from a sense of loyalty and nostalgia, since so many of the poets he had known in his youth. If he erred, this in no way contradicts my claim that he had a far-flung appreciation of different kinds of poetry. The Introduction to the Oxford anthology makes it abundantly clear that his choices were also often governed by certain aesthetic principles (e.g., the failure to include Owen); and it is in the light of these principles that his editorial eccentricities can be understood, if not always justified.

❀ THE VAST DESIGN

Patterns in W. B. Yeats's Aesthetic

I ❋ THE VAST DESIGN: First Principles

> Motions are also symbolic. . . . Going and returning are the typical eternal motions, they characterize the visionary forms of eternal life. They belong to *up and down*, to *in and out*. Ellis-Yeats edition of Blake

> . . . & the circling is always narrowing or spreading,
> because one movement or other is always the stronger.
> In other words, the human soul is always moving outward
> into the objective world or inward into itself;
> & this movement is double because the human soul would
> not be conscious were it not suspended between contraries,
> the greater the contrast the more intense the consciousness.
> Note to "The Second Coming"

Yeats's imagination—if not his talent—was primarily neither lyric nor dramatic but epic. Had he lived in another time he might have been a great epic poet. Regardless of how many dreams possessed his life, the earliest and greatest was to become a modern Homer of Ireland, its mythmaker: ". . . I hated and still hate with an ever growing hatred the literature of the point of view. I wanted . . . to get back to Homer. . . ." In his essay on modern poetry (initially a B.B.C. broadcast in 1936), he had characterized his time accurately as non-epic: "The period from the death of Tennyson until the present moment has, it seems, more good lyric poets than any similar period since the seventeenth century—no great overpowering figures, but many poets who have written some three or four lyrics apiece which may be permanent in our literature."[1] Yeats knew that both time and talent conspired against him: the first denied him the proper soil for epic art; the second seemed better suited for the short, not the sustained effort. The consequent tension between his imagination, with its

[1]*Essays and Introductions*, pp. 511; 491. The first quotation is cited from "A General Introduction for my Work," dated 1937 and published for the first time in the above volume (1961).

protean conceptions of vast designs, and his poetic gifts, which seemed to fall so naturally into the contained and limited forms, produced ultimately the uniqueness and excitement of his aesthetic speculations.

Yeats said often enough that he was in sympathy with the lyric poets, the creators of subtle and ecstatic "songs" that made for the finely controlled intensity of lyric poetry. But, when speaking on these occasions, he sometimes evoked nostalgia and regret for what had been sacrificed: the "tumultuous and heroic," "mankind in their fulness," "old forms, old situations," "heroic and religious truths," "half-philosophical, half-mythological folk-beliefs," "great and complicated images," "vast worlds moulded by their own weight," "the old abounding, nonchalant reverie." He made his point unequivocally in a tercet he called "Three Movements" (1932):

> Shakespearean fish swam the sea, far away from land;
> Romantic fish swam in nets coming to the hand;
> What are all those fish that lie gasping on the strand?

One kind of art which appealed consistently to Yeats has in common a grandeur of conception and form: all heroic and bardic literature; *Parsifal*; Homer; the great Comedies, Divine and Humaine; Shakespeare, whose plays he considered as one vast "myth"; Cervantes; Blake's Prophetic Books; *Faust*; all the "old poems" that had "architectural unity" and "symbolic importance"; Phidias, Michelangelo, Titian; everything that could "mold vast material into a single image." In that last phrase lies the *modus operandi* of Yeats's aesthetic: for the threat that vastness would lose itself in anarchic flood was always to be checked by the assertion of the single image. Through that single image, vastness could become as intense and as focal as a lyric poem, though a lyric poet could not easily attain both the epic grandeur and the lyric compactness which Yeats's ideal suggested.

It must be admitted that, in certain central respects, Yeats's art and his conceptions of art were sometimes at odds; that he did not always succeed in writing the kind of poetry he conceived of as a theoretical ideal. *A Vision* remains his one compensatory effort to write an epic: it fulfilled his great need for the architecture of a panoramic scheme, a "single image," though, lacking both hero and action, it remains—as he lamented—a "System" and not a poem. It has been argued that Yeats's poetry forms a single, long, structured poem, provided we read him with care and sensitivity.[2] But even at

[2]The first to argue this was Donald A. Stauffer, *The Golden Nightingale*; lately the idea has been advanced by John Unterecker, *A Reader's Guide to William*

best this requires some artificiality of effort, for the reading of a grouping of single poems, each poem deriving from a separate occasion, a distinct spot of time, and a special emotional impulse cannot equal a reading of *Paradise Lost* or the *Iliad*. Yeats knew this. While it often illuminates Yeats's poetry, the theory must be accepted autonomously. Testing the poetic achievement against theory does not always yield happy results: it leads to a limitation either of the theory or of the poetry. Yeats's poetry is so various, in conception, technique, form, and theme, that no one representative theory, not even his own, could support it. Often, at the very moment when Yeats's critical prose was pleading one cause, his poetry was objectifying another. Yeats thought as he would; but he wrote as he could.

This is not to suggest that theory and practice were unrelated. On the contrary, it was Yeats's awareness of the disparity between what he wanted and what he could achieve–and his labours to join wish to fulfilment–which guided the direction of his aesthetic thinking. Theory profoundly affected practice and vice versa; and, especially in his mature years, Yeats composed many poems which successfully objectified theory.

But because conception tended to demand what execution could not always deliver, it is not surprising that the shape of Yeats's aesthetic reveals the visible and sometimes violent signs of a struggle to compromise: or, if compromise suggests something too negative, of a struggle to achieve unity through opposition, a method which, as we know already, governed his conceptions of man, life, and history. The need to unify through opposition was not, at first, a thoroughly deliberated philosophic assumption, despite Yeats's early reading of Blake, where the attractive "contraries" were first encountered. Primarily, I think Yeats sought out the contraries when he discovered that certain assumptions about art which he brought to his earliest trials as a poet seemed to oppose what he was doing. As would be normal for any young poet, Yeats was anxious to express himself in a voice made his own; but his powers were not yet equal to the task of attaining the magnitude of the art he consistently admired, and his early reading of Blake and Swedenborg put him permanently on guard against "egoism."

From the first, he felt that great art must be conceived vastly: the

---

Butler Yeats. But perhaps the most convincing account of Yeats's poetry as a carefully arranged sequence of poems that suggests a single work is Hugh Kenner's "The Sacred Book of the Arts," in *Gnomon* (McDowell, Obolensky Inc., New York, 1951), pp. 9–29.

imagination behind it must be capable of expanding itself, as well as expanding the imagination of the audience. This had been Shelley's chief metaphor for describing the power of poetry in the *Defence* (which Yeats knew thoroughly and admired): "Poetry enlarges the circumference of the imagination by replenishing it with thoughts of ever new delight . . . which form new intervals and interstices whose void for ever craves fresh food"; it "bursts the circumference of the reader's mind, and pours itself forth together with it into the universal element with which it has perpetual sympathy"; in tragedy, "The imagination is enlarged by a sympathy with pains and passions so mighty, that they distend in their conception the capacity of that by which they are conceived. . . ." In the presence of tragedy, Yeats wrote, "We feel our minds expand convulsively or spread out slowly like some moon-brightened image-crowded sea. That which is before our eyes perpetually vanishes and returns again in the midst of the excitement it creates. . . ."[3] Yeats quickly recognized that grandeur in art could no longer be achieved quantitatively, by crowding a work with large casts of characters, many plots, a multitude of ideas and emotions; allusion and suggestion, symbol and emblem, therefore soon became central to his aesthetic as techniques of gaining capaciousness and echo, the reverberation of vast worlds rather than the vast worlds themselves. If one might retain the effects of Hugo while wringing the neck of his rhetoric and eloquence, then the lyric of the future could promise a fulfilment of suggested vastness never before achieved.

The expansion metaphor, which Yeats uses in his theoretical prose with marked repetitiousness, suggested that outward surge toward vastness which he crystallized so perfectly in his phrase "emotion of multitude." But the vast design must never lose itself on the periphery of the circle: poetry, said Shelley, is "at once the centre and circumference of knowledge"; poets "measure the circumference and sound the depths of human nature. . . ." The "void" must be continually filled: "That which is before our eyes perpetually vanishes and returns again"; the space left empty by expansion is reoccupied with rhythmic perpetuity. In Yeats's scheme such reoccupation occurs when the echo, having travelled to the limits of form, returns and traverses the space it has cleared in expanding and, by contraction, returns to the centre again. Here, then, the artist gains his "still intensity"; here echo becomes focus, the "vast design" coalesces into the "single image." But the stillness is intense; underneath it "stirs

[3] "The Tragic Theatre," *Essays*, p. 303.

the beast" and always the potential for a repeated gesture of expansion. Yeats, as H. W. Häusermann has written, "considered perfection to lie in a state of balance between the 'flux' and conscious limitation,"[4] between expansion and contraction. Pater had described Greek art and civilization as divided between two "opposing tendencies": "The centrifugal and centripetal . . . the Ionian, the Asiatic tendency, flying from the centre . . . [and] the Dorian influence of a severe simplification . . . calm . . . [promoting] a composed, rational, self-conscious order. . . ."[5] And Northrop Frye has applied this notion to the audience:

> Whenever we read anything, we find our attention moving in two directions at once. One direction is outward or centrifugal, in which we keep going outside our reading, from the individual words to the things they mean, or, in practice, to our memory of the conventional association between them. The other direction is inward or centripetal, in which we try to develop from the words a sense of the larger verbal pattern they make.[6]

All attempts to reconcile expansion and contraction touch somehow on the major issue of the "concrete universal"—an art at once both unique and generic. But for Yeats the question was crucial: in creating the specific and unique, what price did the poet pay for his "originality"—what Blake called "egoism"? This question arose early, in Yeats's first essay on symbolism which he wrote for the edition of Blake co-edited with Edwin Ellis in 1893. Although it is true that in this piece, "The Necessity of Symbolism," Yeats tended to see the problem more metaphysically than aesthetically, the very philosophic bias of the young Yeats reminds us properly that for a poet the realms of thought have no hard and fast boundaries. It is Blake Yeats is explicating but the thought, of course, expresses his own conception as well:

> The mind or imagination or consciousness of man may be said to have two poles, the personal and impersonal, or, as Blake preferred to call them, the limit of contraction and the unlimited expansion. When we act from the personal we tend to bind our consciousness down as to a fiery centre. When, on the other hand, we allow our imagination to expand away from this egoistic mood, we become vehicles for the universal thought and merge in the universal mood.[7]

[4]Häusermann, "W. B. Yeats's Criticism of Ezra Pound," 443.

[5]Pater, *Greek Studies* (London, 1895), pp. 264–265.

[6]Northrop Frye, *Anatomy of Criticism* (Princeton University Press, 1957), p. 73.

[7]*The Works of William Blake, Poetic, Symbolic, and Critical*, ed. Edwin John Ellis and William Butler Yeats, I, 242.

The centre is here equated with the personal, and the personal with the egoistical; and the egoistical, finally, is the opposite of the universal—the finite. This Blakean antithesis was to influence Yeats profoundly. All his life he was to be torn between his conceptual sympathies for "half-anonymous" culture-art—such as the mosaics of Byzantium, in which the individual artist was submerged—and the passionate intensity of his own artistic voice, the "personal utterance" which could so easily turn to egoism or lose itself as an unattached voice singing in the dark like a forlorn nightingale—like the nightingale-poet in Shelley's *Defence*. Yeats's attitude toward individualism as egoism was always equivocal: while he hated the surrender into the multiplicity of the East, which set free the great horrors of the primary, objective age, he pursued with earnest longing the sort of coherence in co-operative ventures in art in which the single voice blended into the choir. Yeats's mask-theory, which permitted a man to possess many selves and anti-selves, seems, when applied to poetic theory, essentially an attempt to escape the tyranny of a single identifiable persona; or to invest the persona with personae that defy a categorical definition or reduction. Originality, he argued, is not the artist's business—it is his share in Cain's curse. But the words must often have tasted like ash in his mouth, for Yeats was a modern and with the inheritance of his modernity, in spite of himself, came the terrible, insistent urge to be original, to be, at any rate, what the people turned enemy least wanted you to be.

"A poet writes always of his personal life," but never as if addressing himself to some single man in the confessional: a poet "is more type than man, more passion than type," and the ascent into higher abstractions here is away from the *cri du cœur*. While the poets of the eighteenth century had their weaknesses, Yeats admired their public stance: "they were not separated individual men; they spoke or tried to speak out of a people to a people; behind them stretched the generations." In a prose that ironically betrays the unique voice of hatred of which Yeats was occasionally capable, he turned on the personal with fury, late in his life: "all that is personal soon rots; it must be packed in ice or salt"; "Talk to me of originality and I will turn on you with rage."[8]

Still, the intensity he sought could not be scored so easily by following the dictates of his epic dreams of vastness and impersonality. The present impinged uncomfortably and made its demands: "Contem-

[8]"A General Introduction for my Work," *Essays and Introductions*, pp. 509–510, 522.

porary lyric poems . . . seemed too long. . . . The English mind is meditative, rich, deliberate. . . . I planned to write short lyrics or poetic drama where every speech would be short and concentrated, knit by dramatic tension. . . ."[9] But this was only one side of the coin: the meditative could become static, or reverie itself might turn dramatic—these were problems he was to solve in the years of trials and failures that pushed him to maturity and control. Meanwhile, not long after he began his career as a poet, Yeats found himself in the exceedingly promising but precarious position of being attracted by opposite ideals: a vast imagination seeking to express itself in tense, short, dramatic poetry. What he needed—and found—was historical support, precedent, for Yeats was in all things conscious of continuity and anxious to make his place in what he later came to call the "procession."

II

Yeats was by nature no purist and his aesthetic, though it is remarkably self-consistent, offers little to the purist critic. The vexing question of genuine "influences," for instance, is nearly impossible to solve with certainty because Yeats was at times an erratic reader and occasionally too cavalier as a reporter of his reading. Yet the shape of the theory itself, with its insistence on epic grandeur, lyric intensity, and dramatic tension was only in part the result of an imagination which found itself frustratingly opposed by its own talents: in part it was also the result of an historical event of which Yeats was well aware—the re-discovery and re-interpretation of Greece and the Renaissance. The earliest encounter with this double revival was probably in Pater's *The Renaissance*, and for a time that book must have been for Yeats what it had been for Wilde: his "golden book."

For Pater, the Renaissance inherited "sweetness" from the Greeks and Romans and "strength" from the medieval world. In addition to "sweetness" the classical world had the quality of *Allgemeinheit*, breadth: its sweetness was part of its naïveté, in the sense in which Schiller distinguished "naïve" from "sentimental" poetry in his famous essay; its *Allgemeinheit* was its power. In addition to "strength," the medieval world bequeathed to the Renaissance—and thus to modern times—a quality of introspection and intensity, of the personal tragedy found in contraction, not expansion, for one contracted in the end upon one's own soul. On the basis of this

[9] *Ibid.*, p. 521.

historical diagram, with its variously apportioned debts and offerings of one age to another, Pater built his basic distinctions:

> *Allgemeinheit*—breadth, generality, universality,—is the word chosen by Winckelmann, and after him by Goethe and many German critics, to express that law of the most excellent Greek sculptors, of Pheidias and his pupils, which prompted them constantly to seek the type in the individual, to abstract and express only what is structural and permanent, to purge from the individual all that belongs only to him, all the accidents, the feelings and actions of the special moments, all that . . . is apt to look like a frozen thing if one arrests it. . . .
>
> That was the Greek way of relieving the hardness and unspirituality of pure form. But it involved to a certain degree the sacrifice of what we call *expression*; and a system of abstraction which aimed always at the broad and general type, at the purging away from the individual of . . . mere accidents of a particular time and place, imposed upon the range of effects open to the Greek sculptor limits somewhat narrowly defined. When Michelangelo came, therefore, with a genius spiritualised by the reverie of the middle age, penetrated by its spirit of inwardness and introspection, living not a mere outward life like the Greek, but a life full of intimate experiences, . . . a system which sacrificed so much of what was inward and unseen could not satisfy him. To him . . . work which did not bring what was inward to the surface, which was not concerned with . . . individual character and feeling, the special history of the special soul, was not worth doing at all.[10]

Michelangelo brought to sculpture "individuality and intensity of expression," and this partially medieval importation is what most clearly distinguishes medieval from classical: "the presence of a convulsive energy in it . . . felt, even in its most graceful products, as a subdued quaintness or grotesque." It is evident where Pater's own sympathies lie: in the conflict which this medieval energy, this "grotesque," brought to the stable Greek ideal. In his essay on Winckelmann, the most revealing of the series in *The Renaissance*, he admits that the Hellenic ideal in which man was at one with himself, nature, and the world was enviable, and the beyond into which man stepped a pit full of danger and uncertainty. But the risk seemed both worth taking and inevitable. If man was to be "saved from the *ennui* which ever attaches itself to realisation, . . . it was necessary that a conflict should come, that some sharper note should grieve the existing harmony, and the spirit chafed by it beat out at last only a larger and profounder music."[11]

[10]Walter Pater, *The Renaissance* (London, 1925), pp. 66–67.
[11]*Ibid.*, pp. 67, 73–74, 222.

Arnold, whom Pater attended, had himself defined Hellenism, after a fashion, as *Allgemeinheit*—a kind of centrality, at least, a state of Being against the ever Becoming flux of Hebraism. Yet was it not Arnold who demanded action from poetry—action specifically committed to the conflict, the commitment against whatever the hero faced in his tilt with a hostile fate? Suffering must find translation in action; "incident, hope, or resistance" must relieve and break "mental distress"; something must be "done." Yeats, we know, approved this passage from the Preface to the poems of 1853, for he used it as a precedent for his rejection of Wilfred Owen and the war poets from the *Oxford Book of Modern Verse*. And, looking back over his life, he writes elsewhere in 1937, "I had begun to get rid of everything that is not, whether in lyric or dramatic poetry, in some sense character in action; a pause in the midst of action perhaps, but action always its end and theme."[12]

At the start of the century Coleridge had made his own distinctions between "Greek" and "Gothic," and reading them in the light of Arnold and Pater and Yeats, we see how germinal Coleridge's remarks were. The terminology of Coleridge's distinction appears at first turned on its head—but only at first:

> The Greeks idolized the finite, and therefore were the masters of all grace, elegance, proportion, fancy, dignity, majesty—of whatever . . . is capable of being definitely conveyed by defined forms or thoughts: the moderns revere the infinite, and affect the indefinite as a vehicle of the infinite;—hence their passions, their obscure hopes and fears, their wandering through the unknown, their grander moral feelings, their more august conception of man as man, their future rather than their past—in a word, their sublimity.[13]

"Sublimity" was a word Yeats used infrequently but its meaning was conveyed by "ecstasy," a word he was very fond of using, and ecstasy is a lyric or dramatic achievement, never an epic one. It is reached

[12]"An Introduction for my Plays," *Essays and Introductions*, p. 530.

[13]S. T. Coleridge, "Lectures on Shakespeare," as quoted by D. G. James, *The Romantic Comedy* (London, 1948), p. 241. James goes on at length to develop Coleridge's distinction, and I am indebted to him for the quotation.

That Coleridge's ideas on this subject were not "original" but were echoes of the Schlegels and of Schiller has been noted by modern critics. See especially Arthur O. Lovejoy's "The Meaning of 'Romantic' in Early German Romanticism," and "Schiller and the Genesis of German Romanticism," both in *Essays in the History of Ideas* (The Johns Hopkins University Press, 1948). Lovejoy traces in great detail the romantic philosophy of finite and infinite, and the romantic distinctions between the Greek and the modern temper. See also René Wellek, *A History of Modern Criticism, 1750–1950* (London, 1955), II, 5–187.

only through tension or action, through ultimate contraction, inwardness, the turning of self toward self. Contraction is, paradoxically, a road toward the infinite, for it is the Self which contains infinite alternatives, infinite mysteries. What makes for conflict is the irresolution of the striving. Whereas the Greeks looked out, the moderns look in: the epic emotion reconciles the individual to the world and the world assimilates and contains him. Epic is always depersonalized, and even Greek sculpture may be said to have striven—in its quest for *Allgemeinheit*—for the epic inclusiveness. Drama and lyric objectify: the individual appropriates the world, not in order to make himself resemble the world but to make the world resemble him. This Romantic conception was initiated and furthered by Kant, Fichte, Hegel, and, above all, by Schopenhauer: "Die Welt ist meine Vorstellung": conscious will becomes self-consciousness and, in Schopenhauer, individual will abdicates to the power of a universal Will. Paradoxically, therefore, though the individual loses in his power to will, the awareness of his own vision of the world gives him a corresponding freedom, unlimited, infinite. This Schopenhauerian doctrine must have influenced Yeats, for he tells us that he had read Schopenhauer "as a young man"—certainly before the 1920's. Art, we must remember, is also a means by which we escape from Schopenhauer's Will, even if only temporarily; the essential point Schopenhauer makes about lyric poetry is its intensely personal nature, though of course such an obvious point is developed with subtlety in Schopenhauer's aesthetic:

> The expression of the Idea of mankind, which devolves on the poet, can now be carried out in such a way that the depicted is also at the same time the depicter. This occurs in lyric poetry . . . where the poet vividly perceives and describes only his own state; hence through the object, a certain subjectivity is essential to poetry of this kind. . . . In the ballad the depicter still expresses to some extent his own state . . . though much more objective than the song [the lyric], it [the ballad] still has something subjective in it. This fades away more in the idyll, still more in the romance, almost entirely in the epic proper, and finally to the last vestige in the drama, which is the most objective . . . form of poetry.[14]

[14]Arthur Schopenhauer, *The World as Will and Representation*, tr. E. F. J. Payne (Indian Hills, Colo., 1958), I, 248–249. "Die Darstellung der Idee der Menschheit, welche dem Dichter obliegt, kann er nun entweder so ausführen, dass der Dargestellte zugleich auch der Darstellende ist: dieses geschieht in der lyrischen Poesie . . . wo der Dichtende nur seinen eigenen Zustand . . . beschreibt, wobei daher, durch den Gegenstand, dieser Gattung eine gewisse Subjektivität wesentlich ist. . . .

When that which is rendered is equivalent to him who renders it, we have lyric poetry; then, in stages, this equation widens until, in drama, the artist and his material are most removed and most finite, since the distance between creator and created in drama necessarily dictates limitations which lyric poetry does not. That Yeats should seek at once the most subjective and objective modes—lyric and drama—is therefore no accident: he desired both.

Infinite and finite were also distinguishable in architecture, where, as in sculpture, once again a culture displayed its ethos: inward or outward. In an essay on cathedrals, while contrasting Cologne with Canterbury, Arthur Symons pits Coleridge's and Pater's conception of Gothic against a cold, reasonable, outward-looking Protestantism which bears curious resemblances to their image of a complacent Hellenism. In Cologne he can find no "ecstasy" but "only a calm certainty." There is grandeur but it is all finished grandeur; Cologne Cathedral everywhere "aspires" but ultimately "only to a sort of emptiness, a vast nakedness of space . . . out of which nothing grows." At Canterbury he gets the sense of "vital expansion," but not the expansion of mere massiveness—that he had found at Cologne; rather "really a kind of soul," a kind of expansion which is, in essence, the result of an inner reflection: "soul in stone" not "mind in stone."[15] This distinction between "soul" and "mind" was, of course, central to Yeats, and it was in the Renaissance—where Pater had gone—that he found one of the crossroads in the history of the issue.

Yeats's conception of the Renaissance, and his frequent habit of paralleling that period to his own time, seem to offer the most effective approach to evaluating his always vacillating attitude toward personal utterance and general myth, subjective and objective. In Yeats's scheme of history, the Renaissance figured crucially both as a culmination and as a seed-bed, a grave and a cradle, a time of unity and of dispersal, the last and the first of frontiers. As early as 1898, in "The Autumn of the Body," Yeats sketched a history of poetry in which the "thingness" of poetry is seem as ascending steadily from pre-Homeric art through Arnold, with a corresponding decline of a universal mythic

---

In der Romanze drückt der Darstellende seinen eigenen Zustand . . . in etwas aus: viel objektiver als das Lied hat sie daher noch etwas Subjektives, dieses verschwindet schon mehr im Idyll, noch viel mehr im Roman, fast ganz im eigentlichen Epos, und bis auf die letzte Spur endlich im Drama, welches die objektiveste . . . Gattung der Poesie ist." *Schopenhauers Sämmtliche Werke* (Leipzig, n.d.), I, 334–335.

[15]Arthur Symons, *The Collected Works of Arthur Symons*, IX, *Studies in Seven Arts* (London, 1924), 107–111. The essay on "Cathedrals" is dated 1903.

comprehensiveness: myth becomes history. Within this scheme, the Renaissance stands at the centre:

The first poets... had not Homer's preoccupation with things, and he [Homer] was not so full of their excitement as Virgil. Dante added to poetry a dialectic which... was the invention of minds trained by the labour of life... and not a spontaneous expression of an interior life; while Shakespeare shattered the symmetry of verse and of drama that he might fill them with things and their accidental relations to one another.

Each of these writers had come further down the stairway... but it was only with the modern poets, with Goethe and Wordsworth and Browning, that poetry gave up the right to consider all things in the world as a dictionary of types and symbols and began to call itself a critic of life and an interpreter of things as they are.[16]

Spenser was perhaps the first poet of the Renaissance to succumb to the separation of "thingness" and "sensuousness." Throughout *The Faerie Queene* Yeats found "a conflict between the aesthetic and moral interests," a quarrel he did not find before the Renaissance. "To no English poet, perhaps to no European poet before his day, had the natural expression of personal feeling been so impossible, the clear vision of the lineaments of human character so difficult. . . ." Escape into allegory was, it seems, Spenser's only solution: he had lost the poet's power to make characters self-sufficient symbols, expressive of the personal feelings of the poet and fitting creations of an individual world view. Poetry's newly acquired courtship with the world of affairs, its now more specifically shaped political nature, burdened it with a public responsibility that rejected the individual ordering, the imaginative affinities that the world of art had always abstracted from the world of reality. "Full of the spirit of the Renaissance, at once passionate and artificial, looking out upon the world now as craftsman, now as connoisseur, he [Spenser] was to found his art upon [Tasso's and Ariosto's] . . . rather than upon the more humane, the more noble, the less intellectual art of Malory and the Minstrels." Overpowered by this new art, minstrelsy died: the Anglo-French Renaissance was superseded by Puritanism, "Merry England" vanished forever, and Bunyan's *Pilgrim's Progress* (the ultimate extension of *The Faerie Queene*) marked the birth of modern England.[17]

In the old bardic spirit, Yeats still found an "imaginative unity" centred on "aesthetic realities," just as the Church had once centred on "moral realities"; independent of all other realities, this bardic

[16]"The Autumn of the Body," *Essays*, p. 236.
[17]"Edmund Spenser," *ibid.*, pp. 445–447, 442, 454.

tradition might create anew a "communion of heroes. . . ." Mankind, Yeats said, plays with heroic masks; in the "ancient story-tellers" we hear of these dream-ideals, of what man might have become "had not fear and the failing will and the laws of nature tripped up [his] . . . heels."[18] Both fear and the failing will are equivalents of scepticism, speculation, secularized intellection, all of which cause a separation between man and man by creating, as in Hamlet, uniqueness: what the sceptic gains in individuality by isolation from belief, he loses in kinship with his fellows by separation from them. The man who questions and contemplates the universe alters his consciousness of it so that his view takes some singular shape, which, in the end, may annihilate him. The cause of this mixed blessing—the urge to question and the consequences of individual vision—Yeats located in the Renaissance.

But, compared with the doting, weakened image of a middle-class imagination—Puritan, allegorical, unheroic—the arrogance of the Faustian man seemed infinitely preferable to Yeats, in art as in life. Better than either was the Greek temper, or writers like Cervantes or Boccaccio, artists who shared a common imagination in that they confronted life and experience directly. For one thing they were not distracted by the world of events, not lured away from the cycle of the seasons, birth, death, joy, sorrow—"all that is the unchanging substance of literature." Without having opened the flood-gates of art by yielding to the onrushing, ever pressing world of circumstance and event, these artists "had not to deal with the world in such great masses that it could only be represented to their minds by figures and by abstract generalisations." Writing "out of their own rich experience," they created symbols for their art drawn directly from the familiar and the immediately apprehended; the impersonality of allegory found no place in their craft or vision: they *saw* the world, saw its splendour in the very detail that had not yet been lost to sense or imagination. For Yeats the loss of this ability to celebrate "the very detail" that sense and imagination once apprehended signalled the end of an age; what followed were the symptoms of our present ills, an emphasis on abstraction, a loss of feeling. Considerably earlier than Eliot, Yeats had diagnosed a "dissociation of sensibility":

> It is the change, that followed the Renaissance and was completed by newspaper government and the scientific movement, that has brought upon us all these phrases and generalizations, made by minds that would grasp

[18]"Lady Gregory's *Cuchulain of Muirthemne*," *Collected Works,* VIII, 137, 157.

what they have never seen.... Theories, opinions... flowed in.... Even our greatest poets see the world with preoccupied minds. Great as Shelley is, those theories about the coming changes of the world... hurry him from life continually... [;] every generation we get further away from life itself.... We lose our freedom more and more as we get away from ourselves... because we... believe that the root of reality is not in the centre but somewhere in that whirling circumference.[19]

From Dante—who brought a well-controlled, individual passion to poetry—through Botticelli, Da Vinci, and Raphael, there appears to be a striving for unity, a confluence of passion and thingness. Soon, however, their intense quietness is disturbed by the awakening "sexual desire" in the art of Michelangelo and Titian; the nervous spirit of the modern temper is now manifest. Shakespeare is an initial culmination—"a man in whom human personality, hitherto restrained by its dependence upon Christendom or by its own need for self-control, burst like a shell."[20] Milton's belated attempts to accomplish a new synthesis of secular and divine, which had defeated, in part, even Michelangelo, end in ultimate failure. Rhetoric, artifice, and a conscious, unnatural dependence on classical myth accentuate the cleavage between sacred and profane. Replacing the former unity is "mechanical force"; the soul is shattered into "fragments," Bacon triumphs, and before us is the Age of Rationalism.[21] And with it comes another age of Roman decadence. Only now the causes are more recessed, more complex; and this accounts for Yeats's ambivalence toward the Renaissance:

I detest the Renaissance because it made the human mind inorganic; I adore the Renaissance because it clarified form and created freedom. I too expect the counter-Renaissance, but if we do not hold to freedom and form it will come, not as an inspiration in the head, but as an obstruction in the bowels.[22]

This two-sided view of the Renaissance constitutes the see-saw of Yeats's own aesthetic balance of anonymity and personal passion, the rest and reassurance of form and the excitement of its violation. Yeats read history as a constant struggle between individualism and abstraction, between the extremes of Western assertive turbulence and Eastern massive passivity. While the Renaissance liberated the artist it gave him the freedom to develop beyond form itself, so that,

[19]*The Irish Dramatic Movement* in *Plays and Controversies*, pp. 96–98.
[20]W. B. Yeats, *A Vision* (rev. ed., 1956), pp. 293–294.
[21]*Ibid.*, pp. 295–296.
[22]W. B. Yeats, *On the Boiler*, p. 27.

paradoxically, his very individualism led ultimately to abstraction—and, as he was to suggest, to the East. This freedom was, in some cases, a kind of suicide: the artist became so individual, so unique, that he surrendered himself to his own novel techniques; when those techniques conquered, the individual disappeared from sight. Eccentricity, a preoccupation of the self for the self's sake, a kind of super-humanism: these carried men into the chasm of abstraction where form was betrayed, tradition denied. In that chasm, Yeats saw—at first—most of his great contemporaries: Eliot, Joyce, Pound, Virginia Woolf.

The Romantics were the last to cope with the assertiveness of heroism short of a transcendence into the abstract: beyond them lay the dissolution. The modern artist has broken with his romantic forbears, for whom man was still the essential hero. Manfred and Prometheus reflect the power of Hegelian idealism, and it is true that they emerge as embodied ethical forces; but somehow the power of heroism still asserts itself in human terms. With the advent of naturalism that too is lost: "The romantic movement with its turbulent heroism, its self-assertion, is over, superseded by a new naturalism that leaves man helpless before the contents of his own mind. One thinks of Joyce's *Anna Livia Plurabelle,* Pound's *Cantos.* . . ."[23]

In almost every kind of modern art, man became a victim of larger and larger abstractions: History, Fate, State, Philosophy. (Yeats was himself aware that his own System was symptomatic, his gyres no less potentially mechanistic devices than Hegel's dialectic.) After our deliverance from nature by the Greeks, "intellect or Spirit . . . began to prevail. . . ." In Hegel came a climax: soon "religion would be absorbed in the State, art in philosophy, God's Will proved to be man's will." Against this tendency Balzac symbolized for Yeats a defender of the faith; into his mouth he put an imaginary refutation. "'Man's intellect or Spirit can do nothing but bear witness; Nature alone is active. . . . I refuse to confine Nature to claw, paw, and hoof.'" Indeed, it is "'men of ideas'" who start civilizations on the road to decline, men like Hegel, "Indifferent . . . to the individual soul"; "'There is a continual conflict . . . the perfection of Nature is the decline of the Spirit,'" and vice versa. Dante's *Divine Comedy* "'summed up and closed the Europe that created Mont Saint-Michel," and the *"Comédie humaine* has closed the counter-movement.'"[24]

From divine to human: this is the topography we have traversed; from human to abstract: this is the road we are about to take—or have

[23]W. B. Yeats, "Bishop Berkeley," *Essays and Introductions*, p. 405.
[24]"The Holy Mountain," *ibid.*, pp. 466–468.

already taken, beginning with the nineties. Essentially Yeats refuses, in his imaginary soliloquy, to let Balzac accept Hegelian optimism, or even to understand it; Balzac's own dialectic, he claims, was far closer to the synthesized Indian wisdom, which does not concern itself with the history of civilizations, but focuses rather on man's unbounded soul in relation to an eternal universe.

The Renaissance, then, began the historical shift from individualism to abstraction by falling victim to its own inner paradoxes: it moved toward Unity of Being through the efforts of individuals, while at the same time it solidified individuality at the expense of that very unity. As in most revolutions, the temporary king, refusing to relinquish the powers given to him, now wishes to remain a permanent fixture: "'the egg, instead of hatching, burst.'"[25] A passage in the *Autobiography* makes this even clearer than it is in *A Vision*. Around the year 1450 men "attained to personality . . ., 'Unity of Being'. . . . Then the scattering came . . . and for a time personality seemed but the stronger for it." In the plays of Shakespeare, the strength of the characters rests in their willingness to let "all things serve their passion," a passion that is total and comprehensive, "the whole energy of their being." Both the world of natural things and the world of institutions and men are "but symbols, and metaphors, nothing is studied in itself, the mind is a dark well, no surface, depth only." For all their individual strength, the artists' visions suggest something final, something consummately unified: "The men that Titian painted . . . seemed at moments like great hawks at rest."[26]

Neither the turbulence of Michelangelo nor the intensity of Titian lasted long. Progressively, the Renaissance is seen as moving toward the "more reasonable, more orderly, less turbulent . . .," until inevi-

[25] *Ibid.*, p. 468.

[26] *Autobiography*, p. 174. A note on my use of the materials in the *Autobiography* is in order. The *Autobiography* was published in separate volumes before being collected for the first time into a single volume in 1938. *Reveries over Childhood and Youth* was published in 1914; *The Trembling of the Veil* in 1922; *Dramatis Personae 1896–1902* in 1935; *Estrangement* in 1926; *The Death of Synge* in 1928; and *The Bounty of Sweden* in 1924. I am aware that in citing Yeats's ideas as recorded in these various volumes, I must use some caution. On the whole, however, I have marshalled evidence from the *Autobiography* as representing Yeats's thought at the time under discussion, not the date of writing (which cannot always be determined accurately), or the date of publication. So, for example, though Yeats published his memories of the eighties and nineties in 1922 and in 1935, I have assumed that, on the whole, we may take them as accurate accounts of the state of his mind during those two closing decades of the last century. It would seem that the opposite risks are greater still: some critics have quoted Yeats's remarks from the *Autobiography* with no eye to date at all, so that at times views meant to represent Yeats's opinions in the nineties have been cited as if, indeed, they were Yeats's views in 1935 or 1938.

tably it is visited by the "sudden change." Gone now is the mind "made like 'a perfectly proportioned human body,'" for the time is now not with but against Unity: it is the beginning of poses and masks, of the artistic imagination as an isolated, disguised force turning in the gyre that runs against history.[27] The seeds of this dissolution were sown in the promising fertile soil of Renaissance individualism. Even as a young man Yeats had wondered about the splintered impression he got from the multiple plots of Elizabethan drama. Compared to the "elaborate unity of Greek drama," the Elizabethan had no intensity to equal it.[28] A lessening of intensity persisted after Shakespeare; the shift in focus was radical. "Imagination" itself "sank"; the "supreme intensity" characteristic of the greatest Renaissance poets and painters and sculptors "passed to another faculty"—discursive reasoning, intellect. It seemed as if Shakespeare, Dante, or Michelangelo "had been reborn with all their old sublimity, their old vastness of conception, but [were] speaking a harsh, almost unintelligible, language." With the advent of science, the greatest efforts of the human mind will cease to be imaginative, and the greatest achievements will be the "movement of philosophy from Spinoza to Hegel."[29]

Shakespeare had already foreshadowed the shift: his originality, the garment of his individual vision, went counter to Yeats's delight in traditional subject-matter. Artistic technique, the executor of originality, interfered with tradition and convention. Because there was something irresistibly attractive in the spectacle of the individual hero Yeats preferred Shakespeare to Chaucer, but begrudged his preference because the dramatist, even more than the poet, had carried the violation of Unity further. "Had not Europe shared one mind and heart, until both . . . began to break into fragments a little before Shakespeare's birth?" In order to make his verse more meditative, even Chaucer had already "robbed . . . [it] of its speed," splitting the unity of music and verse he had inherited from the oral tradition. For the sake of exploring "undisturbed" the "effects of tangibility," "painting [had] parted from religion in the later Renaissance." And, in keeping with the modern temper, painting had, in our own time, sought to "characterize, where it had once personified," rejecting "all that inherited subject-matter which we have named poetry."[30]

Yeats saw his own time as another turn of the wheel similar to

[27] *Ibid.*, pp. 175–176.
[28] *On the Boiler*, pp. 28–29.
[29] "Bishop Berkeley," *Essays and Introductions*, p. 396.
[30] *Autobiography*, p. 117.

that of the Renaissance, repeating the dissolutions of the thirteenth century. The years 1875–1927 resembled 1250–1300: they were both, he says in *A Vision*, periods of "abstraction"—"preceded and followed by abstraction." Standing at the threshold of the first "climax" or "weariness," the modern generation is poised between a conclusion and a beginning, "and when the climax passes [we] will recognize that there common secular thought began to break and disperse."[31] All such change ensues from an age of progress, a time when men still sought to reform, to impose themselves upon the world. Only very recently has a change become apparent. Even Tolstoy could still be guided by "belief" and "preference": the author counted; his position mattered. With Flaubert, the dispassionate objectivity or neutrality of the artist first took recognizable shapes. Yet the unity of an art with no personal point of view was a partial illusion: it was "synthesis for its own sake, . . . books where the author has disappeared, painting where some accomplished brush paints with an equal pleasure, or with a bored impartiality, the human form or an old bottle, dirty weather and clean sunshine." For art the results were both good and bad: bad because the vanished author substituted for his point of view not a cultural but a technical unity; good because, "Having bruised their hands upon . . . limit, men, for the first time since the seventeenth century, see the world as an object of contemplation, not as something to be remade. . . ."[32] Nietzsche had noted, and rejected, this modern preoccupation with objectivity, both in history and in art:

> Might not an illusion lurk in the highest interpretation of the word "objectivity"? . . . We think of the aesthetic phenomenon of the detachment from all personal concern with which the painter sees the picture and forgets himself, in a stormy landscape, amid thunder and lightning, or on a rough sea; and we require the same artistic vision and absorption in his object from the historian. But it is only a superstition to say that the picture given to such a man by the object really shows the truth of things. Unless it be that objects are expected in such moments to paint or photograph themselves by their own activity on a purely passive medium![33]

[31]*A Vision*, pp. 299–300.

[32]*Ibid.*, p. 300.

[33]Friedrich Nietzsche, *The Use and Abuse of History*, tr. Adrian Collins (Library of Liberal Arts, no. 11; New York and Indianapolis, Ind., 1949, 1957), p. 37. "Und sollte nicht selbst bei der höchsten Ausdeutung des Wortes Objektivität eine Illusion mit unterlaufen? . . . man meint jenes ästhetische Phänomen, jenes Losgebundensein vom persönlichen Interesse, mit dem der Maler in einer stürmischen Landschaft, unter Blitz und Donner, oder auf bewegter See sein inneres Bild schaut, man meint

Such objectivity, said Nietzsche, is a "myth," and to pursue it in earnest would result, as Yeats saw, in the worst of abstractions, in a surrender of personality to the "world-process," to use a word that was beginning to be applied to history.

Certain references to modern art and artists in the 1925 edition of *A Vision* were eliminated from the 1937 revision and from all subsequent editions, and the excisions show a significant shift in Yeats's attitude toward his contemporaries. In 1925 he still equated some of them with the sin of abstraction. Placing Pound, Eliot, Joyce, and Pirandello together in a group, he regards them in 1925 as artists who "either eliminate from metaphor the poet's phantasy and substitute a strangeness discovered by historical or contemporary research or who break up the logical processes of thought by flooding them with associated ideas or words that seem to drift into the mind by chance." What he meant by the "poet's phantasy" is uncertain, except that it may be taken, at least in one sense, to be that which the substitutes are *not*: imaginatively reconstructed visions of life that depend neither on current nor on historical fact, nor on the accidental patterns that life is heir to. In 1925 the vanishing artist still bedevilled Yeats. Not yet quite certain whether this non-personal element was indeed the impersonal quality he had himself been seeking, his judgment of contemporary artists tended to be veiled with cautious hostility. Certainly he had not yet fully recognized how close to his own were certain of their aims: that, for one thing, their disruption of unity was made for the sake of rearranging the pattern in a more meaningful unity. Their means sometimes blocked full understanding of what they were doing, though his fear of technical dictatorship was well founded:

> They [Brancusi, Wyndham Lewis and others] are all absorbed in some technical research to the entire exclusion of the personal dream. It is as though the forms in the stone or in their reverie began to move with an energy . . . not that of the human mind. Very often these forms are mechanical . . . mathematical. . . . [They were] . . . masters of a geometrical pattern or rhythm which seems to impose itself wholly from beyond the mind, the artist "standing outside himself."[34]

---

das völlige Versunkensein in die Dinge: ein Aberglaube jedoch ist es, dass das Bild, welches die Dinge in einem solchermassen gestimmten Menschen zeigen, das empirische Wesen der Dinge wiedergebe. Oder sollten sich in jenen Momenten die Dinge gleichsam durch ihre eigene Tätigkeit auf einem reinen Passivum abzeichnen, abkonterfeien, abphotographieren?"

[34]*A Vision* (London: T. Werner Laurie, 1925), p. 211. All previous and subsequent citations from *A Vision* are from the *revised* edition unless otherwise noted.

Pound he held responsible to the end for the "lack of form" and "obscurity" of the new younger poets. They were, he said, elsewhere, all victims of the flood: "Nature, steel-bound or stone-built in the nineteenth century, became a flux where man drowned or swam; the moment had come for some poet to cry 'the flux is in my own mind.'" Such a poet, it turned out, was Turner, riding "in an observation balloon, blue heaven above, earth beneath an abstract pattern." Abstraction seemed now to have reached its limits: nature and the "sensual scene" have been abandoned for technical pattern; "the individual is nothing" in this poetry, only an abstract topography, "objects without contour," remain—"human experience" itself has ceased to be part of specific lives and is "cut off into this place and that place, the flux."[35] Such an art, while it sometimes dazzled him, did not satisfy Yeats's genuine belief in tradition and convention, the type of art he found in Japan—"serene . . . no exasperation, no academic tyranny, its tradition as naturally observed as the laws of a game." What he feared most in the new art—though more strongly in 1925 than later—was its direction toward a dead end. He recognized that for an art to be "transmittable" and "teachable"[36] it had to obey, with grace, certain agreed-upon conventions; in Joyce and Pound and Eliot he found an art too inimitable, and with a conscience sensitive to the need for a line of tradition, he held back his full assent to the end. The arrogance of Renaissance individualism, he felt, had finally transcended the self into what in 1925 seemed almost hopeless abstraction.

But in 1930 Pirandello and Wyndham Lewis excited him once again: they exemplified "the transition from individualism to universal plasticity"[37]—a transition that describes Yeats's own development as truly as theirs. Increasingly, Yeats strove to rid his poetry of "modern subjectivity"—that dragon of Error which, in his own time, has engendered abstraction on the one hand and decadent psychology on the other—what Goethe had called "unhealthy" art. The resurgence of interest in the oral tradition, in song and ballad, in the mid and late thirties was a deliberate attempt to recover the spirit of "universal plasticity." "I want to make a last song," Yeats writes in 1935, "sweet and exultant, a sort of European *geeta* . . . not doctrine but song."[38] But "universal plasticity" was not to be equated with utter anonymity,

[35] *The Oxford Book of Modern Verse, 1892–1935*, chosen by W. B. Yeats, pp. xxv–xxx. To avoid unnecessary notes I refer to these pages inclusively.

[36] *Autobiography*, p. 333.

[37] *The Letters of W. B. Yeats*, ed. Allan Wade, p. 776.

[38] *Ibid.*, p. 836.

nor with the impersonal massiveness of the East. Plasticity would help to soften the rigid features of the stubbornly eccentric, so that one might make an art individual but still teachable and transmittable because that individuality would operate within a procession of universal symbols, like Dante's or Blake's.

Always there has been a contest between East and West: both offered alternatives. From the East came massiveness as well as the exquisitely individual; from the West intellectual abstraction and passionate individuality. Often, in attempts to stave off the "spiritual turbulence" of the West, the artist looked East for the delicate and the subdued—for the perfection of design. In the days of the Cheshire Cheese and earlier, Yeats recalls the "selection for admiration of old masterpieces where 'tonal values,' or the sense of weight and bulk that is the particular discovery of Europe, are the least apparent: some flower of Botticelli's, perhaps, that seems a separate intellectual existence." Even Spenser's "sensuous deliberation," "the magic of *Christabel* or *Kubla Khan*" seem in their "wisdom, magic, sensation" to be "Asiatic." Increasingly, Yeats thinks, "We have borrowed directly from the East and selected for admiration or repetition everything in our own past that is least European, as though groping backward towards our common mother."[39] That "sense of weight and bulk" characterizing the "spiritual turbulence" of a Michelangelo is again the overripeness of a development that began in individual form and ended in abstraction. The movement has not yet abated. Modern poetry, still riding on the crest of this wave, is obsessed with "philosophy." All ensuing ills, all deviations from that point of unity somewhere in the "vast design" of the Byzantine mosaic, are traceable to this undiminished momentum, this surging beyond of what began as a motion toward synthesis. Some have always tried to break out; the Impressionists, for instance, who failed.[40]

The East-West dualism in Yeats was never to be wholly resolved; if one views it sympathetically, it may be considered a profitable irresolution, a tension that gave the poetry much of its intensity. For abstraction was not monopolized by the West. Granted that Hegelian idealism sacrifices the individual soul for the sake of "systems of thought" and a self-conscious sense of history, the East has a way of losing itself in "Asiatic vague immensities." Certain "typical books" of our time Yeats described as being very Eastern indeed: ". . . *Ulysses*, Mrs. Virginia Woolf's *Waves*, Mr. Ezra Pound's *Draft of*

[39]"An Indian Monk," *Essays and Introductions*, pp. 432–433.
[40]*Autobiography*, pp. 334–335.

XXX Cantos—suggest . . . a deluge of experience breaking over us and within us, melting limits. . . ." Essentially this was an art where not only the artist but the man, the object of art, melts, spills, overflows. Here man is "no hard bright mirror dawdling by the dry sticks of a hedge, but a swimmer, or rather the waves themselves." That is the point: man has disappeared into the elements in which he exists —an inversion of classical myth where he often emerges out of those very elements. "In this new literature . . . man in himself is nothing."[41] Written for the Introduction to *Fighting the Waves* this remark suggests at least one of Yeats's own intended meanings of this play: though Cuchulain is defeated he fights the waves, a desperate attempt to avoid the engulfment, the "helplessness" of modern man, in the face of which Yeats himself was sometimes helpless.

Modern art has achieved opposing aims: it has replaced true "Geist" with "Zeitgeist," but it has regained a kind of infinity for man by de-individualizing the individual in the process. Yeats fashioned something of a compromise: subdued by the waves, the single spirit surrenders to the vaster one. This much is defeat. But the waves having "mastered" the swimmer accept him as well, carry him to Byzantium so that he may find his soul again. To die is to have lived through the death. What, therefore, remains genuinely individual in modern art is the spiritual pride inherited from the Renaissance ego, but losing itself in a vastness of its own making even this pride sometimes disappears. Yeats was both caught and repelled by these waves, the Joycean profusion which, however, he eventually preferred to the "pale victims of modern fiction—that suffer that they may have minds like photographic plates."[42] When he glimpsed the purpose behind the "flooding" of minds like Bloom's in *Ulysses,* he suddenly recognized something Asiatic pretending to be European. Prefacing *The Words upon the Window-Pane* he wrote: "to-day imagination is turning full of uncertainty to something it thinks European, and whether that something will be 'arty' and provincial, or a form of life, is as yet undiscoverable."[43] Virginia Woolf, Lawrence, Pound, even Eliot: in them Yeats found the last barrier of art still intact (the realists had given in from another direction), for they at least had style—still that.

All was not lost: "If abstraction had reached . . . its climax escape might be possible for . . . individual men. . . ." Though Chaucer's characters had "disengaged themselves" from the "crowd," had "each

[41]See *Wheels and Butterflies,* p. 65.
[42]*Letters,* p. 827.
[43]See *Wheels and Butterflies,* p. 5.

in turn [become] the centre of some Elizabethan play, and had after split into their elements and so given birth to romantic poetry," must he "reverse the cinematograph?" Yeats asked. Metaphorically, the film image was analogous to the gyres, to the spool, the bobbin, winding and unwinding, discovering its way back. Yeats thought that literature must again embark on this "reversal, men being . . . displayed in casual, temporary, contact as at the Tabard door." Though he might prefer Shakespeare's individual heroes, was it now time to return to Chaucer's "crowd"? A reading of Tolstoy's *Anna Karenina* confirmed "such a turning back" wherever Tolstoy's "theoretical capacity" had given way, wherever abstract philosophy had not interfered. There was still a chance of again following the pilgrims "to some unknown shrine": both nation and individual, "with great emotional intensity," might yet "give to all those separated elements and to all that abstract love and melancholy, a symbolical, a mythological coherence."[44]

In the interim we might contemplate our lot. The man who had passed from Chaucer's great procession through Shakespeare's single hero tragedies to the unique Romantic Manfred had finally become a moribund hero—a decadent. When this accelerated movement away from coherence had reached its point of no return, it left only the rather barren fruits of fragmentation and isolation. Yeats placed part of the blame on the nineties, on "our form of lyric, our insistence upon emotion which has no relation to any public interest." Lionel Johnson's insistence that "life is ritual" stood in mocking contradiction to the ritual of the lives he and the Rhymers actually lived. Pater was the great tempter. His philosophy "taught us to walk upon a rope, tightly stretched through serene air, and we were left to keep our feet upon a swaying rope in a storm."[45] From this experience Yeats learned that the "symbolical . . . mythological coherence" could not be found where, for a time, he sought it: in the "autumn of the body," in Villiers de l'Isle-Adam, who "created persons from whom has fallen all even of personal characteristic."[46] As Yeats was soon to discover, such characters had no energy. The cinematograph had shown clearly that the individual who had slowly disengaged himself from a common culture ended up being, at the turn of the century, a lonely and bloodless creature. True he had transcended both Renaissance egoism and Romantic uniqueness, but his individualism—if one could now call it that—was, alas, no return to Chaucer's crowd but rather a

[44]*Autobiography*, pp. 118–119.
[45]*Ibid.*, pp. 180–181.
[46]"The Autumn of the Body," *Essays*, p. 233.

dehumanization of self. Axel would undertake no pilgrimages except toward death. In time, the shadowy characters of the nineties would become entirely abstract—deliberately so. And in the first version of *A Vision,* Yeats saw this trend exemplified in the turning to myth in Joyce or Eliot: "It is as though myth and fact, united until the exhaustion of the Renaissance, have now fallen so far apart that man understands for the first time the rigidity of fact, and calls up, by that very recognition, myth . . . which now but gropes its way out of the mind's dark but will shortly pursue and terrify."[47] Though, as I have already indicated, he came to understand his contemporaries better, Yeats never entirely retreated from this equation of modern art with abstraction, lacking not only the human element of individuality but the sense of history as well.

By 1937 Yeats is beginning "to see things double—doubled in history, world history, personal history."[48] Increasingly, sometimes against his will, his sense of history deepens—the last poems confirm this; the Europe he is witnessing is no longer what it was, and he knows it. And the knowledge accounts for a temporary bitterness.[49] Some twenty years back, Tolstoy, Dostoevski, and Flaubert were read with pleasure, but to Balzac alone does he return. For, where the French and Russians push a view of life "peculiar to the author," "Balzac leaves us when the book is closed amid the crowd that fills the boxes and the galleries of grand opera. . . ." Because "there is so much history in its veins," that crowd "is always right." With Flaubert or Tolstoy the work becomes a point for scholars to argue: "readers stand above the theme or beside it, they judge and they reject. . . ." Rescued from abstraction by the detailed scope of Balzac's vision, he could see that Balzac's themes "have become philosophy without ceasing to be history." It is not merely bulk and multitude which achieve this: it is "because that first sketch that gives unity is an adaptation to his [Balzac's] need and time of all that moulded Europe."[50] Somehow that Europe had to be recovered. The "main road," he told Dorothy Wellesley, is still the "road of naturalness and swiftness" which for thirty centuries has flourished richly, magni-

[47] *A Vision* (1925 ed.), p. 212.

[48] *Letters*, p. 887.

[49] Karl Jaspers writes: "Two . . . European phenomena are rooted in freedom—consciousness of history, and the will to knowledge"; *The European Spirit,* tr. Ronald Gregor Smith (London, 1948), p. 39. Freedom (as for Yeats) is for Jaspers an essential European drive, and consciousness of history an inevitable consequence; the "will to knowledge" is, of course, a dependent drive of historical self-consciousness.

[50] "Louis Lambert," *Essays and Introductions,* pp. 445–446.

ficently. To "'think like a wise man, yet express ourselves like the common people'"—Lady Gregory had said this to him many years ago: it was still his creed. The others were goldsmiths "working with a glass screwed into one eye," observing and recording, but knowing nothing about being "secret" or how to "exult." In the true procession march the swordsmen—the image is almost melodramatic—and, above all, "we need, like Milton, Shakespeare, Shelley, vast sentiments, generalizations supported by tradition."[51]

In spirit, at least, Yeats dissociated himself from the English tradition—though he knew well enough all his life what his real debts were—and distinguished it from the Irish which he considered to have moved in a different direction, having begun in "folkthought." In England Eliot's "realism" and the "social passion" of the war poets had put an end to romantic art and had opened the way for an "impersonal philosophical" poetry. But the Irish have not succumbed: they have "hardened and deepened their personalities," and through poets like Stephens and Synge have "restored the emotion of heroism to lyric poetry."[52] That heroism, it is clear, is both epic and romantic in spirit, using those terms as Yeats understood them: capacious and "self-asserting." Hard and deep, both these poets were able to make an art at once intense and full of scope: they fulfilled the basic requirements of the aesthetic Yeats was to fashion for himself.

Through methods uniquely his own, Yeats developed an aesthetic of equipoise: epic grandeur (reverie), lyric sweetness (ecstasy) and dramatic intensity (passion). Synthesis—or Unity of Being—was salvation: through a balanced interplay of epic, lyric and dramatic, abstraction might be defeated, egoism avoided, and tradition preserved. Undoubtedly Yeats conceived of himself as one of those individuals "turning back," reversing the cinematograph, seeking the "mythological coherence" which the Renaissance had defeated and the modern period prevented. Meanwhile the juggling was not always without dangers; more than once one element or another slipped through Yeats's fingers, and he was not always aware of it.

III

A theory of art which proposed a surge toward widening dimensions and an opposite narrowing toward a centre or apex of intensity was particularly suited to Yeats, who was to fashion a theory of history

[51]*Letters*, p. 853.
[52]"Modern Poetry," *Essays and Introductions*, pp. 506–507.

and personality governed by the interlocking movement of two gyres and the waxing and waning of the moon. Although this "System," which has gained Yeats a good deal of notoriety, was not completed until 1925, long after the basic aesthetic philosophy had been thought out and promulgated, the generally cyclic nature of both the aesthetic and the philosophy was no mere coincidence—Yeats thought in cyclic metaphors.

In this century, the ancient cyclical views of life and history have again become fashionable: Spengler and Toynbee, Yeats and Joyce—philosophers and writers alike have been tempted. This return to a circular vision of life is more than mere nostalgia: we are attempting to reconcile the indefinite line of progress to the firmer limits of the cycle; to join perpendicular movement to the more static concept of the circle, where movement is essentially carried out in a succession of arcs that lead back to the point of departure. Even Nietzsche found himself somewhat betrayed by his "ewige Wiederkehr," which had the effect of sabotaging Zarathustra's limitless ascent. But, a peculiar restlessness, characteristically occidental, makes the implicit stillness of the circle too hard a discipline to endure for long. Our "passion" —it is Yeats's word—will not let us; the price we pay for our impatience is a submission to the futile, aimless oscillation of the Will that masters the Schopenhauerian universe. So even within the circle there is the open demand for motion, and too often we have ended up like Huxley's furiously pedalling hero at the end of *Antic Hay*, spinning the wheels and going nowhere—an objectification, as W. Y. Tindall suggests, of modern futility. Yet even Huxley's machine is a therapeutic bicycle, and Tindall is right to call a system of cycles "a comforting system. . . ." At least the circle provides the illusion of movement and the certainty of return. Any theory of linear progress, however optimistic in its previsioning of the future, of higher and better things to come, is ultimately pessimistic for the man to whom history is a live continuum: with each step upwards we leave behind us something dead and irretrievable.

Ultimately, the current reaction against the tyranny of progress via linear ascent is no mere expression of restlessness at what seems an endless pursuit of infinity, but a genuine sense of anxiety at not arriving anywhere at the end. To buy a one-way ticket is to surrender a measure of certainty—the old dispensations were more encouraging:

> ...either with the soul from the myth to union with the source of all, the breaking of the circle, or from the myth to reflection and the circle renewed for better or worse. For better or worse according to one's life,

but never progress as we understand it, never the straight line, always a necessity to break away and destroy, or to sink in and forget.[53]

All returns to older traditions are a form of reassurance: man takes fright at the gaping distance between his avowed position of advance and his origins—it is like standing on a ladder whose top and bottom rungs are equally shrouded in a mist. To reassure himself man climbs down, testing his ability to recognize, in spite of distance, his remote beginnings. So with the cycle of a man's life; poets have always used it symbolically as a comforting metaphor, a realization that man's life, having unwound itself, is gathering up once more; that death closes, not widens, the gap between his present and his past. Winding and unwinding motions dominate Yeats's thought and especially his poetry; these motions were, in effect, his defences against the modern urbanized world in endless flight from the past. Yeats himself grew up amongst the ultra-sophisticated, and his efforts to re-establish a relationship with the ancient soil were but one result of the sophisticated dream reversed toward the prelapsarian state. Back to innocence is to bend the straight line into the curve of circle; and that shaping is a creative effort which shows in his art.

In addition to the gyres, Yeats conceived of a different geometric pattern to account for the relationship between movement and stillness: "God is a circle whose centre is everywhere." While the saint resides in the centre, the poet moves to the circumference, to the ring "where everything comes round again." He is not to "seek" but to contemplate the procession with delight: "all that is for ever passing away that it may come again." From his peripheral position the artist must be content with the recurring tides. "Is it," Yeats asked, "that all things are made by the struggle of the individual and the world, of the unchanging and the returning. . . ?"[54] Yeats's poetic landscape offers the answer: tree and roots and branches; sky and soil; dancer and the Great Wheel; and, above all, flood and tide. Cuchulain's struggle with the waves becomes an emblem of man's immersion into and emergence from the flux of motion. When Byron first attempted to swim the Hellespont he was defeated by the tide and the north wind; so he tried again in calmer weather and succeeded. Cuchulain makes no choices of this kind: his tragic expectations are not given a second opportunity, and his plunge into the sea is a final commitment to the dolphin-torn and gong-tormented tide. True, the enchafed flood, the "filthy modern tide," as Yeats called it, is perpetually threatening to

[53]Introduction to *The Cat and the Moon*, in *Wheels and Butterflies*, p. 125.
[54]*Discoveries*, in *Essays*, pp. 356–357.

annihilate us, but its movement (as Conrad understood) is as necessary as the stillness of permanence:

> ...if no change appears
> No moon; only an aching heart
> Conceives a changeless work of art.

The enormous tension of endlessly balancing flux and permanence, motion and stillness, of retrieving the echo and directing it back to the centre—all this was exhausting and risky business, and no one was more responsibly aware of these risks in the balancing of opposites than was Yeats. Modern art, painting and sculpture in particular, had already lost the juggling game, had let the pieces, cubed and split from the perfection of form, fly off in all directions. As late as 1934, however, Yeats seemed still optimistic: "Perhaps now that the abstract intellect has split the mind into categories, the body into cubes, we may be about to turn back towards the unconscious, the whole, the miraculous. . . ."[55] To turn back to these was worth a risk.

IV

The first two major works Yeats wrote exemplified for him the peculiar problem he faced as an artist lured to different roads, both of theme and of method:

> [*The Countess Kathleen*] is an attempt to mingle personal thought and feeling with the beliefs and customs of Christian Ireland; whereas... [*The Wanderings of Oisin*] endeavoured to set forth the impress left on my imagination by the Pre-Christian cycle of legends. The Christian cycle... needed, I thought, a dramatic vehicle. The tumultous [*sic*] and heroic Pagan cycle...expressed itself naturally—or so I imagined—in epic and epic-lyric measures. No epic method seemed sufficiently minute and subtle for the one, and no dramatic method elastic and all-containing enough for the other.[56]

[55]Introduction to *The Cat and the Moon*, in *Wheels and Butterflies*, p. 126.

[56]Preface to *The Countess Kathleen and Various Legends and Lyrics*, 1892, in *Variorum Edition of the Poems*, p. 845. Yeats does not identify what he refers to as the "chief poem" of this volume, but it is clear from the context that he means *The Countess Kathleen*. That play was originally written in blank verse and it is not unusual for Yeats to refer to a play as a "poem"; moreover the play is an apt example of a work attempting to express Christian Ireland. The only alternative possibility would be "The Death of Cuchullin" (later changed to "Cuchulain's Fight with the Sea"); this poem, of less than one hundred lines, is written in couplets, and though we might call it dramatic narrative it is hardly "a dramatic vehicle" and contains nothing particularly Christian in its theme.

Here then were the choices, but Yeats could not go on writing separate works to suit each method: the possibility of combination, had it not occured to him in theory, would in time have forced itself upon him in practice. In fact, he never again wrote anything like *The Wanderings of Oisin* and perhaps nothing quite like *The Countess Kathleen.* But Celtic themes came to interpose and, briefly, to offer some solutions:

There was something in what I felt about Deirdre, about Cuchulain, that rejected the Renaissance and its characteristic metres, and this was a principal reason why I created in dance plays the form that varies blank verse with lyric metres. When I speak in blank verse and analyse my feelings, I stand at a moment of history when instinct, its traditional songs and dances, its general agreement, is of the past.... The contrapuntal structure of the verse... combines the past and present.[57]

It was the same reason that had led Milton to abandon rhyme (thinks Yeats); and he is convinced that rhyme is "one of the secondary causes of that disintegration of the personal instincts" which has filled modern poetry with "deep colour for colour's sake . . . overflowing pattern . . . background of decorative landscape, and . . . insubordination of detail."[58] In other words stylization has supplanted style; what appeared to be "personal" was only falsely so, and the truly "personal instinct" might after all be retained through a blank verse lightened by lyric metres. The combination of past and present would achieve something close to the wedding of anonymity and personal utterance.

For Goethe, wrote Pater in "Winckelmann," the question was: "Can the blitheness and universality of the antique ideal be communicated to artistic productions, which shall contain the fulness of the experience of the modern world?" It was no less a question for Yeats, though he might have phrased it somewhat differently. Unity of Being would be achieved only when anonymous and personal, epic, lyric, and dramatic, join in the making of a new art, an art preeminently European in that it would contain the whole of Europe, including what Arnold somewhat quaintly called the "Celtic" element. For "the Celtic alone," Yeats wrote in 1897, in "The Celtic Element in Literature," "has been for centuries close to the main river of European literature."

As Yeats himself suggested on a number of occasions, the *Comédie*

[57]"A General Introduction for my Work," *Essays and Introductions,* pp. 523–524.
[58]"Edmund Spenser," *Essays,* pp. 443–444.

Humaine—that most European of works—was his prompt book. Balzac, he confessed, was his rescuer:

Is it that whenever I have been tempted to go to Japan, China, or India for my philosophy, Balzac has brought me back, reminded me of my preoccupation with national, social, personal problems, convinced me that I cannot escape from our *Comédie humaine?*[59]

In Yeats's analysis of the structure and meaning of the *Comédie Humaine,* one glimpses at its best the orientation that fed and sustained his beliefs about art. He saw the entire epic as a vast design of society dominated by a Darwinian struggle in which "each character [is] an expression of will." And will is "passion which is but blind will . . . always at crisis, or approaching crisis; everything else seems eliminated, or is made fantastic or violent [so] that the will, without seeming to do so, may exceed nature."[60] Thus the vast epic design reduces itself ultimately to the intense passion of a single, powerful image of will.

Clearly, to achieve the single image one had first to possess the power of creating the vast design. Although "no man believes willingly in evil or in suffering," the "strength and weight of Dante and of Balzac comes from [such] unwilling belief." When he compared modern writers—Balzac excepted—to Dante, Villon, Shakespeare, or Cervantes Yeats found, instead of "strength and weight," something "slight and shadowy."[61] Dante and Balzac move us through their sheer power of expansion which holds inherent in it the promise of intense contraction. The "fiery centre" and the "egoistic mood" which to Blake had seemed so heretical were in the end inescapable. If false egoism masquerading as genuine personal voice were rejected, then Yeats might yet effect a proper relationship between the desire to surrender all for the sake of *Allgemeinheit* and the need to retain more than a mere portion of one's individuality. To wed once again—or for the first time—the strength of the epic with the sweetness of the lyric, the power of dramatic intensity with the ecstasy of personal suffering: such was his aim, still finally Blakean, still European:

...to commingle the ancient phantasies of poetry with the rough, vivid, ever-contemporaneous tumult of the roadside;...[to] dream of...an art that murmured, though with worn and failing voice, of the day when Quixote and Sancho Panza, long estranged, may once again go out gaily

59"The Holy Mountain," *Essays and Introductions*, p. 448.
60"Louis Lambert," *ibid.*, p. 444.
61*If I Were Four-and-Twenty*, pp. 15–17.

into the bleak air. Ever since I began to write I have awaited with impatience a linking all Europe over of the hereditary knowledge of the countryside . . . with our old lyricism so full of ancient frenzies and hereditary wisdom; a yoking of antiquities; a Marriage of Heaven and Hell.[62]

The opportunity of such a marriage between the "rough . . . tumult" of the "countryside" and the "old lyricism" of "ancient frenzies" seemed to await Yeats propitiously at the very outset of his career when, in casting about for a subject-matter, his imagination seized eagerly upon folklore and mythology, Irish peasants and Celtic heroes. But some marriages are preceded by long periods of doubt and struggle and this marriage was not to be consummated easily.

62*Plays in Prose and Verse*, p. 435.

2 ❀ MARKET CART AND SKY: The Two Ways of Art

An art may become impersonal because it has too much circumstances or too little, because the world is too little or too much with it, because it is too near the ground or too far up among the branches. *Discoveries*

Art is a lofty tree, and may shoot up far beyond our grasp, but its roots are in daily life and experience. Arthur Hallam, "On Some of the Characteristics of Modern Poetry and The Lyrical Poems of Alfred Tennyson"

As you know all my art theories depend upon just this—rooting of mythology in the earth. Letter to T. Sturge Moore (1927)

If Yeats might choose a subject-matter that was suitable to both his talents and his artistic ideals, then the aesthetic problems of forging an art out of that subject-matter would be relatively simple to solve. So at least it appeared. Unfortunately the search for a subject-matter was complicated by three major inconveniences: first there was the clamour of a political nationalism seeking a literature that would serve its own ends; second the Celtic Revival offered the poet two rather differing points of interest which eventually he would have to reconcile —the peasant or the king; and third Yeats's new enchantment with some of the recent *symboliste* principles of art made the pursuit of certain sympathies for the common peasant a rather uncomfortable and strained effort. Yeats's first aim was to define what he considered "national"—no easy task; his second was either to make a clear choice between folklore and mythology, or to bring the two together, to combine "two ways of art" by combining two subjects of art, so that he could indeed have an art neither "too near the ground" nor "too far up among the branches" and still retain at least one major *symboliste* attitude: its hostility to the middle class and to realism.

Yeats certainly could not plunge deeply into the aesthetics of poetry until he had settled these preliminary problems, so far as they could be settled; he knew that a choice of theme and subject would shape and modify his method, and he was never technician enough to think of beginning where he knew he should end: with the principles of his craft. The issues were pressing enough, for the young Yeats found himself almost immediately involved in the growing nationalist movement of Ireland which artists and intellectuals were prepared to interpret and to translate into cultural terms; that cultural aims should clash with political realities was inevitable. As an artist, Yeats was little inclined, even at first, to compromise his integrity in exchange for immediate gains; he was, constitutionally, an unpolitical creature. Despite this reluctance, however, he quickly became absorbed in the dream of a Celtic revival, and once his heart was committed he felt free to join the common enterprise.

To his own conceptions of a renewed Celtic culture he brought, besides his loyalty to artistic freedom, a sense of tradition—an edifice largely of his own making, really, which he aimed to erect as a mansion in the New Holy City he envisioned in his dreams. Instead, the mansion became a fortress: tradition, it turned out, was the strongest defence against an encroaching secular nationalism prepared to turn modern Ireland in directions wholly opposite to what Yeats imagined for her. Like one of Spenser's allegorical Houses in *The Faerie Queene*, Yeats's House of Tradition was turned into a place of purgation, standing defiantly and at war in an allegorical struggle against Realism, Political Nationalism, and Secularism. It was his version of Axel's castle, though he could not have thought of it as such until, in 1894, he saw a performance of *Axel* in Paris.

When, in 1921, Yeats published his Noh plays, he had reached—from one point of view—what may justly be called the point farthest from his original intentions. The early dream of a Celtic Twilight had remained a dream only, and the twilight had deepened into a final darkness rather than a new dawn. Hopeful at the start that he might, through a choice of subject, elevate into the common consciousness a genuinely Celtic mythos, bound by both traditional and national allegiances to the Irish past—and present—Yeats had found, by 1915, no sustained support for his efforts, and in that year he wrote the first of his Noh plays, *At the Hawk's Well.* But his note to *The Only Jealousy of Emer* (1919) in *Four Plays for Dancers* still expressed the ideal subject-audience relationship that had governed his initial beliefs: "In writing these little plays I knew that I was creating something which could only fully succeed in a civilization very unlike ours. I think they should be written for some country where all classes share in a half-mythological, half-philosophical folk-belief which the writer and his small audience lift into a new subtlety."[1] True, the audience he envisioned at first was neither so small nor so select as he suggested in 1919, but the "half-mythological, half-philosophical folk-belief" was the assumption on which he had founded his convictions on the subject for the new literature.

By generating an energy of passionate dimensions, the articulated memories of his imagination, originating from a remote but rooted past, would, he thought, recover for Ireland the heroic age that both the cultural tradition and the nationalist necessity could support. Most directly and fruitfully the epic vision was to be fed by the Celtic mythology which was being rediscovered when Yeats first began to write. Vague but grand, remote but exciting, Celtic mythology and peasant folklore unified for Yeats the ideal feudal relationships which were to govern his poetics as well as his politics. The poem, with its internal schemata of obligations and exchanges and its hierarchy of images delicately balanced between the most rooted and earthy and the most rarefied and spiritual orders of experience, would resemble the very society of aristocrat and peasant that had created it as a type.

Without being quite aware of it, Yeats was already shaping his aesthetic from the moment he chose his themes. To see the world of lords and ladies as containing and depending upon the peasants and the soil; to imagine a society of an heroic age that was truly free of class wars: these were the visions of a poet who wished, quite literally, "to sing" of "what is past, or passing, or to come." For the true poet must combine, and surpass, all three functions of the ancient epic bard: historian, contemporary, and prophet.

The demands of such a role seemed naïvely antithetical to the needs of a national renaissance. All but forgotten, the Irish past was no living force in the Ireland of the late nineteenth century—and Yeats knew it. The first aim, he felt, must be to educate the people, to bring them to the knowledge of "the imaginative periods of Irish history... with the heart...."[2] But the discovery of their own culture must lead

[1]Note on *The Only Jealousy of Emer* in *Four Plays for Dancers* (London, 1921), p. 106.

[2]*Letters to the New Island*, p. 107. Many of Yeats's occasional reviews and essays have not been collected, especially those dating from c. 1886–1899. These were published in *The Bookman*, *The Dome*, *The Sketch*, *United Ireland* and other periodicals and newspapers. It might be useful some day to collect all of Yeats's prose, but for the present study I have found the evidence in the collected volumes of essays ample and rich. Certainly the *Letters to the New Island* represent, I think, the best of Yeats's early criticism; most of the remaining uncollected pieces were brief

the Irish beyond it: they must forsake provincialism, weld Catholic and Protestant sensibilities, and acknowledge their European origins. In attempting to bring Irish art to such an embracing consciousness, Yeats made formidable enemies, chiefly among the nationalists and the Catholics. Both insisted on misunderstanding the meaning of the "tradition" which they were eager to resurrect for their own purposes, not the poet's. Art was to serve not to lead. Yet what was art? What was tradition?

"Supreme art," Yeats insisted, "is a traditional statement of certain heroic and religious truths, passed on from age to age, modified by individual genius, but never abandoned."[3] Entered in his diary of 1909, *Estrangement*, and preceding Eliot's "Tradition and the Individual Talent" by eight years, this remark was conventional enough, but its restatement now made it seem novel and, of course, out of date. Written toward the end of his intense participation in the Abbey movement—itself a sharp reaction against prevailing dramatic conventions—Yeats's definition allows, however, for the artist's impatience with tradition, in particular with classical tradition. At the same time he clarifies the tradition which he champions and clearly distinguishes between the two:

> The revolt of individualism came because the tradition had become degraded, ... a spurious copy had been accepted in its stead. Classical morality—not quite natural in Christianised Europe—dominated this tradition at the Renaissance, and passed from Milton to Wordsworth and to Arnold ... until it became a vulgarity ... just as classical forms passed on from Raphael to the Academicians. But Anarchic revolt is coming to an end, and the arts are about to restate the traditional morality. A great work of art ... is as rooted in the early ages as the Mass which goes back to ... folklore.[4]

All literatures, he maintained, were rooted in the life of the "common man," though he never intended simply to endow the masses with poetic imagination; their function was more participation than creation. In all ancient literature he discovered the spirit of improvisation: song, dance, the whole life of a village "mingles with the middle ages until ... [one] no longer can see it as it is but as it was";[5] and so art

---

reviews of little consequence written by a needy young man; and even some of the more important items, written in the nineties, are merely germinal sketches of what was to appear in the more formal essays published in book form.

[3] *Autobiography*, p. 298.

[4] *Ibid.*

[5] "Literature and the Living Voice," *Plays and Controversies*, p. 168.

and audience are at once united in a tradition that stresses their interdependence. This dream of recapturing the middle ages had echoed through the Black Forest of *Axel* and the German romantics, who in turn had looked to the minstrels, Walther von der Vogelweide, *Parsifal* and *Tristan*. For over a century the dream had been an often fertile theme, though for Yeats, as for his predecessors, the appropriation of the middle ages was in no sense historical; it was spirit and essence which were sought. English literature, Yeats claimed, lacked this tradition more than any other European literature; the greatest English writers had always written primarily for an audience fit though few—a cultivated set oriented toward the written tradition. Although one may dispute the validity of his view, the generalization provided Yeats with his real point: that Irish literature had its roots in bardic traditions, while the English had fallen victim to the printing press.[6]

By opposing the written and unwritten traditions, he revealed his line of argument: if great literatures grow from the soil, and if great art must continue in this tradition, if, indeed, it is now necessary to return to it, then what is the tradition for Irish poets writing in English to be? Of one thing he was certain from the start: Irish poets must not begin in the written traditions of England; they must first return to their ancient themes—"heroic" and "religious"—and this would involve them not only with Irish peasants but also with Celtic kings, not only with the folk but with its aristocratic apex.

A serious suggestion that art, and an art shaped presumably in the spirit of a national renaissance, should occupy itself with ancient themes and dated traditions in a contemporary age full of urgent "problems" was bound to meet with considerable hostility. Reclaiming the ancient myths in Ireland also presented a practical problem; Celtic mythology was not Christian, and Yeats himself had realized the discomfiture of the classical tradition in a Christian world. Attempting to meet this issue, he pointed out that "the Irish peasant has invented, or . . . somebody has invented for him, a vague, though not altogether unphilosophical, reconciliation between his Paganism and his Christianity";[7] and, "The Christ who has moved the world was half Indian half Greek in temper."[8]

At the beginning, however, the problem of "paganism" was relatively minor; it was the whole idea of a "revival" that was met in some quar-

[6]*Ibid.*, pp. 169–170.
[7]*Letters*, pp. 297–298.
[8]*Ibid.*, p. 263.

ters with extreme scepticism. Was it even possible to retrieve legends, myths, and folklore from the remotest past so long neglected? Somehow the question was irrelevant, since Yeats's aim was never to revive legends in the spirit of the devoted antiquarian; he was a poet in search of a theme. True, he had said that it was his search for an Ur-tradition, more ancient than Christianity, which had urged him on to study folklore, but he never meant simply to "collect" his lore without subjecting it to poetic transmutations. As early as 1888, he had gently upbraided a volume by Katharine Tynan which had been inspired by Irish ballads: "I do not mean that we should not go to old ballads and poems for inspiration, but we should search them for new methods of expressing ourselves."[9] Throughout his life, he continued, as he does here, to insist on the need for the poet to transcend all traditions from which he borrows with his own voice; and it was precisely this insistence which made his view so difficult to accept. Admiration for translations from the Gaelic came easily, for here the poet would render Irish legends with the fidelity of the historian. But to take poetic licence with these traditions was another matter; after all, some of Yeats's opponents asked, was Yeats interested in Ireland, or in himself? Was he really a "nationalist"? The accusations hit home; Yeats was not yet confident that he had a voice of his own. In dedicating *The Secret Rose* to A. E. in 1897, Yeats wrote:

> My friends in Ireland sometimes ask me when I am going to write a really national poem or romance... [by which] I understand them to mean a poem or romance founded upon some moment of famous Irish history, and built up out of the thoughts and feelings which move... patriotic Irishmen. I on the other hand believe that poetry and romance cannot be made by the most conscientious study of famous moments and of the thoughts and feelings of others, but only by looking into that little, infinite, faltering, eternal flame that one calls one's self. If a writer wishes to interest a certain people among whom he has grown up, or fancies he has a duty towards them, he may choose for the symbols of his art their legends, their history, their beliefs, their opinions, because he has a right to choose among things less than himself, but he cannot choose among the substances of art. So far, however, as this book is visionary it is Irish....[10]

Before the turn of the century, a lively controversy on the future of Irish literature filled the pages of the Saturday issues of the *Daily Express*; on the whole, Yeats was on the defensive end of it. Soon

[9] *Ibid.*, p. 98.
[10] *The Secret Rose*, p. vii.

collected and published under the title *Literary Ideals in Ireland*, these weekly articles resemble a spontaneous symposium to which, besides Yeats, the other contributors were A. E., John Eglinton, W. Larminie. Yeats was first attacked when Eglinton raised the legitimate question: "What Should be the Subject of a National Drama?" The operative sentence—the one which brought on Yeats's challenge—was this: "The truth is, these subjects [Celtic legends]... obstinately refuse to be taken up out of their old environment and be transplanted into the world of modern sympathies." Arguing that the present interest in folklore was nothing more than an echo of sympathies aroused by Herder a century before, Eglinton concludes by insisting that the best thing Irish literature, Irish drama in particular, can do is to build a literature which evolves from a "native interest in life and its problems." Of course, Yeats disagrees; he would not reject a literature made on native grounds, but one which declared its subject-matter to be the problems of contemporary life was unacceptable. In answer he cites *Peer Gynt* and Wagner's *Ring* cycle as examples of old legends successfully revived by and with a modern sensibility. Quoting from one of his own earlier statements, he continues: "All great poets—Dante... Homer and Shakespeare—speak to us of the hopes and destinies of mankind in their fulness; because they have wrought their poetry out of the dreams that were dreamed before men became so crowded upon one another, and... buried in their individual destinies... [so]that every man grew limited and fragmentary." Western tradition, he claims, is after all "weary" both of classical myth and of social literature; and, using Wagner as his chief example, he looks for a rejuvenation of literature in the austerity and vigour of the Celtic myths. That he would eventually find in European tradition something between a degraded classical tradition and a social realism, something that welded Homer with Balzac, was not yet apparent to him.

Eglinton's reply is a dignified but spirited return to his earlier stand: must not a national literature reflect contemporary life? If the old Norse figures are indeed once more to be restored, they must at least be prepared to reflect the exhaustion and fret of the age. By implication Yeats is accused of ignoring life, of seeking to escape from it, so that his art is incapable of expressing either the age or himself: "[it] cannot be representative or national." It is, in fact, an art which is really more sympathetic to philosophy than to art. Wordsworth is then championed as the introspective poet who is both social and contemporary.

As might be expected, Yeats, already biased against Wordsworth by inheritance, objects vigorously. Relying largely upon Hallam's essay on the "aesthetic school," he points out—and rightly—that it is often the Wordsworthian poet (if not Wordsworth) who is weighed down by an excess of philosophical *impedimenta*; his is the poetry of the "utilitarian," "rhetorician," "sentimentalist," "popular journalist," and "popular preacher." Neither "aristocratic" nor the poetry of the "seer," the Wordsworthian art is, on the contrary, the antithesis of the genuinely "philosophical poetry," which is "'A poetry of sensation rather than of reflection'" (the words are quoted from Hallam). It comes to this: if the "renewal of belief" persists, then the arts will be at liberty to "lose themselves in beauty . . . to busy themselves . . . with 'old faiths, myths, dreams,' the accumulated beauty of the age." The question of whether old legends can or cannot be treated adequately in a modern context was, for Yeats, off the mark. Art is not a "'criticism of life'" but a "revelation of a hidden life": what mattered was its sufficiency in certain qualities: "intensity of . . . passion for beauty."[11]

Larminie also takes Yeats to task: for his French taint, his reliance on the school of *Symbolisme*. This prompted him to reply with "The Autumn of the Flesh" (later changed to "The Autumn of the Body"), a defence of his supposed "decadence." The argument of this essay—which Yeats later in part rejected—rests on the notion that the decadence, which Yeats prefers to call an autumn, is a reaction against the merciless realism and materialism of the nineteenth century. Recognizing the need to escape from the weariness and disillusion of autumn to the rejuvenation of spring, Yeats argues that only through "philosophy" can re-birth be achieved. Clearly the term is used unprofessionally; but it hints at the mind which would eventually express itself in *A Vision* and, concurrently, dedicate itself to the aesthetic doctrine of "passionate intensity." Weariness is near sleep and sleep near dreams, where all responsibilities begin. Contemplation—for that is what Yeats means by "philosophy"—guides the dreamer out of the chaos of images to the fixed and intense, the sharply outlined; paradoxically, contemplation will awaken the poet out of nightmare to the recognition of a truer reality.

The views emerging from this controversy draw a fairly representative diagram of the strategic positions of Yeats and his opponents. On the one side are those who envisage for Ireland a national literature

[11]John Eglinton, W. B. Yeats, A. E., and W. Larminie, *Literary Ideals in Ireland*, pp. 11, 13, 18, 27, 34–35, 36–37.

which mirrors contemporary life; on the other stands Yeats, anxious to retrieve and superimpose the traditions of an heroic age. Subject-matter is more the issue than nationalism; but even here there is a further distinction. As primary and ultimate characteristics of all art, Yeats singled out the great, primitive, unattached emotions of the human condition. While the framework may be Celtic, the basic emotions are timeless: they are as contemporary as they are ancient. "I feel," he wrote to Katharine Tynan, "more and more that we shall have a school of Irish poetry—founded on Irish myth and history—a neo-romantic movement."[12] That myth and history were not the same, and certainly not synonymous with folklore, he must have known; but his rapturous praise of folk literature often led him too far in assuming such an identity of meanings. When he writes of an Irish poet, Allingham, to whose bucolic provincialism he is half-willingly attracted, he first raises, and counters with his own favourite antithesis, the then fashionable epithet "cosmopolitanism." Here at last he has found a poet who writes of the countryside: "We—we are of the age. The spirit of the age has never been heard of down there."[13] It is a poetry of no nation, a poetry of "an isolated artistic moment." Was it national? If national meant the espousal of causes or the reflection of contemporary problems, this poetry was as far from being national as it was possible to be. Indeed, perhaps it was too far removed, even for Yeats. He is vexed by the whole business of "nationalism" and "non-nationalism." And having begun his essay with praise he ends it in doubt: "Political doctrine was not demanded..., merely nationalism." If nationalism was neither political polemic nor local colour, what was it? Yeats gropes toward his answer: a "sympathy" with national life; a consciousness of history; a local identity which yet borders on and ultimately dissolves into "universalism" and the "spiritual."

Clarity was hard to come by. For the moment Yeats seems trapped in the very web from which he had only recently struggled to escape. But he saves himself by drawing an inevitable analogy: "You can no more have the greater poetry without a nation than religion without symbols."[14] So he believed in 1888; six years later he discovered that

[12] *Letters*, p. 33.

[13] "The Poet of Ballyshannon," *Letters to the New Island*, p. 164.

[14] *Ibid.*, pp. 172–174. By 1906 A. E. had fully come round to Yeats's view: "If nationality is to justify itself . . . it must be because the country which preserves its individuality does so with the profound conviction that its peculiar ideal is nobler than that which the cosmopolitan spirit suggests—that this ideal is so precious to it that its loss would be as the loss of the soul, and that it could not be realised without

any commitment to nationalism was dangerous. To the politically minded, nationalism—of any stripe—turned into a surrender to public taste, to the mob. Nothing could have been further from Yeats's ideal picture of the artist; even as early as the nineties, though never a devoted "aesthete," he conceived of the artist as a solitary figure. It came naturally to him to reject the mob, and he rejected it in the spirit of Shakespeare, whom he cited as his precedent; he abhorred its taste, its demands, its insularity, its ignorance, its prejudices. "Whitman," he wrote, "appealed, like every great and earnest mind, not to the ignorant many...but to that audience, 'fit though few'...."[15] Here was America's most "national" poet, neglected by the very people whose essence he sought to immortalize. Such contradictions disillusioned him; from the moral of Whitman he drew a prophetic conclusion: great poets often must appeal, not to their own nation, but to the few cultivated men of other nations. Therefore, "the true ambition is to make criticism as international, and literature as National, as possible."[16] In the wake of political activity into which he was, not always unwillingly, drawn, Yeats learned that few would understand that by "national" he meant something deeper than causes, something that would transcend the feverish urgency of the present. Art could not betray itself by becoming national, if that meant compromise with political action.

Tradition was an even more slippery concept than nationalism. On the one hand it meant the best that had been said and thought in the world; on the other it was often confined to Irish, or Celtic, traditions; not always meaning the same as "myth," it quite frequently was conceived of as mere history. Yeats shared in the responsibility for confusing the issues. When he wrote in 1891 that "With Irish literature and Irish thought alone have I to do,"[17] he was writing a half-truth. While it is true that all his life he returned to Irish themes, his concept of tradition was, from the beginning, catholic. A literary chauvinism which elevated Irish traditions at the expense of others was employed most often as a defence and an antidote to the rapidly prevailing view

---

an aloofness from, if not an actual indifference to, the ideals which are spreading so rapidly over Europe. Is it possible for any nationality to make such a defence of its isolation? If not, let us read Goethe, Balzac, Tolstoi. . . ." "Nationality and Cosmopolitanism in Art," in *Some Irish Essays by A. E.* (Tower Press Booklets, no. 1; Dublin, 1906), p. 12. By 1906 Yeats had already read many of the great European masters, and Goethe and Balzac were, of course, to become important authors in his life.

15*Letters*, p. 241.

16*Ibid.*, p. 239.

17"A Ballad Singer," *Letters to the New Island*, pp. 137–138.

of nationalism that would willingly abduct Celtic mythology for political purposes.

Tradition was meant to embrace the whole national culture, but modern society had already gone too far in the direction of fragmentation. Ignorant of their past, the people—the populace at large—were corrupted by vulgar taste. In every way they opposed the heroic and the beautiful; and, in time, the right of the artist to his own vision of themselves. Clearly Yeats's position had eventually to shift from the masses to the "few"; with *The Secret Rose* he openly declared himself on the way toward creating a select poetry for a select audience.[18]

As one reads Yeats's early prose, often mere remarks hastily put together, especially in the crisis years with the Abbey, one detects an uneasiness of tone and an uncertainty of position which were not deliberate, as was the later studied casualness. It was far easier to reject, and vigorously, what he was against; but what was he for? Like Shaw and Joyce, Yeats possessed and often articulated an uncommon ambivalence toward his nation and people; to divide his loyalties equally between art and country was impossible, but the struggles were considerable. In the truest sense an Irish "nationalist," he nevertheless did not flinch from condemning what he felt would be ruinous for Irish life and art; indeed, he thought it his mission, his duty, to protest:

> The poetry of Young Ireland, when it was an attempt to change or strengthen opinion, was rhetoric; but it became poetry when patriotism was transformed into a personal emotion by the events of life.... Literature is always personal, always one man's vision of the world, one man's experience.... If creative minds preoccupy themselves with incidents from the political history of Ireland, so much the better, but we must not enforce them to select those incidents.... I am a Nationalist... and this made certain thoughts habitual with me, and an accident made these thoughts take fire in... dramatic expression.... and I made *Cathleen ni Houlihan* out of this....[19]

It is to Yeats's credit that he was able to withstand the pressures and temptations not only of others but also of forces within himself; and it was his final, irrevocable rejection "of that movement towards externality in life and thought and Art"[20] which in the end made

[18] *Letters*, p. 186.
[19] "An Irish National Theatre," *Plays and Controversies*, pp. 55–56.
[20] "The Theatre," *Essays*, p. 209.

a personal victory possible. In short, his rejection of a socially conscious problem literature saved him from some inevitable pitfalls that awaited an idealistic "nationalist."

Yet Yeats was no mere romantic, rejecting the present because it was ugly and replacing it with the past simply because it was beautiful. It is true that for some time Yeats cherished an ideal "disembodied beauty" as the sole aim of all art, a belief which he subsequently repudiated, but it is just as true that this "aesthetic doctrine" was always anchored in some personal reality. Since he did not choose to interpret the world as a materialist, he did not seek to make his art from observation alone. But "life"—the meaning of that word was crucial. If "life" meant the recording of mere events, then Yeats certainly would oppose an art based on it; for to him "life" was at least half-spirit, half-soul, and fidelity to "truth" was precisely the recognition of the unseen. Art was not only a mirror but a lamp and events, once illuminated, took on the lustre of transformation: "All changed, changed utterly...." To Yeats the realists were liars; for telling only of what they saw, how could they conceivably convey the whole truth? This he knew even before he found confirmation in Berkeley and the Platonists. Struggling with an Abbey Theatre steadily turning away from his own ideals toward comedy and realism, he wrote:

> Literature is ... the great teaching power of the world, the ultimate creator of all values.... Literature must take the responsibility of its power, and keep all its freedom: it must ... describe the relation of the soul and the heart to the facts of life ... as it is, not as we would have it be.... It must be as incapable of telling a lie as nature....
>
> I would sooner our theatre failed through the indifference ... of our audiences than gained . . . popularity by any loss of freedom.[21]

These sentences are certainly full of integrity. They reveal also some basic convictions about art and society which Yeats had to formulate before he could really come to terms with aesthetics. The great bulk of prose he wrote in his early years, and the corresponding decline of critical essays in the later years, are a matter of natural development. He could be an artist only after he had been a critic. And once he was an artist, the criticism would become more casual, more subtle, less definitive.

Even some of his fellow-artists insisted that art came second to the nation, an argument which he answered by saying, in effect, that the

[21]"An Irish National Theatre," *Plays and Controversies*, pp. 57–59.

two could not be put into a hierarchical order. He knew and understood the fundamental weaknesses of an art devoted to patriotic causes, or an art seeking to satisfy popular tastes, two aims that were not dissimilar. Invariably, the first resulted in failure; the second in dry, sterile stereotypes. Whenever a public demands "typical" or representative characters on the stage, he warned, it wants nothing but "personified opinions."[22] Ballads were not enough; Irish literature had never created a "Personality," a Goethe, or Dante, or Shakespeare: a European. For such a man to flourish, the air must be free of all constricting influences: patriotism, and political culturism, clerical censorship, and social causes. As the "voice of the conscience," literature was never to support the morality of others but, on the contrary, to "affirm its morality" against the vested interests of both the secular and the religious arms of society, against all official and doctrinaire powers.[23] If literature were given absolute freedom to furrow its native soil, the kind of nationalism that was in some sense even patriotic would come of its own accord.

Like Eliot's, Yeats's approach to tradition derives its force from its insistence that those who "create" traditions are themselves the most original of artists. Tradition, unlike convention with which it is often confused, is living history: "The great myth-makers and mask-makers, the men of aristocratic mind ... have imitators, but create no universal language. Administrators of tradition, they seem to copy everything, but in reality copy nothing, and not one of them can be mistaken for another...."[24] When he discovered Byzantium and the Noh drama, he would need to modify this view, but for the present the point that tradition fed on and was fed by original genius required the accentuation Yeats gave it.

For a time the prospects of becoming a poet looked hopeless, and lesser men gave up. But Yeats had the happy capacity to see his own struggles and defeats, his failures and illusions, in the light of a greater design. It often saved him from personal pessimism and cosmic optimism. No desire for martyrdom persuaded him that the "fascination of what's difficult" was, after all, necessary. Everything ultimately was "unified by an image . . . symbolical or evocative of the state of mind, which is of all states of mind ... the most difficult to that man, race, or nation...." The difficult brought tragedy but tragedy, as he was later to say, was "joy," "because only the greatest

22"First Principles," *ibid.*, p. 93.
23*Letters*, p. 356.
24*Autobiography*, p. 334.

obstacle that can be contemplated without despair rouses the will to full intensity." Attacking all poetry which depended for its reputation on moral or political polemics, Yeats was himself attacked for depending so little on either. Against "the greatest obstacle" his last line of defence was tradition: it was his birthright, his ancestral home. He capitalized on the analogy "between the long-established life of the well-born and the artist's life." Like the true aristocrats the poets "come from the permanent things and create them"; the "old blood" of the aristocrat is paralleled by the artist's "old emotions." And both "despise the mob and suffer at its hands...."[25] It was a happy analogy —it allied poetry once more to patronage. But it was also to alienate it from a potential audience.

In an unpublished journal Yeats wrote: "We, even more than Eliot, require tradition and though it may include much that is his, *it is not a belief or submission, but exposition of intellectual needs... the need of old forms, old situations....*"[26] When tradition serves as a "need" it fulfils the spiritual function of ceremony through aesthetic means; as Eliot might say it takes the place of belief. Although Yeats appears to deny tradition the status of belief, he means, more probably, to distinguish between the conception of a fundamentalist tradition and that of a continuing revelation. This he needed to do precisely because he wished to reject much of the classical and Christian tradition so central to Eliot. To convince Ireland of this "need" of its ancient heritage became his first missionary aim.

Yet the need of a tradition and the demands of nationalism could never be resolved completely, though to be exposed to the choice of a subject was to touch close to the basic problems of an aesthetic. If a poet chooses myth or folklore, he must clearly abandon realism as a method; and if he is prepared to reject what is popularly in demand, he must himself face rejection. "We cannot," Yeats insisted—the "we" was prematurely inclusive—"discover our subject matter by deliberate intellect, for when a subject matter ceases to move us we must go elsewhere.... We must not ask is the world interested in this or that, for nothing is in question but our own interest...."[27]

Still Yeats's position was far from clear: he wishes to have an "inherited subject-matter known to the whole people" in order to create a literature that would be "'distinguished and lonely.'"[28]

[25]*Ibid.*, pp. 119–120, 287–288.
[26]Quoted by Ellmann, *The Identity of Yeats*, p. 240.
[27]*Discoveries*, in *Essays*, p. 358.
[28]*Autobiography*, pp. 116, 62.

Intent on reviving an art sustained by a dream of a feudal relationship which never existed—peasant and lord in ideal harmony—he found it difficult to explain his contempt for the people and to justify his insistence on the artist's right to a personal vision. In a nation determined to lead its belated revolution to the ultimate establishment of a republic, Yeats's admiration for the aristocratic values—in spite of his balancing worship of the peasant—did not rally much support. Caught in a society in which both aristocracy and peasant were, in different ways, decadent and moribund, he faced the inevitable strength of the urban middle class who wanted no part of aristocratic ceremony or peasant lore. The middle class wanted realism and an art devoted to mirroring its own problems and aspirations; Yeats wanted a "spiritual" literature which would find its "reality" in the universals of myth and in the history of the soil. Here Yeats fought his Armageddon. When he emerged from it, the fate of the battle was difficult to determine: it was only certain that he was alone. What he salvaged was neither a reclaimed tradition nor a culture-conscious nationalism, but the provocative discovery that as an artist he now faced two distinct directions which he would have to choose between, unless he could develop a method that would permit him to make use of what was for him essential in both.

II

It had never been Yeats's intention to sacrifice "the people" in the abstract. But those who became hostile had no more knowledge of or sympathy for art than Yeats had for *their* immediate problems. To preface the *Poems* of 1895, Yeats had written reassuringly: "I would, if I could, add to that majestic heraldry of the poets, that great and complicated inheritance of images which written literature has substituted for the greater and more complex inheritance of spoken tradition, some new heraldic images, gathered from the lips of the common people."[29] Dublin, he realized at once, was cosmopolitan; the old traditions, if they were to be found at all, were in the country.

What is popular poetry? The question provided Yeats with a title for an essay he wrote in 1901,[30] and for its date it seems peculiarly irrelevant. At a time when the sophistication of *fin de siècle* and the social realism of Shaw and Ibsen had, at either end, flattened the

[29]Preface to Poems (1895), revised 1901; see *Variorum Edition*, p. 847.

[30]This essay first appeared in the *Cornhill Magazine* (March, 1902) though it was later included in *Ideas of Good and Evil*. Yeats dated it 1901.

notion of art as a "popular" activity, Yeats's attempts to recover the essence of folklore seem gauche and naïve. In spite of some good regional poetry, and in spite of Hardy's Wessex and Kipling's "ballads," few writers (and fewer readers) were taking the peasant very seriously in 1900. Then, as now, folklore was apt to be regarded as a quick headline or a quaint gesture of somewhat limited and temporary interest to the overly urbanized, a pleasant anti-image for the sophisticated. But Yeats was in earnest. In retrospect, moreover, the question appears much less anachronistic. If the nineties in England were to some extent echoes of the continent's rococo and early romanticism a century earlier, Yeats's attraction to the cottages may be paralleled to Goethe's youthful field trips to collect *Volkspoesie*. More quickly than either had suspected both Yeats and Goethe discovered that folk art is not what they had thought it was. But, for Yeats at least, the recognition was sobering without corroding the essential mythos which related art and folk. As late as 1906, when he had learned many answers to the question he posed himself in 1901, he still maintained a characteristic stance on the issue of popular poetry. Towns, books, specialization, and fragmentation: these were the blighting influences which had made it "more possible to produce Shelleys and less and less possible to produce Villons. The last Villon dwindled into Robert Burns. . . ."[31] Despite Yeats's qualified admiration for Shelley, the antithesis between the romantic rebel and the true vagabond poet was quite consistent. In 1925 Yeats articulated his own difference from Shelley in a note on *The Rose*: "the quality [I] symbolised as The Rose differs from the Intellectual Beauty of Shelley and of Spenser in that I have imagined it as suffering with man and not as something pursued and seen from afar."[32] It is a primary distinction: embodiment of the ideal rather than distance from it necessarily alters the ideal itself, making it less distinct as an ideal yet more recognizable.

The essay of 1901 asks a rhetorical question. "I wanted," Yeats confesses, "to write 'popular poetry' . . . for I believed that all good literatures were popular . . . and I hated what I called the coteries. I thought that one must write without care, for that was of the coteries, but with a gusty energy. . . ." Confusing creative labour with the sterility of academic rules, he felt that all conscious effort in art was hostile to the *furor poeticus*; and so prejudiced he had resolved—the consciousness of the resolve was itself ironic—to become a "popular" poet. The misinterpretation of "popular" had led him rapidly to the

[31]*Discoveries*, in *Essays*, p. 330.
[32]See *Variorum Edition*, p. 842.

vaporous, the shadowy, the pursuit "from afar"; it very nearly wrecked his earliest poetry. Fortunately he saw through his illusions quickly, eliminated the "reds and yellows Shelley gathered in Italy," and set to work on a "wintry" style. Poetry considered as a faithful imitation of folkways steered him close to the disastrous errors of the realists, whom he had censured for their naïve confusion of art and life. It was urgent, too, that he discover quickly the hollowness of poets who cultivated "folk-poetry" self-consciously, the pseudo-popular poets: "I had been busy a very little while before I knew that what we call popular poetry never came from the people at all." Convinced that poetry must reflect, nevertheless, "the colours of one's own climate and scenery," and that such poetry is then properly sung or spoken to music, Yeats early conceived of a poetry possessing two necessary qualities: regionalism (nationalism in the cultural sense) and suitability for public performance. If the modern public proved to be ignorant of the subject that was the fault of the public, not the poetry. From this point of view Yeats's later poetry is "private" only because the Irishness he had built into so many of his poems was not yet a part of the Western consciousness. In time, he hoped, Cuchulain might become a symbol of the West no less than Odysseus, Hamlet, or Faust.

About the pseudo-popular poets, then, Yeats had no illusions. Poets like Longfellow or Campbell wrote a middle-class poetry, contrived and unnatural. They had already forgotten the unwritten tradition without having learned the written: they were not poets. And between the written tradition (which he had at first distrusted) and the unwritten he began to see affinities, that the one had built on the other. Both traditions were, in their way, valid; both were "alike strange and obscure, and unreal to all who have not understanding, and both, instead of that manifest logic, that clear rhetoric of the 'popular poetry' [the Longfellow variety], glimmer[ed] with thoughts and images. . . ."[33] Villon and Milton were not incompatible; each wrote poetry that was, however differently, rooted. Moreover distinctions had become blurred; Yeats discovered—to his delight—that sometimes the genuine ballad did not differ greatly from the *made* poem, that coterie and popular poetry had so intermingled that the folk themselves could scarcely tell them apart. In any case, the speculations about popular poetry guided him toward a clarification of his own, rather confused, sense of the origin and history of poetry. Essentially it was a view not very far from Dryden's distinction between Homer and Virgil: the

[33]"What is Popular Poetry?" *Essays*, pp. 5–6, 10.

intuitive and visionary, the grand and the spacious, was neither better nor worse than the Virgilian elegance, the refined and the subtle. It was history that had made the division; one of Yeats's aims was to reunite the two kinds of poetry or, at least, to make their opposition serve as a useful tension that would be profitably dramatic.

Still, the divisions fall into place: the ancient and unwritten poetry places little between itself and its audience—it is direct. Opposite to it stands the conscious poet, who selects and alters, shapes and is in turn shaped by, the world of his art. Broadly the distinction divides body from soul. The desire to have the best of both worlds was not a mere confusion; Yeats saw precedence even in the Renaissance, in Spenser. In his essay on Spenser he writes: "His religion, where the paganism that is natural to proud and happy people had been strengthened by the platonism of the Renaissance, cherished the beauty of the soul and . . . the body with . . . an equal affection." Because he was naturally delighted with Spenser's Acrasian islands, Yeats's interest in Spenser has seemed to be clearly the romantic affinity of one lyric poet for another. Such an explanation is only partial. In Spenser's peculiar blend of paganism and Platonism Yeats recognized the "double fountainhead" which, he felt, would feed Irish literature. Catholic and Celtic Ireland was, in some way, nearer to the Renaissance than to any other age. Poised between the "heroic" and the "religious" truths, Ireland was potentially in the ideal position of annunciating a double tradition that had served Spenser and Milton. But given this opportunity the poet must avoid what Yeats considered Spenser's failures. Specifically, he must sidestep allegory, the official morality that is bound to be passionless. Spenser had tried too hard "to be of his time"; he had succeeded only in replacing the Church with the State—he was moved by "expedient emotions." In any final assessment he must be judged as an artist of the coteries, a poet who had not, ultimately, been able to surrender his contriving consciousness. The conflict between the moral allegorist and the sensual mythographer prompted Yeats to generalize: "Is not all history but the coming of that conscious art which first makes articulate and then destroys the old wild energy?" In the end, as he was to write in "The Statues," "knowledge increases unreality"—the artist's fall from innocence begins with articulation. The expression, in conscious form, of a Dionysian impulse leads inevitably to its self-destruction. Yet even consciousness could salvage some of the "old wild energy" so long as it did not turn into self-consciousness. Synge had successfully articulated a peasant simplicity that was no less artless than the plays which gave it life. Had

Spenser gone to Ireland, not as a government official but "as a poet merely," he would have discovered in the soil, in the people, in "wandering story-tellers," all of the Fairy Kingdom "unfaded" and fresh. He would, in fact, "have found men doing by swift strokes of the imagination much that he was doing with painful intellect, with that imaginative reason that soon was to drive out imagination altogether and for a long time."

Folk art and coterie, inspiration and labour, naïveté and sophistication, body and soul, imagination and intellect: the pairings keep multiplying. Clearly there were two great ways of art, two directions, two traditions, two methods. The art that followed the Renaissance revealed to Yeats a conspicuous decline of heroic grandeur, a diminution from the epic to the lyric, from the grand to the subtle. "Imaginative reason" has steadily forced the poet to retreat to smaller ground where, with increasing subtlety, he has wrought an exquisite art. But the price has been a loss of "marching rhythms"; poetry, says Yeats in the Spenser essay, has "ceased to have any burden for marching shoulders, since it learned ecstasy from Smart...and from Blake['s] . . . joyous little songs . . . of almost unintelligible vision[s], and from Keats, who sang of a beauty so wholly preoccupied with itself that its contemplation is a kind of lingering trance."

Now the poet, he continues, "must sit apart in contemplative indolence playing with fragile things." Though this sounds like a weary echo of decadence, the conjunction of contemplative with indolence spelled out a philosophical intensity that, however limited its manifestation, was still of sufficient strength to give the lyric some passion. What has faded out of poetry is its "sanguineous temperament," its energy; the fragmented civilization inherited from the Renaissance no longer permits the poet a free and nonchalant choice of subject, and the "poetical will" itself has been surrendered. Abdication of such freedom has naturally reduced the poet to writing "out of those parts of himself which are too delicate and fiery for any deadening exercise." The image of the artist bent on self-preservation, existing only within the limits of his inner self which he dare not expose to a hostile world, is peculiarly contemporary. Johnson, Dowson, Thompson, Wilde—the "tragic generation"—had lived and died that way. Immunity against the world is gained by submersion in the destructive element; isolation weakens and ultimately starves the poet who, like Kafka's hunger artist, feeds only on himself. To compensate for its loss of vigour, poetry has, with each succeeding generation, "more and more loosened the rhythm . . . broken up and disorganised, for the sake of subtlety of detail, those great rhythms which move . . . in masses of sound." What poetry has gained in refinement it "has lost in weight and measure and in its power of telling long stories and of dealing with great and complicated events."[34]

In the Atlantis time of poetry the poet could be subtle without being obscure, symbolic in a public, not a private, idiom. Any image he used was known to the "common people," every thought came from the "common thought." If the legends of Irish myth and folklore fail to inspire a new faith in the "common ploughland," poetry stands to be doomed forever to producing fragmented poets: "we may never see again a Shelley and a Dickens in the one body, but be broken to the end."[35]

The cycle was tellingly vicious. In order to regain unity, to make contact once more with the essential soil that nourishes the imagination, the poet had to assume an audience willing to take him back. Too long an absence had, however, widened the breach, so that it seemed all but unbridgeable. A society that had rejected the poet left only a few who would listen, and the limitation of his audience would again force the poet to retreat. And if the poet—for better or for worse—suddenly wished to impose upon a society no longer receptive to its own past, was this not a violation of the interplay between artist and audience which had once given freedom to both? If the Abbey went the direction of social realism and comedy rather than Celtic myth, was this a betrayal or, to the contrary, an attempt to renew a contractual obligation? To his surprise Yeats often found himself trapped in his own confusion, like the poet in one of Eichendorff's romantic novels, who having indicted the written tradition for bringing an end to innocence proceeds to write a poem on the subject. Only with time was Yeats able to differentiate between real contradictions and legitimate antinomies. And the "entanglements of moods," on which he blamed all the sorrow of life, were often a real shirt of Nessus on his back. In order to make his own vision of art adequate he needed peasant and king, folklore and myth, the passions of the soil and the ecstatic spirituality of some Platonic heaven. If the soul travelled through spirit and mire, as with the arrow of Zeno's paradox, it was impossible to say where it was at any given moment—whether, indeed, it ever *was* anywhere.

It is fortunate that Yeats's first critical prose survives, for through it already speaks (and not always faintly) the voice of the later poet,

[34]"Edmund Spenser," *ibid.*, pp. 454, 460–461, 463, 462, 470, 470–472.
[35]*Discoveries*, in *ibid.*, pp. 366–367.

at times with an astonishing foreshadowing of subsequent positions. When in the thirties he provided an introduction for a collection of these early reviews, written mostly in the late eighties and early nineties, Yeats himself remarks: "I . . . noticed that I had in later life worked out with the excitement of discovery things known in my youth as though one forgot and rediscovered oneself."[36] Most of the poems he wrote about are now forgotten, but, taken together, these "letters" to New England newspapers are the perfect prelude to the later exfoliation of Yeats's insistent themes when he wrote on the nature of poetry.[37] Reviewing William Watson's *Wordsworth's Grave and Other Poems*, in 1890, he formulated the fundamental dichotomy of art in terms of poetic intention: " . . . the mind of man has two kinds of shepherds: the poets who rouse and trouble, the poets who hush and console. It is often pleasant to turn to the latter; to turn, when bewildered by the gigantic, to men who have nothing extravagant, exuberant, mystical; to turn from the inspired to the accomplished." Inspiration and accomplishment seem here to parallel epic grandeur and lyric subtlety, though "accomplished," in this instance, carries more the overtones of coterie scholarship than of the ecstatic. Watson's book is a hushing and consoling one, though it "has sprung from the critical rather than the creative imagination," something to tip the scales against it from the start. "Scholarly," "cultivated," without a single "ragged or slovenly line," it is still a poetry deficient, not only in passion, but in spiritual refinement as well.

Yet the choice is not rigid: the poet must not be full of either Ossianic passion or scholarly perfection. Somewhere between them is the art of lyric effusion and Whitmanesque energy, neither epic nor lyric. Yeats found it sometimes in some of the minor Irish poets who made a momentary ripple in the sea of the "revival." What counted was not always the genre but the poet's approach to his subject. In two works by John Todhunter he saw again outlines of a division. One work reflected the "art poet": it was "scholarly" and "poetical," though not without its own dignity. Compared to it a second work was "unelaborate," "almost too simple." The first was "cosmopolitan" and written in the "most artificial if most monumental" of metres, blank verse; the second was "fluid" and full of "barbaric measures." In describing the latter work Yeats used essentially the language of the anti-coterie critic: "simple," "breezy," "free aired" and "too altogether

[36]*Letters to the New Island*, p. vii.

[37]Quotations in this and following paragraphs are from *ibid.*, pp. 205, 208, 212, 177, 186, 190–191.

different from the close back parlor atmosphere of nineteenth century life." But the faults of such poetry had been avoided: there was no "rhetoric," "personal ambition," "posing," no "trying for effect"; the "sadness" of the poetry was "nature's, not man's—a limpid melancholy." Youthful and exuberant, it resembled the spirit of Greece, while its opposite was "Old with words and thoughts and reveries . . . complex with that ever-increasing subdivision of thought and complexity of phrase that marks an old literature." Both works fell into a final pattern: the one as "young as nature" and belonging to "Ireland and youth"; the other "as old as mankind" and belonging to "old England and old age."

The distinction was noteworthy for its opposition of the naïveté of youth to the wisdom of old age. By definition a renaissance is a rebirth, a new dispensation, and Yeats was justified, as was the young Nietzsche, in clamouring for the fresh breath of youth. Yet passion (youth) and wisdom (old age) became increasingly necessary as a combination in achieving the highest climax in the search for Unity of Being. First, however, Yeats had made particular note of the division, which a century earlier Schiller had set down in his classic essay on naïve and sentimental poetry. Because the society from which it sprang was still unified, Greek art, Schiller had pointed out, was "naïve"; the Greek artist did not really "imitate nature." In so far as his unified culture permitted him to create ideal forms without being conscious of *striving* for perfection, the artist was at one with his model—he was identified with nature. These naïve artists did not dream nostalgically of returning to essences; their art was essence. "They are," wrote Schiller, "what we were: They are what we again ought to become" ("Sie sind was wir waren: sie sind, was wir wieder werden sollen"). On the other hand, the "sentimental" artist, self-conscious of his distance from his culture—a modern and fragmented culture as Yeats himself had observed—seeks to resurrect and to reach out for the vanished ideals of a Golden Age. Naïve poets "felt naturally; we feel the natural" ("empfanden natürlich; wir empfinden das Natürliche"); and naïve poets "move us through nature" ("rühren uns durch Natur") while the sentimental poets "move us through ideas" ("rühren uns durch Ideen").

Dorothy Wellesley had observed that Yeats rarely spoke of nature, that he did not seem to see it really, and that it was certainly absent from his poetry. It would be tempting to ascribe this to Yeats's "naïve" poetic nature—in Schiller's sense—particularly after Yeats had passed through the initial stages of the "sentimental" poet—"The woods of

Arcady are dead"—which Schiller would have classified as Sentimental-Elegaic. Certainly Yeats did linger at the start in that position where the poet feels a yearning for a Golden Age; but, according to Schiller, the sentimental poet could express himself in only three modes: idyllic, satiric, and elegaic. While he could mourn for some vague past, Yeats was temperamentally unsuited to becoming either satiric, where the poet is aware of the disparity between past and present, or idyllic where the poet is wishing away present for a substituted future. Schiller's distinctions cannot be pushed too far, but they remain perhaps the most useful ways of approaching modern poetry. And Yeats, one feels, is closer to being at times the "naïve" poet of our age than any other, for the acute awareness in his criticism of the distance between present and past, man and nature, made it possible to rid his poetry of the same issue. The poetry is seldom a lament (though often angry), or, when it is, almost always accompanied by the reassurance of the new gyre:

> All things fall and are built again,
> And those that build them again are gay.

Or there is an acceptance of change and the necessity of illusion:

> Man is in love and loves what vanishes,
> What more is there to say?

Also, Schiller's distinction between nature and ideas is essentially the same as Yeats's between emotion and intellect. Dissociation was relative to the poet's separation from the world, the first step toward providing him with an object for imitation and, thereby, diminishing his immediacy. In one of the reviews Yeats writes:

> As a literature ages it divides nature from man and sings each for itself. Then each passion is taken from its fellows and sung alone, and cosmopolitanism begins, for a passion has no nation. But [in the "younger" of the two works under discussion] . . . man and nature are one, and everywhere is a wild and pungent Celtic flavour. When a literature is old it grows so indirect and complex that it is only a possession for the few. . . .

By appealing to a minority, literature was faced in the wrong direction, but the difficulty was that the majority were no longer the folk but the mob. Written and unwritten traditions must merge and both must, in the process, avoid the middle—the middle class as subject and audience. Though opposite in intention and method, the scholarly literati and the folk might ally themselves against a common enemy and strive toward a common goal. So Yeats envisioned it in 1900, when he hoped for an audience of "few"—"a few simple people who understand from sheer simplicity what we understand from scholarship and thought."[38]

With age a literature becomes not only separated from man; in the consciousness of that separation, it will also begin to compensate by turning mellow (and, in the nineties, yellow) through falling victim to an overripe romanticism. When such excess becomes overrefined and analytical it produces the heroes of Wilde and Huysmans. Ancient passions are metamorphosed from masculinity into effeminate, sensual impulses. As Yeats grew weary of "that overcharged colour inherited from the romantic movement," and began to reshape his style, he took care not to abandon the emotions with a compensatory irony, a spiritual dryness of statement for which he had equal contempt. What he sought, he explained in characteristically paradoxical language, was "an impression as of cold light . . . an emotion which I described to myself as cold."[39]

Repeatedly in the early reviews I have been analysing, Yeats was apt to mark out two directions that the artist might take and, just as consistently, he was hesitant to make hard and fast commitments. Both ways had their attractions and dangers. One poet's verses were "meditative and sympathetic, rather than stirring and energetic"; there was no thunder, only the "viol and the flute." "It is easy," he admitted, "to be unjust to such poetry, but very hard to write it." Again, it was a poetry emerging "straight out of the [*sic*] nature from some well-spring of refinement and gentleness," making for "half the pathos of literary history." Another poet was praised for mingling "austerity and tenderness[,] a very Celtic quality"; while "precise, definite thoughts . . . sheer intensity" were favourably compared to the "world sadness" of two very sentimental young ladies.[40]

Everywhere, however, there was an insistence on some hardness of tone and fabric; at the time Yeats was a harsher critic of others than of himself. For example, in 1894, he wrote to Olivia Shakespear, having read her novel, *Beauty's Hour*: "I think Gerald wants a slight touch more of definition. A few lines . . . would do all . . . [;] he develops into rather a plastic person . . . but you should show that this is characterization and not a limitation of knowledge." A second novel was criticized still more vigorously: "I wonder how you would fare were you to pick out some eccentric man . . . from the Villiers de

[38]"The Theatre," *Essays*, p. 204.
[39]*Autobiography*, p. 45.
[40]*Letters to the New Island*, pp. 123, 96, 88.

Lisle Adams and Verlaines, and set him to make love to your next heroine?" Mrs. Shakespear's novels were too subjective, passive, and plastic; he advised her to make her men "salient, marked, dominant," thereby trebling the "solidity" of her work. Shadowy, vague, her heroes were "too passive . . . driven hither and thither by destiny . . . refined, distinguished, sympathetic"—sentimental: he might just as well have said it.[41] From his earliest experiments with the drama Yeats learned quickly that without intensity, without some "cold emotion," passivity becomes a mere burden on the plot. A latent, explosive passivity would at least suggest the "beast underneath," as he was later to phrase it. To shore up one's poetry with something "salient, marked, dominant" was itself a protection against weakness, and such weakness, Yeats noted, was never visible in genuine folk art. Through all its tenderness penetrated always the severer touch, sometimes even the cruel.

But the mark of certitude and self-assurance was never a private matter alone; one never felt "the poet" had, self-defensively, taken a manly stance. Indeed, "the poet" hardly came to mind. Yeats was thinking of the ancient culture-creations, specifically the tombs of Mausolus which he had seen in the British Museum: "In . . . that ruined tomb raised by a queen to her dead lover, and finished by the unpaid labour of great sculptors . . . we cannot distinguish the handiwork of Scopas from . . . Praxiteles; and I wanted to create once more an art where the artist's handiwork would hide as under those half-anonymous chisels. . . ." He wanted "simple emotions which resemble the more, the more powerful they are, everybody's emotion. . . ."[42] Such "simple emotions," before they could resemble those of others, had initially to be wrested from one's own nervous system. No poet of intelligence, seeking to restore singlehandedly the ancient lineaments to a literature that had abandoned them, could fail to see the paradox of his dream. For the very act of restoration was, of course, intensely personal, and for a single poet to undertake the conscious burden of what had once been the collective and unconscious pattern of a culture was to court all the passionate pain of effort and the strain of conflict characteristic of the lone voice. Anonymity, striven for with the intensest personal effort, provided Yeats with only a temporary solution (though in the Noh plays he was to turn to it again); it gave him respite in the eye of the storm but in its safety he was deluded. When the storm subsided he was close to shipwreck, for the opposite extreme

[41] *Letters*, pp. 233–234, 240–241.
[42] *Autobiography*, pp. 92–93.

of that personal utterance which his father so notoriously hated was abstraction, which Yeats hated and feared even more.

The solution was, as ever, to unite, and he "was soon," he tells us in the *Autobiography* "to write many poems where an always personal emotion was woven into a general pattern of myth and symbol," thereby escaping the "sterile modern complication" of originality without surrendering his private voice, but securing the half of anonymity that would not lead to the horrors of abstraction. It seemed to be his lot, then, to be confronted with alternatives in contrary directions; to endure it, quite willingly, Yeats began now to "drift"—the word is his own—toward a theory of masks.

Intense and passionate, his imagination full of epic emotions, he was still the sensitive young man with a delicate sense of beauty and a passion for the rose. Moreover, the aesthetic conflict was for some time paralleled by personal conflicts, for the unhappy, unrequited love for Maud Gonne required the most strenuous efforts at self-control. The wounded ego struck, as it alone can, and demanded self-pity; in turn, the father's masculine values shamed excess of emotion into submission, though at great cost. After the first three volumes of poetry, in 1899, Yeats felt defeated as a lyric poet. Nothing short of abandoning the lyric, for the time being, could rescue him as a poet, and his failure to harden his verse significantly after his public pronouncements following *The Wanderings of Oisin* undoubtedly brought him that much nearer to drama.

Again it was a move of self-preservation, only this time the choice was more conscious, not an escape from the alien world but a measure to regain strength. Premature exhaustion was the leading symptom of the tragic generation:

> They had taught me that violent energy, which is like a fire of straw, consumes in a few minutes the nervous vitality, and is useless in the arts. Our fire must burn slowly, and we must constantly turn away to think, constantly analyse what we have done.... Only then do we learn to conserve our vitality, to keep our mind enough under control and to make our technique sufficiently flexible for expression of the emotions of life as they arise.

In view of his undisputed poetic achievements in old age, it would seem that Yeats had learned the art of conserving. Thinking and analysis are functions of the intellect; and as defences against poetic dissipation Yeats found them useful and necessary. How to harness "violent energy" and to make fires "burn slowly" become eventually aesthetic principles of a high priority. Containment of a too individual emotion is achieved by an intellectual intervention, saved from being pure rationality by assuming the qualities of philosophical reflection, "reverie" and "contemplation." Nothing in these words was intended to suggest inaction; quite the contrary, a proper philosophic interlude would lead to action. "Does not all art come when a nature, that never ceases to judge itself, exhausts personal emotion . . . [so] that something impersonal . . . suddenly starts into its place . . . ?"[43] Perhaps life was too full of "unbounded emotion" and "wild melancholy" to be a useful source for art: "it may be the arts are founded on the life beyond the world, and that they must cry in the ears of our penury until the world has been consumed and become a vision."[44] If this were true how could Yeats achieve what he so ardently called the delight of life which is as "personal" as Villon's poetry? Vision itself would need to exclude, or at least to surmount, the artist's immediate, sensory perception of the world; yet every artist must begin by placing faith in his own vision of his object before he turns it into subject. And such faith issues only from a belief in the object as well—a loyalty to life. Yet, paradoxically perhaps, the more the artist confined himself to his art, proceeding on the assumption that art is not life, the more likely would he be to strike the deeper reality.

By 1899 Yeats had committed himelf to an art of "primary emotions," derived from the "experiences and duties of life,"[45] but he rejected decisively the realism that Ibsen and Shaw were already heightening into a formidable aesthetic and a philosophy of life. Always different from life, art must never try to compete; the solution lay elsewhere. If "poetry is founded upon convention, and becomes incredible the moment painting or gesture remind us that people do not speak verse when they meet upon the highway,"[46] then the safety of art depends on the frontiers of convention, not in attempts to penetrate beyond, and therefore outside, them. Once the artist, especially the dramatist, accepts convention without apology, he can alter it with his individual genius to create freshness and change. But in order to keep possession of his art, the artist must always work from within, not from without: he must adjust life to art not art to life. Of course Art as an Hegelian absolute was as dangerous as the realist's Life. To limit the imagination to an enclosure of art, to protect it from

[43]*Ibid.*, pp. 93, 191, 200.
[44]"The Celtic Element in Literature," *Essays*, p. 227.
[45]*Letters*, p. 315.
[46]"The Theatre," *Essays*, p. 209.

life, was once more the sort of preventive measure that would kill by over-immunization. "A vision of reality": it was a way Yeats defined art, both in poetry and in prose. But Vision needed clarification, needed to be distinguished from the connotations of vagueness and religious mysticism. Echoing Blake's bias for sharp and definite lines, Yeats soon discarded "vague forms, pictures, scenes, etc"; for "All ancient vision was definite and precise."[47] The earliest attempt to mark out a clearer identity for a concept of vision comes in a letter about *The Wanderings of Oisin*:

> I have corrected the two first parts of "Oisin." The second part is much more coherent than I had hoped.... It is the most inspired but the least artistic of the three. The last has most art. Because I was in complete solitude...when I wrote it....It really was a kind of vision....With the other parts I am disappointed—they seem only shadows of what I saw. But the third must have got itself expressed....Yet the second part is more deep and poetic. It is not inspiration that exhausts one, but art. The first parts I felt. I saw the second.[48]

The first distinction is between the art of the seer and the poet as maker: the former creates inspired poetic depth, the latter vision and art. Of the three parts of *Oisin* the second was the "most inspired but the least artistic," while the third, which had "the most art," came as "a kind of vision." Understandably Yeats was somewhat nagged by the insistent intuition that the second part, though the most artless, attains poetic depth. Moreover it is not inspiration which exhausts but art and craftsmanship; what he "saw" came more easily than what he "felt." And, contrary to expectation, it was vision that he felt. If this seems somewhat confused or puzzling, Yeats's choice of terms may be partially responsible. It is clear, at any rate, that he distinguishes between two possible pairings: vision and art; inspiration and poetic depth. The problem was how to get depth and poetry into art and vision. Puzzled that vision should result in an art less deep than that born out of inspiration, Yeats is obviously suspicious of pure inspiration: it produces an art more seen than felt, something ultimately non-artistic, belonging more to the mystic's vision than the poet's. For in this context, vision suggests the poet's toil, the laborious shaping process by which he transmutes personal experience into art. So exhausting was the task that when he had at last completed the third part of *Oisin* he was close to physical and mental collapse.

[47] *Letters*, p. 343.
[48] *Ibid.*, p. 87.

Yeats had been to art school before he turned poet; the discipline was arduous, the "rules" were fundamental and precise, and he had had to learn them. The exhaustion of *Oisin* came, one suspects, from the continuous efforts of the artistic-critical discipline to keep him from the brink of impressionistic mysticism, that deadly intrusion into art which eventually hoisted A. E. to obscurity. Not without a certain sympathy Yeats had written: "The poetry of 'A. E.' . . . finds its symbols and its stories in the soul itself, and has a more disembodied ecstasy than any poetry of our time."[49] It was not to be the place, exclusively at least, where Yeats would find his stories and symbols; by turning to the great traditions of folklore and myth he was turning to life, turning to it, he felt, with a more honest and a deeper insight than the proponents of realism or the poetic mystics. In *A Vision* he understood these problems better, and A. E. became typed as a kind of poet. Placed in the twenty-fifth phase, A. E. belongs to those artists who "eliminate all that is personal from belief," but replace the personal, not with artistic impersonality, but with motives outside of art altogether. "There may be great eloquence, a mastery of all concrete imagery that is not personal expression, because . . . there is an overflowing social conscience." As "Poets of this Phase are always stirred to an imaginative intensity by some form of propaganda," all that poetry of A. E. "where he is moved to write by some form of philosophical propaganda, is precise, delicate and original."[50] For poets of this phase the price of clarity is alliance with special causes, spiritual or political. Artistic vision was preferable.

If Yeats felt the life of the soul (unattached to the body) to be unsatisfactory material owing to its tyrannical, propagandistic impersonality, he was equally displeased with essence, with pure colour. No doubt the azure of Mallarmé and the yellow of the nineties had overfed the sensibilities even of a painter's son, but as early as 1888 he criticized Katharine Tynan for having "described things from without." Hence she had achieved the picturesque, rather than the poetical, sacrificing too much to colour "for its own sake": "Your love of colour too was made to serve a real vision. . . . Your best work—and no woman poet of the time has done better—is always where you express your own affectionate nature or your religious feeling, . . . your worst, that . . . where you allow your sense of colour to run away with you and make you merely a poet of the picturesque." Just as the poetry of A. E. was a kind of philosophical propaganda this poetry

49"Modern Irish Poetry," *Collected Works*, VIII, 126.
50*A Vision*, pp. 173–176.

was a picturesque propaganda; but, while the emphasis appears to be on art it is really on life: where the personal is eliminated for the sake of some effect outside both the poet and his vision of reality, art loses its sense of being art and, one might say, its sense of being human. "We both," he cautioned in the same letter, ". . . need to substitute more and more the landscapes of nature for . . . art."[51]

In the earliest of Yeats's conceptions of the artist, his individuality and his loyalty to life—body and soul—are inseparable. Life is a multiple of individuality, and anonymity, like that in the Byzantine mosaics or the statues and tombs of Mausolus, never separates that multiple from the many selves it embodies: it is, after all, an art only "half-anonymous." As a spiritual objectification in the natural world, the soul was never rejected; difficulties arise when, like A. E., the artist detaches the soul for a disembodied existence. Before the turn of the century Yeats suggested that the rarer subtleties of the soul could be beautified only when, and if, the artist was assured that the soul will live beyond the body; but it is the conviction of the soul's immortality, not its ultimate life in another world, which makes art possible. It had always been the classic dilemma, for critics and artists alike: to find the via media between body and soul was to solve, in some measure, the most pressing aesthetic problems. In his own early criticism, Yeats had consistently valued experience above observation, ranked emotion higher than fact. Clearly, then, imagination was higher than fancy and, concurrently, symbolism was richer than allegory. A symbol could animate an "invisible essence," but allegory was limited to representing one of several interpretations of some "embodied thing"; growing out of the imagination a symbol revealed while allegory, born of fancy, could merely amuse.[52] Fancy became an equivalent of phantasy. A. E. was severely criticized for writing of a "fiery footed" planet, for the imagination deals with "spiritual

[51] *Letters*, pp. 98–99.

[52] *Collected Works*, VI, 138. This passage on symbolism and allegory, appearing at the beginning of "William Blake and his Illustrations to *The Divine Comedy*," differs in one respect from the passage as reprinted in *Essays*: instead of calling a symbol "the only possible expression of some *invisible* essence," Yeats has changed this to read: "visible essence" (italics mine). It is possible that this is a misprint, but just as possible that Yeats wished, in the later version, to emphasize the concreteness of the artist's vision even more sharply: essences were not necessarily invisible, and therefore vague and abstract. (See *Essays*, p. 142.) The idea of "visible essence" undoubtedly came from Shelley. In his essay on Shelley (1900), Yeats attributes to Shelley the idea that " 'the body is a garment' not only about the soul, but about all essences that become visible, for 'the heavens are . . . a veil . . . the vestments of the celestial gods' " (*Essays*, p. 102). The word "invisible" is restored in *Essays and Introductions*, p. 116.

things symbolized by natural things"[53]—by birds and towers, by dancers and swords, by tables, ancestral houses, and swans. Despite the unavoidable admixture of symbolism and allegory each can be recognized where it has come to its special "perfection": Michelangelo's "Moses" has stirred the mind of modern man; Tintoretto's "Origin of the Milky Way," pure allegory, is both ephemeral and fanciful.[54]

The rejection of allegory rested chiefly on its lifelessness, its lack of resonance, its capacity to be at once too full of meaning and yet without any meaning at all. Generations might ponder the multiple suggestiveness of a symbol, but the precision of allegory left nothing unsaid. Only occasionally, when allegory rises to vision, is it great. Since allegory was not "natural" for him, Spenser fell short of such perfection; in the midst of his deadly sins and his elaborately wrought architectural allegories, he seems preoccupied with "quivering" lovers.[55] Like Shelley, Spenser had not sufficiently accounted for the insistence of the "gong-tormented" sea of life, though in his art it often engulfed, with amoral frenzy, his allegorical topography. By the time Yeats had completed *The Secret Rose*, his most obvious allegory, he was already "weary" of it, charging that it had severed his imagination from life, allegorized the passions until they were no longer passions at all. However, symbols were not exempt from censure, particularly when symbol was confused with mere image. For his lack of the sharply defined, for his "innumerable images that have not the definiteness of symbols,"[56] Shelley was found guilty of vagueness.

Yeats was more keenly aware of the dangers of abstraction inherent in a misuse of symbols, and aware of it much earlier, than is often assumed. To look only at the poetry is misleading; theory always preceded it, often by as much as a decade. Recognizing the need to combat abstraction and to prevent it from interfering with true vision, Yeats, with increasing awareness, searched for discipline—through style, form, and a choice of subject. If allegory was too precise, symbolism, unless checked, could become too vague. That such an interplay of checks and balances was inherently dramatic Yeats recognized at once as an advantage. Shelley remained too long in reverie, awaited in some "chapel of the Star of infinite desire" the passion of life.[57] Though the forests of *Axel* could yield the right secrets, one must

[53]*Letters*, p. 343.
[54]"Symbolism in Painting," *Essays*, pp. 182–183.
[55]"Edmund Spenser," *ibid.*, pp. 457–459.
[56]"The Philosophy of Shelley's Poetry," *ibid.*, pp. 95–96.
[57]*Ibid.*, p. 116.

not, in the end, relinquish the responsibility of living to his servants. Art was the tree whose higher branches were fed by the lowest roots. The significance of the analogy did not become wholly clear until Yeats began to write drama. Meanwhile, to have found a subject was, he discovered, only the beginning of the artist's problems. Everywhere he was confronted with choices and alternate strategies, and the question of Symbolism and *symbolisme* would eventually become crucial; it is, of course, a complicated and essential issue, and Yeats's solutions require a careful analysis (which I shall attempt in the fourth chapter). In the meantime we must continue to follow Yeats's struggles with preliminaries.

In the years before the Abbey Theatre experience had effected definable changes in his poetic imagination, Yeats vacillated continually between the desire to become a conscious craftsman and the conviction that a surfeit of consciousness removes the poet from his source; between the necessity of maintaining a lyric cry, personal and ecstatic, and the need of a widening enclosure, an impersonal, culturally identifiable anonymity. At some point all the opposing lines would meet in Unity of Being, but meanwhile choices had to be made, and the glamour of Unity could not yet have been very consoling to a poet so fundamentally divided. For one thing, not all roads led to Unity; realism, for instance, was pointed in the opposite direction, with its characteristic specialization and the necessarily partial view of life that was inherent in a philosophy of verisimilitude. Moreover, Unity could not be achieved by a diligent concentration on the aim of achieving it. Choice alone would not suffice—indeed, it would hinder; for the unified man had not put himself together by fitting so many pieces of a puzzle into place, or "through a multitude of deliberately chosen experiences": it could be done only "emotionally, instinctively." Nor was such unity achieved in isolation from one's culture and, in the years Yeats first sought to gather the fragments, personal and cultural, that confronted and impeded his way, culture was hardly amenable to unification. ". . . I [did not] understand as yet," he confessed, "how little that Unity . . . is possible without a Unity of Culture in class or people that is no longer possible at all."[58]

But equally as dangerous as choosing too self-consciously was not to choose at all. Having behind him the disillusion with the Abbey, Yeats wrote in 1913 that he felt most sympathetic now with poets who had "tried to give to little poems the spontaneity of a gesture or of some casual emotional phrase." It was all one could ask for from

[58]*Autobiography*, p. 212.

these fragmented times: "Meanwhile it remains for some greater time, living once more in passionate reverie, to create a 'King Lear,' a 'Divine Comedy,' vast worlds moulded by their own weight. . . .[59] By 1929 he had gone even further: "I have come to fear," he wrote to Olivia Shakespear, "[that] the world's last great poetic period is over,"[60] and he enclosed his four-line requiem for the heroic ages, which he called "The Nineteenth Century and After":

Though the great song return no more
There's keen delight in what we have—
A rattle of pebbles on the shore
Under the receding wave.

To pin Yeats to these scattered utterances, as if each announced an irrevocable step in a well-defined direction, would be a mistake. He was often weary, often pessimistic about his own failures, surely more than often disillusioned with the state of the world. Yet his changing position testifies to the eventual return to a kind of lyric intensity after the dramatic adventures—and misadventures. Although by 1906 the dreams of a real epic revival were, practically speaking, shattered, Yeats still faced, in his own words, "the choice of choices" between the two ways of art which seemed at the time irreconcilable and—what was worse—equally attractive, equally necessary:

There are two ways before literature—upward into ever-growing subtlety, with Verhaeren, with Mallarmé, with Maeterlinck, until . . . a new agreement among refined and studious men gives birth to a new passion . . . or downward, taking the soul with us until all is simplified and solidified again. That is the choice of choices—the way of the bird until common eyes have lost us, or to the market carts; but we must see to it that the soul goes with us, for . . . the traditions of modern imagination, growing always more musical, more lyrical, more melancholy, casting up now a Shelly . . . a Swinburne . . . a Wagner, are, it may be, the frenzy of those that are about to see . . . the Crown of Living and Melodious Diamonds. If the carts have hit our fancy we must have the soul tight within our bodies, for it has grown so fond of a beauty accumulated by subtle generations that it will . . . be impatient with our thirst for mere force . . . for the tumult of the blood.[61]

But even the choice of choices might be evaded if the "either-or" were surmounted with a "both." In drama, up and down, the way of the bird and the market carts might combine by bringing "the whole

[59]"Art and Ideas," *Essays*, pp. 439–440.
[60]*Letters*, p. 759.
[61]*Discoveries*, in *Essays*, pp. 330–331.

of life to drama, to crisis, [so] that we may live for contemplation, and yet keep our intensity."[62] The dramatic poet might remain personal while confronted with however select a public. "All that is greatest in modern literature is soliloquy," Yeats wrote in 1889 (perhaps echoing Mill: "All poetry is of the nature of soliloquy"); to avoid a "muddy torrent of shallow realism," both the poet and the audience must come to the theatre to be inspired, to be instructed. The "modern author . . . is a solitary":[63] it is his fate and his commitment. But his solitariness transcends itself toward a public art.

Where other men might be broken or paralyzed by irresolution in the face of opposing alternatives, Yeats thrived on them. In the end, the various manoeuvres in search for a proper subject led him into the aesthetic of expansion and contraction, the sweep outward and the gathering toward the centre. For if Celtic mythology and folklore were indeed to become his subject-matter, he would have need of the impersonal distance of history and the countryside; but the passion and ecstasy of the commitment to them, the pitch of dramatic intensity which the troubador needed to sing his remote and earthy lays, would force him into personal utterance as well. The song might be of far-off things, but the singing had to commence from where all the ladders start—in "the foul rag-and-bone shop of the heart." Market cart and sky, the ways of earth and heaven, embraced between them the whole of the world's drama. And it was to drama that Yeats turned next.

[62]*Autobiography*, p. 165.
[63]*Letters to the New Island*, p. 176.

3 ❋ PICTURE AND GESTURE: The Illusion of Motion

> I think the whole of our literature as well as our drama has grown effeminate through the over development of the picture-making faculty. The great thing in literature, above all in drama, is rhythm and movement. The picture belongs to another art. Letter to Frank Fay (1905)

When Yeats began to write for the stage in earnest just before the turn of the century, he saw at once that the rejection of realistic techniques, which had been easy for him as a lyric poet, was not simply transferable to his new role as a dramatist. In some way drama had achieved an alliance with realism that was difficult to break: mimesis was the oldest law of the theatre. He knew, of course, that the great dramatists had always managed to transcend a mere imitation of reality without abandoning the familiarity with life that gave their art sweep and depth. But the Greeks and Shakespeare had written in special cultural climates, and Yeats would have to find his own way of escape from the banalities of a servile realism. If he could unite his lyrical gifts with the passionate intensity that drama demanded, then he might achieve a union between "picture" and "gesture," between what he called in another context "marmorean stillness" and "overflowing turbulent energy." Through such a fusion it would be possible to create a non-mimetic art, not shadowy but sharply focused with a "manful energy" and a "clean outline, instead of those outlines of lyric poetry that are blurred with desire and vague regret."[1]

The most fundamental problem, then, which Yeats needed to solve in the theatre was how to set lyric poetry, with its pictorial fixity, into motion without losing beauty amidst the noise of modern "vitality" to which he always objected. Poetry moved in time, but the stage offered space, a space that became itself a kind of picture,

[1]Preface to *Poems, 1899–1905* (1906); see *Variorum Edition*, p. 849.

limited, framed. If the dramatist insisted on retaining poetry, he had at least to compromise with that space so as not to leave it entirely vacuous: if not literal motion, then perhaps the *illusion* of motion; perhaps that same illusion of motion which sculpture at times achieved. For all the emphasis on the "soul" insisted on by the new doctrines of *symbolisme*, and by what Symons called the "doctrine of Mysticism," Yeats very early recognized that the soul has its "image"—its reflection. That mirroring of abstract soul had to push beyond the languishing stasis of itself, so that we might "rejoice in every energy, whether of gesture, or of action, or of speech, coming out of the personality...." Indeed, Yeats had to learn, slowly and painfully, the business of the dramatic poet, and the most important lesson, it seems, was to recognize the essential role of action, a role that was not diminished though one wrote in verse rather than prose:

> . . . I have been getting some practical knowledge of the stage in our Irish dramatic movement, and I have spent a good part of the time shaping and reshaping some half-dozen plays in prose or verse. After I had learned to hold an audience for an act in prose I found that I had everything to learn over again in verse, for in dramatic prose one has to prepare principally for actions, and for the thoughts or emotions that bring them about or arise out of them; but in verse one has to do all this and to follow as well a more subtle sequence of cause and effect, that moves through vast sentiments and intricate thoughts that accompany action, but are not necessary to it. It is not very difficult to construct a fairly vigorous prose play, and then, when one is certain it will act, as it stands, to decorate it and encumber it with poetry. But a play of that kind will never move us poetically, because it does not uncover . . . that high, intellectual, delicately organized soul of men and of an action, that may not speak aloud if it does not speak in verse.[2]

Once the dramatist rejected the simple solution of realistic movement upon the stage—actors merely walking or running across space to simulate reality—some kind of sculptured gesture seemed the only alternative. Of course it might be argued that sculpture had the same stasis as the pictorial rest of lyric poetry, but then Pater had already discovered that the greatest sculpture, as the greatest painting, achieved the powerful motion which moved in the art itself and moved the spectators of it: "Greek sculpture could not have been precisely a *cold* thing; and, whatever a colour-blind school may say, pure thoughts

[2]*The Irish Dramatic Movement*, in *Plays and Controversies*, pp. 123–124; Preface to *Poems, 1899–1905* (1906), *Variorum Edition*, p. 849.

have their coldness...which has sometimes repelled from Greek sculpture, with its unsuspected fund of passion and energy in material form, those who cared much...for a similar passion and energy in the coloured world of Italian painting." Egyptian sculpture, Pater contended, was truly motionless; the Greeks, however, considered the human form as "a living organism, with freedom of movement... infinite possibilities of motion, and of expression by motion" but "full also of [the] human soul."[3] It is from sculpture (and painting), from Greece, Byzantium, and Italian art, that Yeats learned motion: how to wed poetry to action, and yet retain the sovereignty of soul and beauty.

Charm, said Lessing, speaking of the powers of poetry in the *Laocoön*, is beauty in motion: "Reiz ist Schönheit in Bewegung." In view of Lessing's insistent distinction between poetry and the plastic arts, the conception of a beauty in motion in poetry was, we remind ourselves, motion in time and not space. But as Joseph Frank has suggested, modern literature—both poetry and the novel—has adapted the spatial forms of sculpture and painting to express its own space-bounded configurations.[4] Yeats, whom Frank does not include in his group of modern spatial poets, had indeed a spatial imagination, though he remained always hostile to the extremer forms of a spatial art, such as Pound's, wishing himself to balance spatial form with temporal intrusion: to balance the pictorial image in space with the linking design of temporal progression, with action. So, it seemed to him, the Greeks had managed their sculpture at its best, in the riders atop the Parthenon, who "had all the world's power in their moving bodies, and in a movement that seemed...that of a dance...."[5]

As in early Byzantine art, the pictorial aspect of the poem would be kept from becoming fixed and static by denying it the conventional spatial room. The Byzantine artists knew that the danger of a totally frontal view was a paralysing stillness which would carry the whole design out of relationship with the beholder: a mere picture could not move either itself or others. And so they developed the modified three-quarter view in their mosaics and paintings; it avoided the indifference of profile and caught figures simultaneously facing each other and the audience. This was achieved, in part, by placing the

[3]Walter Pater, *Greek Studies* (London, 1895), pp. 198–199, 250.

[4]The revised version of Joseph Frank's essay "Spatial Form in Modern Literature," is reprinted in *Criticism: The Foundation of Modern Literary Judgment*, ed. Mark Schorer, Josephine Miles, and Gordon McKenzie (New York, 1958), pp. 379–392.

[5]*A Vision*, p. 276.

figures on the curvatures of niches at either end of a dome, say: it became their version of beauty in motion:

Intensity of action was preferably conveyed by locomotion. The figures run towards each other with outstretched hands and flying garments. . . . There is a definite tendency in this method of rendering action to point forward in time, to make the result of the action apparent together with the action itself, and so not only to connect the figures of one picture among themselves, but also to establish a relation between the successive pictures of a narrative cycle.[6]

For Yeats Greek and Byzantine art were consistent models, and when he turned to drama he applied those models toward the achievement of his own aims.

"It was," Yeats reported, "certainly a day of triumph when the first act of [Synge's] *The Well of the Saints* held its audience, though the two chief persons sat side by side under a stone cross from start to finish. This [was a] rejection of all needless movement. . . ." Yeats goes so far as to assert that, in tracing his thought to its source, he discovers "two dominant desires"—"to get rid of irrelevant movement" and to have "vivid words."[7] The "vivid words" would animate the picture in space: *ut pictura poesis*, though this was no mere confusion of the two arts. Yeats realized that any energetic intrusion, unchecked, is likely to break "the proud fragility of dreams"—hence his crusade against irrelevant movement; yet he knew as well the danger of too much silence and confessed that, at first, in the theatre, he was "driven into teaching too statuesque a pose, too monotonous a delivery," for fear that "vitality" would crush the "sleepwalking of passion."[8]

The "statuesque" quality Yeats refers to reveals perhaps the extent to which he was influenced by sculpture and sculptural techniques in shaping his dramaturgy. And here again he must have been struck by Pater's treatment of sculpture, which coincided so perfectly with the conception of balance between movement and repose. For Pater, Michelangelo perfected in his work the union of "elements of tranquillity, of repose" and "an intense and individual expression. . . ."[9] Of all the arts the least "self-analytical," sculpture is suffused with a "spirituality" though it is true that "Discourse and action [poetry] show man

[6]Otto Demus, *Byzantine Mosaic Decoration* (London, 1948), p. 9. My description of Byzantine techniques is based on Demus's excellent discussion of them, pp. 3–14.

[7]"An Introduction for my Plays," *Essays and Introductions*, pp. 528, 527.

[8]*Plays for an Irish Theatre*, p. x.

[9]Pater, *The Renaissance* (London, 1925), p. 69. For a discussion of Yeats and sculpture see F. A. C. Wilson's analysis of "The Statues" in *Yeats's Iconography*, pp. 292 ff.

as he is, more directly than the play of the muscles and the moulding of the flesh...." Sculpture, then, is "pure form," but this limitation, this starkness, this lack of dependence on anything but its own form, is its strength and power: it gives it its *Heiterkeit* or repose, which the Greeks learned to modify with a "mobile, a vital, individuality." Further, in presenting the "type, the general character," sculpture purges from its domain all that is accidental, and achieves its effects "not by accumulation of detail, but by abstracting from it," not by pure mass but by a deliberated density. According to Pater, Hellenic sculpture fulfilled yet another requirement essential to Yeats's aesthetic scheme: restraint. "In every direction it is a law of restraint. It [Hellenic sculpture] keeps passion always below that degree of intensity at which it must necessarily be transitory.... It allows passion to play lightly over the surface of the individual form, losing thereby nothing of its central impassivity, its depth and repose." With its "archaic immobility... stirred, its forms... in motion," it is always a "motion ever kept in reserve, and very seldom committed to any definite action." Even Yeats's "vague Grecian eyes gazing at nothing" find a precedent in Pater's description of them as eyes "wide and directionless, not fixing anything with their gaze, nor riveting the brain to any special external object...."[10]

Such statuesque qualities, properly modified, were what Yeats in the end sought in drama, in its form, staging and poetry. To achieve just enough motion in time—or the illusion of it—and just enough picture in space was his ultimate aesthetic for the theatre. "No breadth of treatment," he wrote in his preface for *The Green Helmet*, "gives monotony when there is movement"; but all movement must be disciplined with the proper decorum of momentary arrest—the "pause" in the midst of action which he always acknowledged as part of dramatic form.

II

Even before his experience with the theatre, Yeats had striven for some kind of dramatic conflict in the long poem. Length, he felt, would increase his opportunities for introducing conflicting positions, working his tale toward some dramatic resolution. There would at least be enough space to juxtapose opposing elements, symbolically and allegorically. To explicate *The Wanderings of Oisin* he wrote: "There are three incompatible things which man is always seeking—

[10]Pater, *The Renaissance*. All the quotations come from the essay on Winckelmann, pp. 211–218.

infinite feeling, infinite battle, infinite repose. . . ."[11] Each of the three islands in the poem was meant to symbolize one of the three incompatibles. But, as islands will, they stood in isolation; they were static. (Much later, in 1933, Yeats embodies this triad more successfully in his poem "Three Things.") Yeats quotes Synge as proposing for his own dramatic ideal the confluence of three conflicting directions: "'There are three things any two of which have often come together but never all three; ecstasy, asceticism, austerity; I wish to bring all three together.'"[12] Asceticism and austerity are certainly close and Yeats later changed "austerity" to "stoicism," a word clearly more suited to his own concept of drama as the "more...cheerful aceptance of whatever arises out of the logic of events."[13] More related to philosophy than to artistic means, "stoicism" also described more accurately the quality of contained passion rather than its absence, which "austerity" might suggest. Capable of embodying all three of these qualities, drama was obviously the most useful of genres for reconciling opposites or maintaining a tension among several forces which the dramatist could strategically place in the development of his action. Ultimately the "three things" represented such a configuration of tensions, and they resembled closely the "two ways" of art which Yeats had set forth in 1906, when he was already well under way as a dramatist. Through drama, then, Yeats hoped to find an equilibrium, a balance between the remoteness of a Shelley and the immediacy of a Villon. In search of precedent and tradition, he learned from an unusually comprehensive company: Shakespeare and Maeterlinck, the Greeks and Villiers de l'Isle-Adam, Racine and Synge, and, eventually, the Japanese Noh dramatists.

It is no surprise that Yeats's early writings on the drama suffer from some confusion and a sense of uncertainty. While disliking realism, he could not sanction what often masqueraded as its antidote—a shadowy, insubstantial art. An admirer of the sparseness of Greek and, later, Japanese art, he could not disown the power of passion in Shakespeare; and although his attitude toward representational art was marked by suspicion, he conceded that Synge mastered the realistic form so that it became something higher than an "imitation of life." Also it became increasingly clear that the drama of kings and queens,

[11]*Letters*, p. 111. In "The Circus Animals' Desertion" the line reads: "Vain gaiety, vain battle, vain repose."

[12]*Autobiography*, p. 208. On p. 310, in *The Death of Synge*, Yeats changes the terms to read: "stoicism, asceticism and ecstasy." The same words are applied to Lionel Johnson in a lecture-essay; "Lionel Johnson," *Collected Works*, VIII, 186.

[13]Preface to *Poems, 1899–1905* (1906), *Variorum Edition*, p. 849.

of Celtic heroism, would be difficult to write in "common idiom." To gain a certain measure of poetic intensity he would need to sacrifice the language of the street; but in order to avoid the vaporous style that began to repel him even before he came to the theatre, the lyric had always to be subdued, but not eliminated. The severe strain of checking his own impulses seriously undermined Yeats's confidence, and for a time he assumed a pose far more didactic and certain than he actually was. But all the struggle was worth escape from the "muddy torrent of shallow realism,"[14] a phrase he had already coined in 1889.

The primary objection to realism was levelled against its working premise: to create an illusion of reality. Like all romantics, Yeats was —at times almost snobbishly—derisive about the theatre in the claptrap or "peep show" sense, in its sometimes absurd attempts to make an audience feel they are witness to a "real" experience. All such attempts to substitute the illusion for the reality were, Yeats felt, betrayals of art; if art had to apologize for its own existence it was not art at all. He cited "that saying of Goethe's which is understood everywhere but in England, 'Art is art because it is not nature.'"[15] Shakespeare has Touchstone tell Audrey in *As You Like It* that "the truest poetry is the most feigning." In the commercialism that so often accompanied realism Yeats recognized a deliberate effort to hide art with the spurious claim of presenting *une tranche de vie*, but the slice itself was a sign of a partial vision, a separation, a cutting away from some centre. Symbols, though they were by definition abstractions themselves, would at least retain a fulness, a suggestiveness that might bring to the audience a richer and more ample image of life. However, even symbols were dangerous and could mislead the artist, from a false sense of spaciousness, to a limitation as restrictive as that of realism. In introducing a book of drawings by W. T. Horton, in 1898, Yeats remarked that the symbolist, making his symbols only from the things he loves, is bound to fall into a "certain monotony"; there are Botticelli's and Rossetti's faces, and the well or the lighthouse in Maeterlinck's plays.[16] In a society where the audience would be entirely familiar with recurrent symbols, the monotony of repetition would strengthen the dramatist's art rather than bore his public. But Yeats knew that those who would fill the seats of the Abbey would come with no such knowledge, no common sense of recognition

[14]*Letters to the New Island*, p. 176.

[15]*The Irish Dramatic Movement*, in *Plays and Controversies*, p. 21.

[16]W. T. Horton, *A Book of Images*, with an Introduction by W. B. Yeats (London, 1898), p. 15. This Introduction is in three parts; the first two only were later reprinted as "Symbolism in Painting."

to share with him. Yet symbolism remained a way to salvation. When, four years earlier, in 1894, he had written an enthusiastic account of his experience with *Axel* in Paris, he was understandably delighted with the victory of *symbolisme* over the "'photographing of life'"—he had found a play "in which all the characters are symbols, and all the events allegories." It was a false start. Thirty years later in a preface to a new translation of *Axel* he admits, despite his continued admiration for the play, that his earlier "revivalist thoughts" leave him now "a little ashamed."[17] Although *Axel* had avoided all the realistic fakery he hated, it did not substitute all he loved—and needed—in art.

Nor was Maeterlinck's static drama a better example; it, too, was only half the unity he dreamed of realizing for himself. Maeterlinck's chief defect was in the unbroken silence that never moved. In all his plays Yeats noticed the conspicuous absence of that quality he admired most in Shakespeare, "that ceaseless revery about life which we call wisdom." It is a reverie accented by some dramatic intrusion. "In all the old dramatists... one feels that they are all the time thinking wonderful, and rather mournful, things about their puppets, and... they utter their thoughts in a sudden line or embody them in some unforeseen action."[18] While "revery" became a term filled with subtle meanings—Yeats used the word with remarkable insistence—in the present context he equates it with "wisdom," that sublimity and grandeur of archetypal thought which is the harvest of great minds. The phrase "mournful things" expresses more than the *dolorisme* of the nineties; Yeats always glimpses the eternally sad nature of all wisdom. Moreover, the word "puppet" refers not to Maeterlinck's puppets but to the objectified characters controlled by the "disinterested" dramatist. Motivated from within, not from without, these "puppets" live their own lives on the stage; they move with a freedom denied the characters in bondage to a dramatist who takes more interest in effect than in truth. Yeats once asked Verlaine whether it was not true that Maeterlinck too often struck the nerves when he should have touched the heart; to which Verlaine answered, not without malice, that Maeterlinck was "'a little bit of a mountebank.'"[19] Yeats quite frankly admitted that he was attracted to the Belgian less by his plays than by his method.[20] As early as 1898 he had described the symbol-laden characters of the plays as "faint souls, naked and

[17]Jean Marie Matthias Philippe Auguste, Count Villiers de l'Isle-Adam, *Axel*, trans. H. P. R. Finberg, with a Preface by W. B. Yeats (London, 1925), p. 9.

[18]*Letters*, p. 255.

[19]*Ibid.*

[20]*Ibid.*, p. 375.

pathetic shadows already half vapour and sighing to one another upon the border of the last abyss."[21] An over-ripeness had so softened Maeterlinck's plays that his art seemed drained of all energy. Yet *Axel* and Maeterlinck attracted Yeats, and to fill their dreaminess with a startling reality still seemed a possible goal: "reverie" could be wedded to "passion."

The fundamental alternatives were simple enough: a drama of character and action (plot); Shakespeare's infinite variety and passion; the stark, statuesque qualities of Greek art; the symbolic-allegorical drama of the *symbolistes*. If no clear choice was possible, or even desirable, the problem was how to avoid combinations of methods that would thin out and weaken their special quailities. One had first to neutralize the extreme effect of a dramatic method—and so change it entirely in the process—before joining it with another. So Synge, for example, had not entirely rejected realism, but in appropriating some image of reality had rounded the edges of that reality with a poetic rhythm that was almost contrapuntal to the mimetic aspects of plot and character. Whatever the gamble, Yeats's hope was to produce something altogether new from the roots of the old. *The Shadowy Waters*, from its beginnings in 1894 (the year of *Axel*), when Yeats still persists in calling it a "poem," to its final acting version at the Abbey in 1906, tells a history not only of a play but of a lyric poet's successive struggles with dramatic theory.[22]

At the time *The Shadowy Waters* was being subjected to final revisions in 1906, Yeats read, and was obviously impressed with, Arthur Symons' essay "The Ideas of Richard Wagner." Actually the essay is all Wagner: a paraphrasing, and more often actual quotations, of Wagner's salient principles of aesthetics. "The Wagnerian essay," Yeats wrote Symons, "touches my own theories at several points, and enlarges them at one or two. . . ." A certain passage in *The Shadowy Waters* had given him considerable difficulty; it had struck a wrong note. From Symons' essay he singled out Wagner's insistence that "a play must not appeal to the intelligence, but by being . . . a piece of self consistent life directly to the emotions."[23] Although the points where the Wagnerian aesthetic touched on Yeats's own were numerous, the largest single area of agreement was this distinction between the emotional and rational appeal of art. The masculine artist,

21"The Autumn of the Body," *Essays*, p. 233.

22See the excellent article by Thomas Parkinson, "W. B. Yeats: A Poet's Stagecraft, 1899–1911," *ELH*, XVII (1950), 136–160, where that history is given in detail.

23*Letters*, pp. 459–460.

said Wagner, in Symons' words, must be immersed in life, and "from life [he] derives the new material which he will turn into a new and living art." A "living art" had the vitality of "bodily motion" and "rhythm"; all the arts, Wagner argued, had a common impulse, "lyric drama." Once poetry was "spoken and sung" and was born anew always from "the midst of the people"; now the "art poets" have ruined the marriage with deliberate divorce. Even the problem of stasis and flux Wagner had considered in terms that closely resembled Yeats's: "Christian legend can only present pictures, or, transfigured by music, render moments of ecstasy. . . . The essence of drama is living action. . . ." To Wagner drama is "'the emotionalising of the intellect,'" the point to which Yeats acknowledged his special debt; the dramatist, said Wagner, must find his action in "a new creation of myth, and this myth must arise from a condensation into one . . . image of all man's energy . . . nature apprehended, not in parts by the understanding, but as a whole by the feeling . . . [a] strengthening of a moment of action. . . ."[24] In the same year, 1906, Yeats prefaced his *Poems, 1899–1905* with the remark that "All art is . . . an endeavour to condense as out of the flying vapour of the world an image of human perfection. . . ."[25] And in a letter a year earlier he concluded that "all the finest poetry comes logically out of the fundamental action"[26]—that poetry and action cross-fertilize each other, for poetry without action would lead to the complete paralysis of movement, while action without poetry would cause movement alone to dominate. Neither result was desirable.

It was a mistake, then, to envision the lyric impulse as self-sufficient and unattached to the gesture of action, just as Wagner had argued it was inconceivable to think of music without poetry. The nineties had clung too tenaciously to the theory that "some things are inherently poetical" and might be packed into "the scene at every moment." Such poetical things "wear out"; "My Shadowy Waters," Yeats confessed, "was full of them . . . and that gave the whole poem an impression of weakness."[27] "Diana Vernon," his mistress and oracle, had told him what he already knew: stay away from artifice and live close to the "simple, popular, traditional, emotional."[28] By sheer

[24]Arthur Symons, "The Ideas of Richard Wagner," *Collected Works of Arthur Symons*, IX, *Studies in Seven Arts* (London, 1924), pp. 151, 156–157, 168, 170–171.

[25]See *Variorum Edition*, p. 849.

[26]*Letters*, p. 460.

[27]*Ibid.*

[28]*Autobiography*, p. 223.

coincidence this oracular advice just preceded his departure for Ireland on the journey that was to lead him to Lady Gregory and, eventually, to Coole, where in microcosm he found the society from which simple, popular, traditional, emotional had once been able to evolve and take shape. Certainly no realistic problem literature, like Ibsen's or Shaw's, would suit such ideals.

III

Throughout his early struggles as a dramatist, Yeats was a fairly isolated figure, intent on overcoming all the inherited obstacles that stood in his way: he would have a drama neither wholly symbolic nor wholly realistic, not "popular" in the middle-class sense but representative of folk and mythic traditions. Its rhythms were to be sufficiently expansive to allow for passion and yet simple; its language full of style but not artificial; its emotions grand but not abstract. By 1897 he had already formulated something approaching a theory, though essentially it took account only of peripheral effects. Scenery must be symbolic, not realistic; and "the acting should have an equivalent distance to that of the play from common realities."[29] Two years later, several days after the founding of the Irish National Literary Theatre, Yeats wrote a long letter to the *Daily Chronicle*, in which he elaborated his earlier suggestions. Foremost is his resistance to anything that might aid the illusion or delusion of realism; both are rejected: the first by implication, the second on principle. For Dr. Johnson's assertion that we always know we are in the theatre as well as Coleridge's "willing suspension of disbelief" are indirectly encumbrances on pure imaginative indulgence. Although the sentiment; "I want to be able to forget everything in the real world" is slightly *fin de siècle*, the "real world" must not be confused with reality. Every attempt, through representational props, to remind us of the "real world" destroys, in Yeats's language, the moment of "imaginative glory," the instant at which art annunciates its selfhood. Already he is thinking of scenery with a "severe beauty, such as one finds in Egyptian wall paintings"; the symbolic backdrop is not to be shadowy and remote but distinct and austere. Modern theatre has not failed because imagination and intellect have disappeared, but because the spoken word has lost all prestige, theatre has been created all for the eye rather than the ear, and commercialism must attract, or divert, its audience with finery and glitter.[30]

[29] *Letters*, p. 280.

[30] *Ibid.*, pp. 308–311.

Although Yeats's efforts to rid the stage of eye-catching scenery naturalistically designed to aid the illusions of the audience (to *delude* them, really), suggest the substitution of a monotonous emptiness, he was aware that a measure of relief was desirable, here and there, to startle and surprise. In an essay on Rodin, Arthur Symons had argued that the "living representation of nature in movement" needs some "deliberate exaggeration" and that "the form must be awakened."[31] Gordon Craig, who later staged some of Yeats's plays, was at the turn of the century in the *avant-garde* of his field. Paying homage to Craig's innovations in another essay, Symons described Craig's method:

> He drapes the stage into a square with cloths; he divides these cloths by vertical lines, carrying the eye straight up to an immense height, fixing it into a rigid attention. . . . He prefers gestures that have no curves in them, the arms held straight up, or straight forward, or straight out sideways.

Clearly this geometric, linear pattern of arrangement has all the bearings of primitivistic painting: the lack of curves, the vertical and horizontal gestures of the arms, resemble closely the figures of Yeats's "Egyptian wall paintings." Like Yeats, Craig aimed "beyond reality [realism]," attempting to offer instead of a naturalistic pattern "the pattern which that [naturalistic world] evokes in his mind, the symbol of the thing." With a naturalistic stage, the audience is expected to envision the reality of the illusion and to delight in the affinity between them; Craig wanted to give them the abstracted vision of that reality—here was the "beyond"—to make them conscious of the very disparity between that vision and the reality. Where the realist did his utmost to convince the audience it was not in the theatre, Craig and Yeats would do their best to convince them that they were.

Apparently Craig thought in terms very close to Yeats's ultimate picture-gesture conception; he would arrange his bounded stage and then animate it: "The picture is there; the stage director then lights his picture. He then sets it in motion. . . ."[32] To remove a play "out of time and place" Yeats was to use schemes of contrasting colours on the stage. In this way he hoped to accentuate the necessary exaggerations while maintaining the essential decorum: "One wishes to make the movement of the action as important as possible, and the simplicity which gives depth of colour does this. . . ."[33] He has spent his life, he

[31]Symons, "Rodin," *Studies in Seven Arts*, pp. 4–5.
[32]Symons, "A New Art of the Stage," *ibid.*, pp. 224–232.
[33]*Plays for an Irish Theatre*, p. 217.

says in his introduction to his plays (dated 1937, only published in 1961), getting rid of "every phrase written for the eye" and re-establishing a syntax "for ear alone"; but the assertion is somewhat misleading: he wished to disengage the audience from visual delusion, but in doing this he substituted a visual illusion which would coincide, rather than interfere, with the auditory power of the spoken words.

In an address at Harvard, in 1911, Yeats set forth in great detail some of the techniques which he saw fitting for the staging of the new drama, the "theater of beauty." Familiar already was the disowning of scene-painting as a realistic simulation of reality; but Yeats now makes clearer why painting must not substitute for what is on the stage. "Now the art of the stage," he said, "has three things which the easel painting has not. It has real light and shade, it has real perspective, and it has the action of the player." Because the stage provides the reality of what painting must create as illusion, it has distinct advantages; to undercut these with painting would merely be a replacement of something real with something unreal. He urges that even light be shed upon the stage "as Nature does: from a single point." That light will then diffuse, with great effect, over the entire stage and create precisely the shades wanted. If a bare wall seems too monotonous, do not paint windows on it—place "a shaft of light across it," and watch how alive that light can be, how animated that wall will become. Of particular interest is Yeats's special partiality for what he called the curved dome effects, which consisted of re-shaping the stage as if it were a cathedral, flooding it with coloured lights. The curve eliminated the "wings" effects, the conventional methods of giving continuity. Yeats mentions Reinhardt and Fortuny, in particular: "They use a great hood of canvas, a half-dome, that curves from one side of the proscenium to the other, and from the back of the stage to the top of the proscenium arch. Nothing is visible but a great curved surface, much like the dome of the sky, upon which lights in color may be thrown." What Yeats stresses is that these effects enhance, rather than violate, nature: the dome-effects aim, he says, to give us the "beautiful, realistic effect, reproducing as exactly as possible the sense of the open air," and he likens these effects to the Japanese theatre, where the "interior will be exactly represented . . . but an exterior is only suggested." Considering himself a writer of poetic drama and of tragedy, Yeats casts his lot with "suggestion," "symbolism" and "pattern," though he does not fail to see the legitimacy of realistic drama, even admitting that it, too, may "be beautiful," but that "it is well that its mechanism be made perfect." Meanwhile, he would continue to hope for a revolutionary change, perhaps even a change in the shape of theatres themselves—and on almost all these points he would eventually be proven right.[34]

Of course, the dramatist needed an audience prepared to be cheated of the expected delusions, and Yeats was aware that his audience in Dublin would come neither from the peasant cottages nor the streets of the city, and still less from the aristocratic houses already in steady decline. In an essay in 1899, "The Theatre," he clearly indicated that he sought an élite audience, though through bitter experience some eight years later he was to discover that some of the "simple people" he wished for became the most effective rioters against the *Playboy*. With the exception of his own plays, his prophecy of the kind of drama which the "movement" would foster was equally off the mark: "Our plays will be . . . remote, spiritual and ideal." In his assertion that the aim of all culture is "to bring again the simplicity of the first ages, with knowledge of good and evil added to it," he echoes Herder and Rousseau, though the good and evil come from the *Zeitgeist* of Baudelaire and Nietzsche. Drawing upon both the romantics and the Pre-Raphaelites, he proclaims an identity of art and religion; the drama must be given back to the "artist-priests" and they will once more make "their Art the Art of the people."[35] Having originated in ritual, to it alone the theatre must return.

But who gave any serious thought to ritual? " 'How,' " Yeats asked in 1906, after much disillusion, " 'can I make my work mean something to . . . simple men . . . not given to art but to a shop. . . ?' " Little more than six years had convinced him that despite his awareness of reality he had somehow lost touch with those elements of the populace that he had most favoured as sustaining art—his art had perhaps become so anonymous it was entirely private. It is, after all, he now admitted, the "intensity of personal life" which moves men, but this "personal energy . . . must seem to come out of the body as out of the mind." It was all too possible for the dramatist to threaten his characters by placing them in a world they could never survive. He must always ask himself, " 'Have I given [my characters] . . . the roots . . . of all faculties necessary for life?' " It was his initial commitment to an art of "personality"; he was discovering the "dissociation" which

[34]W. B. Yeats, "The Theater of Beauty," an address delivered before the Dramatic Club of Harvard University, published in *Harper's Weekly*, LV (November 11, 1911), 11. I am indebted to Professor Marion Witt for calling this useful essay to my attention; while certain sections of it echo Yeats's essay "The Tragic Theatre" (1910) other parts have not been reprinted elsewhere.

[35]"The Theatre," *Essays*, pp. 205–207.

so persistently was to impress itself on the modern imagination. Language was losing prestige, and there was also a loss of personality: "We have lost in personality, in our delight in the whole man—blood, imagination, intellect, running together—but have found a new delight, in essences, in states of mind, in pure imagination. . . ."[36] Essences without bodily energy: it was the weakness of Maeterlinck, a tendency of the subtle path that needed to be checked before it removed art from its source beyond reach and reconciliation. Drama had been intended as the exuberant vision of a multiple fulfillment. As he had prophesied in "The Autumn of the Body," it was to be the promised regeneration, the awakening from the weariness that had put art to sleep. Synge must have been in his mind when he described the ideal conception of the future art as: "joyful, fantastic, extravagant, whimsical, beautiful, resonant, and altogether reckless."[37]

By 1905 Yeats's interest in heroic legend had decisively supplanted his earlier enthusiasm for the folk. The excitement of decision and a measure of certainty produced a flurry of dogmatic assertions, not altogether lacking in charm: "All good art is extravagant, vehement, impetuous . . . beating against the walls of the world"; "All art is founded upon personal vision . . .; and all bad art is founded upon impersonal types . . . accepted by average men . . . out of imaginative poverty and timidity . . .";[38] "The greatest art symbolises not those things . . . we have observed . . . [but] those . . . we have experienced"; "All fine literature is the disinterested contemplation or expression of life"[39]—the prose, like the pronouncements, has the energy that was to rescue the drama from the threat of pictorial stasis. He had already foreseen the issue in 1904:

> There are two kinds of poetry, and they are commingled in all the greatest works. When the tide of life sinks low there are pictures, as in the *Ode on a Grecian Urn*. . . . The pictures make us sorrowful. We share the poet's separation from what he describes. It is life in the mirror . . . but when Lucifer stands among his friends, when Villon sings . . . when Timon makes his epitaph, we feel no sorrow, for life herself has made one of her eternal gestures, has called up into our hearts her energy . . . the imagination of personality . . . drama, gesture.[40]

[36]*Discoveries*, in *ibid.*, pp. 328–330.

[37]*The Irish Dramatic Movement*, in *Plays and Controversies*, p. 123.

[38]*Ibid.*, pp. 153–154.

[39]*Ibid.*, pp. 157–159.

[40]*Ibid.*, pp. 114–115. It is possible that the conception of "picture" and "gesture" (if not necessarily the terms) came to Yeats from Symons' essay "The World as Ballet" (1898). Describing the effect of the ballet, Symons writes: "Nothing is

In the extravagance of art, in its recklessness—its "gesture"—the artist could regain his foothold on life without insisting on a photographic imitation. Style, in its broadest sense, would transcend language and give to the whole dramatic configuration a force and *liveliness* of a higher order than the merely *lifelike*. In 1914, in a letter to his father, Yeats conceived of style as embodying the "two elements" of picture and gesture or, as he put it, the "one impersonal and generally in great poetry sorrowful, and the other personal and pleasurable." Both exist side by side in the best poetry.[41] With ease the dramatic aesthetic proliferated, and by the end of the first decade of the Abbey experience, in 1910, dramatic theory had become a way—and a new way—of looking at all art.

Among Yeats's several self-confessed failings, the tendency to beautify seems to be most outstanding, even before the theatre experience. It was a natural fault inherited from the nineties. Early he became convinced that "We should write out our own thoughts in as nearly as possible the language we thought them in, as though in a letter to an intimate friend."[42] Such was the intimacy John Butler Yeats had in mind in a letter to his son in 1909, which Yeats answered with approval. The opposite of intimacy was "'generalization,'" for intimacy was "experience" and "life" itself; the non-intimate becomes the rhetoric of Kipling's poetry or the essays of Macaulay.[43] Great art is miraculous because it is only *half*-anonymous, intensely personal and intimate, and yet rooted in tradition and evocative of the profoundest common passions. Only a sense of "personality" could achieve the personal universal, the lyric poet's epic and dramatic resonance. In 1910 Yeats prepared three lectures, each of which, he wrote his father, constituted a "plea for uniting literature once more to personality, the personality of the writer in lyric poetry or with imaginative personalities in drama."[44] Such an ideal would take issue with the "philosophical propaganda" (abstraction) of A.E., which obliterated not only intimacy but reality as well. In one of his lectures Yeats divided literature into two camps: the "old writers," who were pre-

stated, there is no intrusion of words used for the irrelevant purpose of describing; a world rises before one, the picture lasts only long enough to have been there: and the dancer, with her gesture, all pure symbol, evokes, from her mere beautiful motion, idea, sensation, all that one need ever know of event." *Studies in Seven Arts*, p. 246. Professor Kermode makes good use of this essay in his chapter on the dancer in *Romantic Image*, pp. 72 ff.

[41]*Letters*, pp. 586–587.

[42]*Autobiography*, p. 63.

[43]*Letters*, p. 534.

[44]*Ibid.*, p. 548.

occupied with their own sins, and the "new writers," who were busy with the sins of the world. Among the old he placed Shakespeare, among the new Milton.[45]

The point was that Shakespeare, out of his own Vision of Evil, could seize and then objectify sin in some of his great dramatic personages—Timon and Macbeth, Claudius and Iago. Milton, however, proceeded from a traditional Vision of Evil, imposed, as it were, by divine order; the sins of the world became necessarily abstract. Seen in the context of the greatest writers, this dichotomy works clearly enough. Paradoxically, the Reformation individualized sinning but abstracted the sin. Though Yeats did not elaborate, this literary dualism explains his reluctance to accept the particular visions of such poets as Baudelaire and Wilde. For Baudelaire and Wilde, too, had their eyes on the sins of the world; and their method of coping with them ultimately deprived each, as much as it had Milton, of personal and intimate drama. Baudelaire's disgust and Wilde's irony were, in the end, superimposed moralities; what was personal in their poetry was only the remains of a conflict, the ashes of the warfare between personality and the hostile world which consumed it. The new writers were chiefly moral, as distinct from ethical; whether in support of traditional moralities, like Milton, or against them, like Baudelaire or Wilde, the motivating force of their art depended largely on a Vision of Exil extended from the single individual to society. No less concerned with order and an aggregate moral framework, the old writers nevertheless were more confident in choosing the individual as sole possessor, executor, and actor of his Vision of Evil, facing this Vision in the isolation that made him a tragic hero.

Dealing with the same subject in a different context, Yeats was obviously thinking of the Protestant Ethic which, having shifted the focus from Hell to Earth, found itself faced with Evil that no individual could any longer bear himself once he stood outside the framework of rewards and punishments in the Dantesque universe. Like Shelley (whom Yeats accused of having no real Vision of Evil), many post-Renaissance poets were forced to abandon the final agonies of a Faustus—man pulled by opposing forces, neither of which was in *this* world. They socialized evil, diminished the hero's share in it, and by spreading Evil over a collective society lost both the horror and the passionate glory that had made the older art so intense. "A soul shaken by the spectacle of its sins, or . . . in tragic delight, must offer to the love that cannot love but to infinity a goal . . . while a

[45]*Ibid.*, p. 555.

soul busied with others' sins is soon melted to some shape of vulgar pride."[46] These, it seems, were at least the possibilities of Yeats's distinction which, though he did not himself draw them out, are certainly suggested in his hesitant and vacillating treatment of Wilde. For Yeats, Wilde always fell short of the tragic dimension because the personal passion was too much distilled, the irony too dominant, the comedy too obviously a grotesque distortion of the underlying tragedy. An art troubled by the intensity of a genuine Vision of Evil would arouse a higher order of passion than an art disturbed by "the trembling of the veil"—Mallarmé's phrase—or by the ironic tremors of comedy.

IV

"The trouble with all . . . modern poets and painters," wrote John Butler Yeats in a letter replete with capitals and italics, "is that they are TRIFLERS. *The have never been forced into a close relation with life*. . . . Fancy Sargent forced into a close relation with life like Millet, like Michael Angelo. . . ."[47] When, in the *Autobiography,* Yeats stops an account of the history of art to focus on a comparison of a Sargent painting with a Strozzi portrait, he unmistakably allies himself to his father. Strozzi's painting of a Venetian gentleman and Sargent's portrait of President Wilson (see Plate I) hung, for some reason, on the same wall in the Dublin National Gallery. Yeats observed the two paintings and from them intuited a complete aesthetic cleavage in principles that separated the two periods of history:

> Whatever thought broods in the dark eyes of that Venetian gentleman, has drawn its life from his whole body; it feeds upon it as the flame feeds upon the candle . . . his whole body thinks. President Wilson lives only in the eyes, which are steady and intent; the flesh about the mouth is dead, and the hands are dead, and the clothes suggest no movement of his body . . . but that of the valet, who has brushed and folded in mechanical routine. There [in the Strozzi portrait], all was an energy . . . here [in the Sargent portrait], all is the anxious study and slight deflection of external force; there man's mind and body were predominantly subjective; here all is objective, using those words not as philosophy uses them, but as we use them in conversation.[48]

This confirmed the way of the old masters who, working outward from

[46] "Art and Ideas," *Essays,* pp. 435–436.
[47] John Butler Yeats, *Letters to his Son W. B. Yeats and Others, 1869–1922* p. 139.
[48] *Autobiography,* p. 175.

their own nature, their own sin, were the more completely subjective artists; modern art served morality and was divorced from life. Yet such conclusions were vastly oversimplified; Yeats was suggesting far deeper, far subtler differences.

Energy and the "thinking body" are not new: he had insisted on them for years; but the metaphor of the flame feeding upon the candle is more precise than any he had used before. If the thought feeds upon the body as the flame upon the candle, then thought has intensity and heat; it is not mere intellect. Also the thought in the Strozzi portrait is not self-consuming but consumed with that which it was nourished by, exactly as Shakespeare suggests in his sonnet, youth is consumed by the body. In the Sargent portrait, President Wilson, who is animated only by the fixity of his eyes, has no longer a body that can feed or be fed: he has frozen into a picture save for the eyes which, instead of expressing some inner vision, seem only to stare upon an outer. The two paintings clarify the difference between the energy of an inner dramatic projection and the passivity of response, the articulate and the vague "vision." "You, long ago, said Poetry is creation," writes John Butler, ". . . that it has its source in vision and in vision only."[49] "I think with you," wrote Yeats, "that the poet seeks truth, not abstract truth, but a kind of vision of reality which satisfies the whole being." Of course, abstractions could not be eliminated entirely; art was itself abstract. Though he cursed them Yeats admitted that in some dialectical fashion abstractions were part of art, of passion with its indefinite resonance, "one half its life and yet its enemy."[50] It was inevitable that the correspondence should eventually turn to the most fundamental question: what *is* art?

Thinking like a portrait painter, John Butler suggested that, within the framework of definitions hitherto agreed to, all art was "imitation." Yeats did not so much refute as enlarge. Art, he felt, "uses the outer world as a symbolism to express subjective moods." In its way, it is an ingenious compromise between romantic and classic. By and large the romantic cherishes subjective mood; but his mood ranks highest, so that ultimately its self-expression is shaped not as a correspondence to the outer world but as a self-sufficing emotion. The mood is its own symbol. For Yeats the outer world always remains rather majestically essential: it is from it that symbols are drawn and find affinity with inner revelations. Yeats's hawks and herons are not one with Coleridge's albatross. The symbol chosen from the outer

[49] *J. B. Yeats: Letters*, p. 178.
[50] *Letters*, p. 588.

world—for its outer worldliness—rings the work of art, unites the artist with his world, the subjective with the objective. Imitation is proportionally governed by the degree of subjectivity: "The greater the subjectivity, the less the imitation." But the subjectivity itself is sometimes inherent in the object of nature. "You [John Butler] say that music suggests now the roar of the sea, now the song of the bird, and yet . . . the song of the bird itself is perhaps subjective, an expression of feeling alone." Object and subject are not simply separable as the dead reality which the imagination appropriates and then makes live. Essentially it is, of course, in execution that art separates itself from the imitative process: "The element of pattern in every art is . . . not imitative, for . . . there will always be somewhere an intensity of pattern . . . never seen with our eyes. In fact, imitation seems to me to create a language in which we say things which are not imitation."[51] Believing that nature provides her own patterns, the realist, at his simplest, would indicate mere imitation; but abstraction of nature's patterns always creates anew patterns of art itself. By the time imitation is expressed, pattern has so altered the original that, in the final product, it is difficult to speak of imitation at all. Though subtly evasive and circular, this separation of the object from the process that creates it was fully consistent with Yeats's conception of art as vision, while the artist was, not a visionary, but a maker.

But John Butler was not entirely satisfied; theoretical prevarication irked his common sense. He wrote back and asked for examples of the imitation-theory Yeats had proposed. In his answer Yeats returned to his "picture"-"gesture" dualism of twelve years earlier, though the perspective this time was different:

> You ask for examples of "imitation" in poetry. I suggest that the corresponding things are drama and the pictorial element and that . . . those who lack these are rhetoricians. I feel in Wyndham Lewis's Cubist pictures an element corresponding to rhetoric arising from his confusion of the abstract with the rhythmical. Rhythm implies a living body . . . while the abstract is incompatible with life. The Cubist is abstract. At the same time you must not leave out rhythm and this rhythm is not imitation. Impressionism by leaving it out brought all this rhetoric of the abstract upon us.[52]

Pattern itself, then, here called "rhythm," is the life-giving element of art, though non-imitative. Yeats finds precedent in a book of

[51] *Ibid.*, p. 607.
[52] *Ibid.*, p. 608.

Japanese paintings, where he saw everywhere a "delight in form, repeated yet varied, in curious patterns of lines, but these lines are all an ordering of natural objects though they are certainly not imitation." What impressed him most was the sense of conscious arrangement, a deliberate attempt to pattern the outer world, to suit it to some inner mood perhaps. In the Impressionists' philosophy such arrangement was considered to be "unconscious and instinctive," and it is to this that he credits the vigorous reaction of Cubism. By striving to regain consciousness of arrangement, the Cubists have taken the right direction; their weakness, their error, has been to replace "conscious feeling" with "abstract scientific thought": it is this which encourages the confusion of rhythm with the abstract. Abandoning the outer world, Cubism has done away with more than art could afford to give up, for rhythm is perfectly compatible, though not identical, with nature: "If I delight in rhythm I love nature though she is not rhythmical. . . . The more I express [rhythm] the less can I forget [nature]."

Because he makes pictures one cannot forget and sees them "as full of rhythm as a Chinese painting," Keats is a greater artist than Shelley, certainly greater than Swinburne, whom Yeats again found hopelessly abstract. Carlyle has only "ideas, never things . . . worn out images"; they have cast him into oblivion. Flooded with moral zeal and abstractions—"'God,' 'Eternity,' 'Work'"—he could be neither dramatic nor pictorial. "I separate," Yeats concludes, "the rhythmical and the abstract"; though "they are brothers . . . [rhythm] is Abel and [the abstract] is Cain."[53] The analogy was meant to be appalling; life and art both are slaughtered by the abstractions without which neither could be complete. It was the artist's responsibility to prevent, if he could, the fratricide that would cancel his art altogether; though he must acknowledge the kinship of Cain, he must banish him ultimately from domination of his work. For to Yeats it was after all Abstraction that had criminally assaulted, and subdued, Victorian poetry.

However right Yeats may have been in his periodic outbursts against the dangers of abstraction, his judgment that Cubism had no rhythm, or confused it with abstraction, seems odd, especially in view of his own training as an artist. One explanation is that, for him at least, Cubism was too abstract. Bound always to a sense of reality, he depended on signs from the objective world which he must have missed in the more mathematical proportions of a Cubist's canvas. Allusion and suggestion were sufficiently distanced from the real world; but

[53] *Ibid.*, pp. 608–609.

to abandon that world altogether for "technique" was, in painting and in poetry (one recalls the criticism of Pound as a pure technician), to lose sight of the essentially human transcendence of significant form. Also it is likely that, at least in Wyndham Lewis, Yeats saw an arrested rhythm, the rather violent brushwork that always stops short of completion and appears to fall into accidental patterns, like the sudden turn of a kaleidoscope. Later in life he was to see more clearly the tension that such partial pattern induces, but he could never reconcile himself to it, never embrace it as a way to unity. Beyond the pattern and the rhythm there had to be form, of course, but not the form of abstractions which threatened to be no form at all. "Measurement began our might": the classical proportions, with their inherent sense of movement (perhaps first recognized by Winckelmann in his famous phrases, "noble grandeur and still magnificence") were closer to what he asked of art. Such statues, as he said in his poem on them, "moved or seemed to move."[54]

Picture and gesture: Yeats continued to describe art in terms of this dialectic throughout his life. What he once called "still intensity" would always be animated by the "emotion of multitude"—the poetic focus would be rescued from paralysis by the poetic echo. Like the image-begetting sea in "Byzantium," the abundance of "life . . . trembling into stillness and silence,"[55] was to be aesthetically set in motion by the very "ecstasy" of the epiphany; and was this not like "some fulfilment of the soul in itself, some slow or sudden expansion of it like an overflowing well?"[56] Unlike the aesthetic that Stephen Dedalus offers in *A Portrait of the Artist as a Young Man*, Yeats's demands on art did not stop with the "arrest" of emotion. Dedalus' (or Joyce's) insistence that art is never kinetic but induces "the luminous silent stasis of esthetic pleasure," is precisely what Yeats struggled to escape from when he turned to drama. A "silent stasis" resembled too clearly the space-bound pictorial image of which word-painting was a direct ancestor. Like the souls in "Byzantium," art was committed to both "trance" and "dance."

There are several examples in Yeats's poetry of his successful fusion

[54]See an article by Hazard Adams, "Yeatsian Art and Mathematic Form," *Centennial Review*, IV (Winter, 1960), 70–88. Since writing this chapter, I have also discovered that Giorgio Melchiori has an "Excursus" entitled "Yeats and Abstract Art" in his recent book, *The Whole Mystery of Art: Pattern into Poetry in the Work of W. B. Yeats*, pp. 271–273. Melchiori makes some interesting observations on Yeats's views of rhythm and abstraction in relation to the Vorticists.

[55]"The Tragic Theatre," *Essays*, p. 301.

[56]*Autobiography*, p. 286.

of picture and gesture, among which "Lapis Lazuli" comes most obviously to mind. But perhaps it is not the classic example because the picture there is set in motion too conceptually, too obviously. Of all poems "A Bronze Head"—also a late effort—most successfully illustrates the fusion and equipoise of turbulence and stillness, the intensity that rouses to passion. Essentially the poem attempts to explore the possibly superhuman qualities of Maud Gonne, at whose bronze head Yeats is apparently gazing as he stands at the entrance to the museum. At first he sees only "a bird's round eye,/Everything else withered and mummy-dead." The circle of the eye dominates and holds his vision until that vision seems to grow so spacious that the following lines repeat in essence the same image (a centre surrounded by empty space), only in vast proportions:

> What great tomb-haunter sweeps the distant sky
> (Something may linger there though all else die;)
> And finds there nothing to make its terror less
> *Hysterica Passio* of its own emptiness?

But once she was not so immense: "her form [was] all full," though in human terms. Yet already the poet saw circle within circle, saw a "sterner eye [that] looked through her eye," an eye with sight powerful enough to survey the whole passing scene of the world's decline. In the words, "Heroic reverie," which appear in the penultimate line of the poem, Yeats suggests the synthesis of passion and intensity that brings to one final image the drive and the repose of the poem: the image is the eye, which stares so hard it seems almost to be staring beyond reality at nothing, like the eyes of Sargent's Wilson; but half in terror, half in exultation, fixed by its merciless stare and yet passionate by means of that very stare, the eye is alive after all: the bronze head—like the poem—assumes the depth and vigour of the Strozzi portrait.

A year after the exchange of letters on "imitation," Yeats turned more sharply than he ever had in the direction of "personal utterance," in theory and in practice. Nourished by his experience with the drama, he was now able once more to assume the role of lyric poet, convinced that he had learned the secrets of strength, the recklessness of extravagance, that will keep his art personal but not egoistical; dramatic, but not therefore deprived of all lyricism; symbolic—still that—but not vague or abstract. Once more, and with increasing emphasis, he subscribed to the union of picture and gesture, only in future the equilibrium would apply beyond drama to the whole realm of poetry. His faith, he wrote in 1913, is in ecstasy; the commitment came as a relief, for at last he could utter the word without evoking the goose-flesh response of the nineties: he had made himself a context. "Of recent years," he wrote in the same letter, "instead of 'vision', meaning by vision the intense realization of a state of ecstatic emotion symbolized in a definite imagined region, I have tried for more selfportraiture . . . to make my work convincing with a speech so natural and dramatic that the hearer would feel the presence of a man thinking and feeling." Two kinds of poetry, he concluded, have dominated literary history: the Keatsian vision and the Burnsian drama (though he found Burns too obvious). Compared with French poetry, the English have lacked most in this dramatic tension.[57] He had read Donne's poetry the year before with enthusiasm and in a state of discovery; the drama of personal struggle he found there would force the poet to intrude upon his own decorative pattern which, left to itself, like one of Spenser's gardens, was in danger of becoming utterly detached.

The resultant changes of style that followed the Abbey Theatre experience and profoundly affected the whole nature of Yeats's poetry have been explored at length. It is true that the immediate effects of coming upon the dramatic passion of motion—however controlled—were to make Yeats utterly suspicious and wary of the pictorial. But it is useful to remember that the drama had a catalystic effect, and that the dramatic aspect of self-portraiture would, in the end, not eliminate the intensely imagined region of vision. Picture, it is now clear, was several things: it was the over-emphasis on pattern, the intricacy of Victorian "design" from the Pre-Raphaelites to the tapestries of Morris; it was allegorical word-painting, in Lessing's sense; it was a stage of representational scenery. But for all that Yeats never surrendered the essential quality of repose and fixity that picture provided—though he later found better words for "picture." In the letter to Frank Fay which heads this chapter, he speaks of the necessity of rhythm in literature and this rhythm became one form of his conception of "gesture." In the end picture could only be eliminated at the cost of shattering the work of art with a reigning rhetoric, a "vitality" so strong it would be supreme. And intensity would be sacrificed as well, for all gesture must have a limit against which it strains. Gesture became, eventually, a kind of reaching into the frame of pictured form, almost an illusion, almost "Schönheit in Bewegung." Pater had emphasized the increasing tendency toward

[57] *Letters*, p. 583.

motion in the history of sculpture, and Yeats was sensitive to it; Nietzsche had brought him even closer toward fulfilling his desire for a stirring passion by going beyond Pater to explain the meaning of the irrational element in Greek art: Apollonian form fruitfully disturbed by a Dionysian undercurrent. For Yeats the discovery was crucial, and it is easy to see why, having been bound so firmly to an art threatened by pictorial stasis, he would at first exaggerate his discovery of dramatic gesture. But until he found the full resolution between immobility and motion he "suffered continual remorse, and only became content when [his] abstractions had composed themselves into picture *and* dramatisation."[58]

Once the din of the first decade with the Abbey receded, Yeats faced a loneliness, both as person and as artist, which almost forced upon him the reconsideration of silence. It was a realm he was now prepared to enter:

> Like a long-legged fly upon the stream
> His mind moves upon silence.

[58] *Autobiography*, pp. 115–116. Italics mine.

4 ❊ EMOTION OF MULTITUDE AND STILL INTENSITY: The Echo of Silence

> ... the nobleness of the Arts is in the mingling of contraries, the extremity of sorrow, the extremity of joy, perfection of personality, the perfection of its surrender, overflowing turbulent energy, and marmorean stillness. . . . "Poetry and Tradition" (1907)
>
> A swift or a slow movement and a long or a short stillness, and then another movement. "Certain Noble Plays of Japan" (1916)
>
> Intensity is all. Letter to Edith Shackleton Heald (1938)

The resolution between picture and gesture solved a fundamental problem for Yeats: as dramatist or lyric poet, he could now strengthen his work with "masculinity" and with the "rhythm" of movement to balance the pictorial effects that no poetry could entirely do without. But such a resolution, while it brought him far beyond the early uncertainties, still left some major issues unresolved. Gesture was at best a reckless, passionate, *dramatic* intrusion, but it did little to create a sustained resonance, depth, the epic vastness that Yeats still wished to get into his art, and which he so much admired in the old great masters. Yeats's own return to the mythology of Ireland brought him close to that vastness inherent in all ancient mythologies. Pater had spoken of it in the Greece of Hesiod, the "still fluid world, of old beliefs . . . a world, the Titanic vastness of which is congruous with a certain sublimity of speech . . . of motion or space. . . ."[1] But Poe and the *symbolistes* had deprecated the long poem as an impossible form; and Yeats, exhausted from his one attempt to write a long work, must have wondered whether he possessed the sheer physical stamina to attempt another. It would be better if one could discover a method

[1]Pater, *Greek Studies* (London, 1895), pp. 28–29.

of capturing that reverberating, enlarging echo without actually creating it—that is, by again achieving the illusion and effect, rather than the thing itself. Yeats came to call this illusion the "emotion of multitude," though he had first to work through what he meant by "Symbolism"; and to check that multitude from overflowing beyond the frontiers of form, he would find ways of recalling that resonance to the centre, to its "still intensity." By such a two-way expansion-contraction method, he would achieve what, according to Pater, the greatest of Greek sculpture had combined—inner and outer strength: "not merely . . . the profound expression of the highest indwelling spirit . . . but . . . the expression also of the great human passions, of the powerful movements as well as of the calm and peaceful order of the soul, as finding in the affections of the body a language, the elements of which the artist might analyse, and then combine, order, and recompose."[2]

Both multitude and intensity are explicit in the epigraphs heading this chapter, which range over a period of thirty years. In the first Yeats states his theory of art as a "mingling of contraries" already alluded to in the previous chapter. Turbulence and stillness, it is clear, form a set of terms he was already working with as early as 1907. Eventually, he was delighted to discover the characteristic oscillation between movement and arrest in the Noh plays. Certainly the "swift or slow movement" was not precisely the same as the "overflowing turbulent energy" described earlier, but Yeats recognized—long before he came upon the Noh plays—that even the overflow of turbulence had to be subdued, not only by its contrary but in its essence.

The introduction to the Noh plays did not, as has sometimes been assumed, cause a radical about face in Yeats's position, a shift toward entirely new directions. In certain respects, as I have already indicated, the Noh undoubtedly brought Yeats farthest from his dreams of a popular theatre, a folk art which he had hoped would draw on a larger audience than the severely restricted aristocratic Noh. But aesthetically the Noh was confirmation, not conversion: in Professor Parkinson's words the Noh "encouraged and strengthened, it did not shape and change"; its "basic structure . . . had already been present in . . . *Plays for an Irish Theatre* (1911). . . ."[3] I would add that the basic aesthetic doctrines of the Noh were already in embryonic form at the turn of the century—certainly at the end of 1901. To

[2]*Ibid.*, p. 267.

[3]Thomas Parkinson, "Yeats and Pound: The Illusion of Influence," *Comparative Literature*, VI (Summer, 1954), 262, 261.

demonstrate this will involve a careful tracing of the contending claims of multitude and intensity, the solution to which posed for Yeats the most challenging and complex aesthetic questions.

The desire to achieve a resonant multitude was an early one, but at the turn of the century, in the essays on symbolism in painting and poetry, Yeats already recognized the difficulties of bringing such resonance to perfection in the art he was most suited to create and in keeping with certain loyalties, both those inherited from his youth and those which he had recently sworn his artistic self to preserve. The latter were the loyalties to the new "mystical" movement, *symbolisme,* and the canons were clear: no bulkiness, no gross realism, no cramming your work with the impedimenta of "ideas," philosophic or any other. Yet how could the artist achieve a sense of vastness without delineating it? How could that vastness keep its links with the past, retain its own historical and associative multitudinousness? And how could Yeats reconcile his attachment to the Pre-Raphaelites, which came very early; the allegiance to Blake, culminating in the joint edition with Ellis in 1893; and his new enthusiasm for *symbolisme*, which seems to have reached its peak between 1894 and 1900? These are not simple questions and I do not propose that the answers to them will be simple. But to understand Yeats's development from 1894 to 1915—when the Noh theory began to bear fruits in Yeats's plays for dancers—it is necessary to attend most carefully to the various shifts in Yeats's attitude; if we overlook them, we are confronted with rather puzzling and unexplained changes that will appear to be far more sudden and revolutionary than in fact they were.

Yeats's visual experiences in the drama, as early as 1901, will prove to be of great importance, for in the theatre he first saw—literally—that multitude could be suggested by means that the poetry of *symbolisme* had not offered. Both painting and sculpture were further stimulants and examples. In 1902 Nietzsche's Dionysian-Apollonian dualism, with its solar and lunar divisions, proved extraordinarily useful. A re-reading of Shakespeare culminated in the central essay "Emotion of Multitude" in 1903; and by 1911, when Yeats and Pound first became intimate, Yeats had, as Professor Parkinson notes, already "outgrown the early Yeats,"[4] and the principles for the later revisions of his early poetry were already well established. These revisions achieved many different ends, but one certainly was to solve, for lyric poetry, the union of multitude and intensity. Certain poems Yeats wrote in the last half of his poetic career, particularly

[4]*Ibid.*, p. 258.

"Among Schoolchildren" and "Byzantium," illustrate with what success he was eventually to put this resolution to use, and it is to some of these poems that I shall turn in the sections which follow, for it is worthwhile to remind ourselves that there were also fruits to all this busy speculation.

II

In the 1903 essay "Emotion of Multitude," Yeats suggested how the great dramatists of the past had achieved multitude through a variety of means, from the use of the chorus to the resonance of language itself. But, as he was careful to point out, "checks" were always employed; what these "checks" were to be in his own art he did not yet know: to suggest multitude was one thing, but to keep it from becoming mere rhetoric or physical intrusion was more difficult. Of one requirement he was certain, even in 1903: in order for expansion-contraction to take place, in order to attain a sense of multitude surging outward which could then be recalled to the intense centre, the artist must have space in which to move. And that space had long been occupied, especially in the fine arts, by pattern or by bulk, by the intricacies of design in such an artist as Beardsley, by the massive realism of Academy art, even by the weightiness of Blake's designs. Though Yeats had recognized this restrictive sense of occupied space in 1903, he did not in "Emotion of Multitude" work out definitive solutions; that essay, therefore, stands as both a culmination of earlier and tentative theories and a starting point for subsequent resolutions. To understand the pivotal nature of this essay, it is best to postpone a closer examination of it and first look before and after.

Partly because his father was a painter and partly because his own imagination was highly visual, Yeats responded deeply and very early to painting, and it was in painting that he seemed initially to find some of the answers to his aesthetic problems as a poet and later as a dramatist. It is worth noting that of his two essays on symbolism, the essay on painting (1898) preceded that on poetry (1900) by two years; and that before 1900 he had also written his important essay on Blake's illustrations to *The Divine Comedy* (1897).[5] Painting, then, was a primary interest, and Yeats's conceptions of symbolism between 1896 and 1913 are best traced by paying close attention to his changing attitudes toward two antithetical artists, each of whom had something attractive to offer to the young poet: Blake and Whistler. (See Plates II and III.) It is through the Blake-Whistler

[5]The essay was first published in *The Savoy*, July, 1896.

BERNARDO STROZZI:
Portrait of a Gentleman
(page 85)

JOHN SARGENT:
President Wilson
(page 85)

[46]

And *Earth*, and *Ocean*, pay their Debt of Man,
True to the grand Depoſit truſted There?
Is there no Potentate, whoſe out-ſtretcht Arm,
(When rip'ning Time calls forth th' appointed Hour,)
Pluckt from foul *Devaſtation's* famiſht Maw,
Binds *Preſent*, *Paſt*, and *Future*, to his Throne?
His Throne, how glorious, thus divinely grac'd,
By germinating Beings cluſt'ring round,
A Garland worthy the Divinity!
A Throne, by Heav'n's Omnipotence in Smiles,
Built, (like a *Pharos* tow'ring in the Waves,)
Amidſt immenſe Effuſions of his Love,
An Ocean of *communicated* Bliſs.

An all-prolific, all-preſerving God!
This were a God indeed. And ſuch is Man
As here preſum'd: He riſes from his Fall.
Think'ſt Thou Omnipotence a naked Root,
Each Bloſſom fair of Deity deſtroy'd?
Nothing is dead; nay, Nothing ſleeps; each Soul
That ever animated human Clay,
Now wakes; is on the Wing: And where, O where,

5 Will

WILLIAM BLAKE:

Illustration for Young's *Night Thoughts*

(page 96)

PLATE II

JAMES A. MCNEILL WHISTLER: *Nocturne: Blue and Silver, Battersea Reach* (page 96)

PLATE III

PLATE IV

J. M. MILLAIS: *Ophelia* (page 101)

SIR EDWARD BURNE-JONES: *King Cophetua and the Beggar Maid* (page 101)

PLATE V

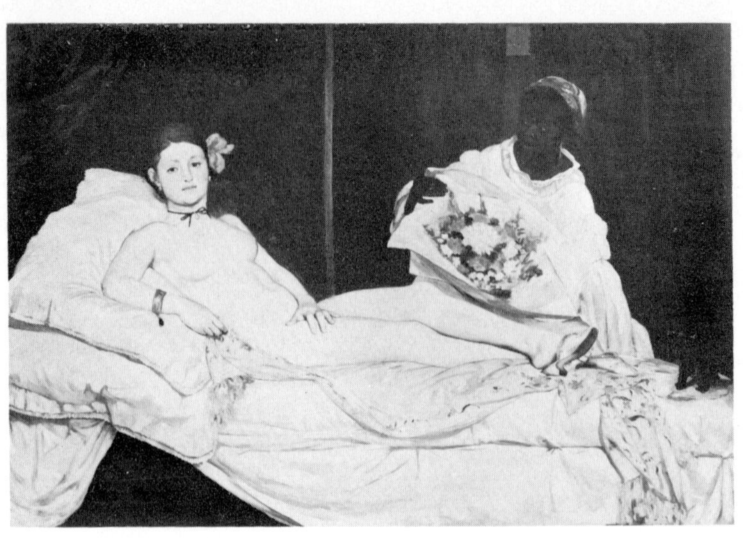

E. MANET: *Olympia*
(page 158)

E. MANET: *Eva Gonzales*
(page 158)

GEORGE F. WATTS: *William Morris*
(page 192)

PLATE VII

PLATE VIII

TITIAN: *Portrait of a Man* (page 192)

PALMA: *Portrait of a Poet, Probably Ariosto* (page 192)

antithesis that Yeats seems to reach toward some final conclusion on the nature of symbolism and of art itself; the route toward certainty is by no means stable and, at the start, the conflicting loyalties to the art of two such different craftsmen as Blake and Whistler visibly divided and confused Yeats for, as was so often the case, he wished to have it both ways. Art and ideas, pure poetry and philosophic impurities, the function of the intellect to balance mere sensuousness —these were the issues that constituted a montage of conflicts and shifts, qualifications and commitments in Yeats's aesthetic, culminating in a theory of symbolism that would finally join multitude and intensity.

Symbolism was, understandably, an initially attractive solution for, in order to create space, the artist (whether in painting or in poetry) had to find a substitute for mass, and the obvious answer seemed to be the symbol. But the use of symbols and their choice was no simple matter: symbolism did not always achieve a clearing of space, especially if that symbolism tended more toward allegory than true symbolism. Despite Blake's elaborate Symbolic System, which Yeats had studied carefully and sympathetically, not all of his graphic art satisfied, partly because its assurance, its aggressive and powerful postures, diminished the subtler effects which Yeats had lately come to appreciate. In the essay on Blake's illustrations to *The Divine Comedy*, Yeats already registered his dislike for the "great sprawling figures" illustrating Young's *Night Thoughts*; they were "a little wearisome even with the luminous colours of the original water-colour, [and] became nearly intolerable in plain black and white. . . ."[6] Yeats's position in this essay—as I shall presently illustrate—is a very curious one: he seems caught in the dilemma which, at the outset of this study, I tried to indicate by setting his epic imagination against his lyric talents. The situation in this essay is further complicated because Yeats had recently been to Paris (1894) with Symons, seen *Axel,* and returned a convert —with reservations. It is these reservations which make him apologetic and defensive about certain aspects of Blake's theory of art, and he had already been devoted to Blake for years; this defensiveness is of great interest and, I think, of great importance, if we recognize that Yeats was at the time also attracted to an artist like Whistler.

Whistler's paintings were at this time a *succès de scandale,* for a variety of reasons: Whistler's ungentle art of making enemies, the general atmosphere in the Academy which was still officially at war with the French, and the lingering memory of the Ruskin-Whistler

[6]"William Blake and his Illustrations to *The Divine Comedy,*" *Essays,* p. 153.

trial. But some of the hostility toward his paintings was undoubtedly part of a counter-attack against the very real threat they posed—the implicit and explicit efforts to make more plastic the rigidity of design that had gone so far as to clutter the canvas beyond the point where objects could be discriminated. One way of creating space was to remove objects altogether. At their most characteristic Whistler's paintings achieved such a dissolution of objects, making for a total impression by "arrangement" of forms and colours which prevented one from being lost in hopeless detail. Painting, he demonstrated, might be both fluid and impressionistic and still have form. In an approving essay on Whistler—which Yeats must have known—Arthur Symons speaks of "these twilight aspects, these glimpses in which one sees hardly more than a colour, no shape at all, or shapes covered by mist or night, or confused by sunlight. . . ."[7] But atmospheric fog such as this might lead to a complete abandonment of all pattern, a dissolving of outline in exchange for shadow. In either direction one was apt to encounter dangers: too much delineation, too many objects, and the result was a cluttered canvas; too little and one had nothing but vagueness. Blake had insisted on outline as the *sine qua non* of the genuine artist; and, according to Yeats, Blake held that the "imperishable lineaments" should never be obscured by "shadows and reflected lights."[8] But, as a young art student, Yeats had himself "longed for pattern, for Pre-Raphaelitism, for an art allied to poetry," convinced that beauty alone was fit for the canvas and that, presumably, beauty *was* pattern.[9]

Outline and pattern were neither synonymous nor antithetical: outline might be thought of as circumscribing pattern, so long as pattern still yielded separable objects. According to Yeats, Blake considered outline "the line that divides . . . [form] from surrounding space. . . ."[10] There is nothing either cluttered or shadowy about Blake's engravings, and they do not lack pattern of a kind. It was only when outline disappeared almost entirely that the painter perhaps stood to lose some of the traditional effects expected of him. One disadvantage of a surrender of outline might be the loss of what Yeats called the "ecstasy awakened by the presence before an ever-changing mind of what is permanent in the world. . . ." The artist "will think less of what he sees and more of his own attitude towards

[7]Symons, "Whistler," *Collected Works of Arthur Symons*, IX, *Studies in Seven Arts*, (London, 1924), p. 79.

[8]"Blake," *Essays*, p. 149.

[9]*Autobiography*, pp. 49–50.

[10]"Blake," *Essays*, p. 148.

it," and his art will be ruled by "an essentially critical selection and emphasis." Such art Yeats attributed to Whistler and Degas (though he certainly disliked Degas more and for further reasons), artists in whom, he felt, "we all feel the critic"; it was an art "that is not the greatest of all."[11] But this was in 1906, in *Discoveries,* and it certainly represented a shift from an earlier estimate of Whistler in "Symbolism in Painting" (1898), where Whistler's name is included in a long list of symbolists (Keats, Wagner, Blake, Calvert, Rossetti, Villiers de l'Isle-Adam, Beardsley, Ricketts, Shannon, Maeterlinck, Verlaine) who "accepted all symbolisms," and "all the Divine Intellect." Even in this essay Yeats distinguishes between whole and "fragmentary" symbolists, between Blake and Wagner on the one hand, and Keats and Calvert on the other. The "fragmentary symbolist," though able to evoke "infinite emotion," lacks the power to place his symbols in the "great procession."[12] In what category Whistler belongs he does not say, but it is likely that he would have assigned him the place of fragmentary symbolist, even at this date. In any case, by 1906 Whistler is clearly too personal an artist lacking the vision of the "permanent," Blake's "imperishable lineaments."

Blake had "cursed all that has come of Venice and Holland," but in 1897 Yeats sees this as too restrictive a view, not only because of his recent enthusiasm for *symbolisme*, but also because he is still filled with memories of the Pre-Raphaelites (and what would Blake have said of Rossetti's "Lilith" or "Pandora"?):

> The limitation of ... [Blake's] view was from the very intensity of his vision; he was a too literal realist of imagination, as others are of nature; and because he believed that the figures seen by the mind's eye . . . were 'eternal existences,' symbols or divine essences, he hated every grace of style that might obscure their lineaments. To wrap them about in reflected lights ... and to dwell over-fondly upon any softness of hair or flesh was to dwell upon that which was least permanent and least characteristic....

We can see that some nine years later, Yeats was less inclined to see Blake's view as a limitation, classifying the art of personal "attitude," which in Whistler's case certainly produced "grace of style," as diminishing "what is permanent in the world." In 1897 Yeats felt the need to defend Blake's view:

> What matter if in his visionary realism, in his enthusiasm for what, after all, is perhaps the greatest art, he refused to admit that he who wraps the

[11] *Discoveries*, in *ibid.*, p. 355.
[12] "Symbolism in Painting," *ibid.*, pp. 184–185.

vision in lights and shadows, in iridescent or glowing colour, until form be half lost in pattern, may . . . create a talisman as powerfully charged with intellectual virtue as though it were a jewel-studded door of the city seen on Patmos?[13]

Outline, therefore, if we think of it in part at least as the border circumscribing pattern, served as a useful safeguard against the vagueness of too individual a vision, too critical a selection, both in painting and literature. But just as that critical selection, leading to vagueness of delineation, might destroy the "permanent" that outline preserved, so pattern itself, once it came to dominate the canvas, would spill over its proper boundaries and also obliterate outline. Pattern might strangle art with the very means intended to give it form, order, and freedom. As the experience of the Pre-Raphaelites demonstrated —in paintings like Hunt's "The Scapegoat" or Rossetti's "Cassandra"— pattern might develop into a kind of super-realism, an art dominated by the *camera obscura* characteristic of the Flemish painters ("all that has come of . . . Holland," which Blake hated), not Giotto or Botticelli. If the artist did not step back, as it were, to leave room for the imagination to roam, his art might become Brobdingnagian, an art Yeats disliked, "too much concerned with the sense of touch, with the softness or roughness, the minutely observed irregularity of surfaces."[14] If pattern was, as Yeats wrote his father in a passage already quoted in the previous chapter, the non-imitative portion of art, then it had a responsibility to check itself from becoming too self-conscious; a pattern so intricate or cluttered that no space was left was as undesirable as no pattern at all. Whistler at least used "arrangement"— a pattern of shapes and colours; if he sometimes lost himself in the dissolution of the "permanent in the world," this was perhaps preferable to the methods of those who lost themselves permanently, the realists, for example, who substituted sheer bulk for pattern and outline both. In any event, it was clear that intricacies of line and minutely patterned objects, provided there were enough of them, encroached upon the demarcating outlines of painting as damagingly as—or more than—Whistler's dissolution of them.

While painting was to find solutions in a number of rich and daring movements—Cubism, Futurism, Vorticism—the situation in literature was less dazzlingly and more slowly resolved. For the literary artist "ideas" were a great inconvenience since it was in the nature of language to compel the intellect to attention and involvement; Fenol-

[13]"Blake," *ibid.*, pp. 146–147, 149.
[14]*Autobiography*, p. 96.

losa might be right in objecting to the Western habit of abstraction in the use of "to be" verbs, but the most famous soliloquy in English was hard to forget. Ideas kept naggingly hanging about, like cast-out orphans demanding to be taken back into the fold. One solution for achieving multitude in literature was obviously to re-admit ideas; and Yeats rather gingerly began to realize the necessity for this early in his career, though in time he became fairly bold and dropped the need to be apologetic about such revisionism. If they were permitted into the work by a careful process of screening to make certain they had the proper credentials and were not mere excess baggage, ideas had every right—every necessity—to be in art.

It would be false, however, to suppose that the problem was an easy one for Yeats; his early associations with the Rhymers, the French *symbolistes,* and the "aesthetic doctrines" of Hallam initially disposed him unfavourably toward any intellectual or philosophic content. Such content was, to quote Pound's *Mauberley,* what "the age demanded," and the age be damned. Yet Yeats soon tired of the effort to attain "pure" form. True, even Keats and Shelley had escaped the fate of Wordsworth, and had not "intermixed into their poetry . . . elements from the general thought, but wrote out of the impression made by the world upon their delicate senses."[15] Then followed the Pre-Raphaelites and their delicate senses. Yet, for all their emphasis on pattern and sensuousness, the Pre-Raphaelites had never abandoned "ideas." In 1913 Yeats was re-discovering the Pre-Raphaelites, seeing in Rossetti's faces the same power that had occasioned him to remark in 1898 that they made "one's thoughts stray to mortal things, and ask . . . 'What predestinated unhappiness has made the shadow in her eyes?' "[16] the kind of questions Pater had asked of the Mona Lisa.

There was, after all, history in this Pre-Raphaelite art, fullness, resonance. Yeats wonders "if my conception of my own art is altering, if . . . I praise what I once derided." The essay in which he so wonders is called "Art and Ideas"; and he tells how he had gone to the Tate, just several days before taking pen in hand to write down his impressions, and had been overpowered by an "old emotion," by Millais' "Ophelia," by Rossetti's "Mary Magdalene," by Burne-Jones's "King Cophetua and the Beggar Maid." (See Plates IV and V.) Anyone familiar with these paintings knows how typical they are in

[15]"Art and Ideas," *Essays,* p. 431. This essay is dated 1913 and was first published in 1914.

[16]"Symbolism in Painting," *ibid.*, p. 185.

bringing to perfection the intricacies of pattern or rendering multitude sometimes by crowding the canvas with groupings of figures and incidental symbolic objects. Was this essentially what attracted Yeats? I do not think so; he himself describes what moved him: the "painting of the hair, the way it was smoothed from its central parting, something in the oval of the peaceful faces" (most likely a reference to "King Cophetua and the Beggar Maid")—they evoked in him "memories" of his youth when he had naturally loved these paintings. And so now, many years later, he "forgot the art criticism of friends" and once again took delight, unabashedly, in his youthful enthusiasms. Why had he once "derided" this art? What had the "art criticism of friends" attacked? He does not say, except to indicate that he had "always loved these pictures" in which the people could be associated "with the poems or the religious ideas that [had] most moved [him]"—"the traditional images."[17] Ideas and the literary element of painting, both certainly evident in Pre-Raphaelite art, were no longer the fashion in the nineties. The early discipleship of aestheticism had eventually made him hostile to every art which failed to promote what was then fashionably called the "pure work."[18] Even Pre-Raphaelitism, with its intensely religious and mystical subject-matter, its pointed allegorical "stories" on canvas, its literary impurities, fell in the wake of this hostility. Too often the Pre-Raphaelites were still imitating life or literature—or at least imitating.

"I developed," Yeats writes, "these principles [of the aesthetic school] to the rejection of all detailed description, that I might not steal the painter's business, and indeed I was always discovering some art or science that I might be rid of . . . [as] painters who were ridding their pictures, and indeed their minds, of literature." Yet once he had exhausted these "delighted senses" he was left "discontented": "Impressions that needed so elaborate a record did not seem like the handiwork of those careless old writers one imagines squabbling over a mistress, or riding on a journey, or drinking around a tavern fire, brisk and active men."[19] True, Blake had "preferred to any man of intellect a happy thoughtless person," but this came from his hatred of "abstract things" and his "praise of life"—intellect need not be equated with life as a subject-matter.[20] That was the equation which rendered the "tragic generation" so impotent as poets. Homer, Dante, Shakespeare—each "used all knowledge . . . of life or of philosophy,

[17]"Art and Ideas," *ibid.*, pp. 429–431.
[18]*Autobiography*, p. 102.
[19]"Art and Ideas," *Essays*, p. 432.
[20]*Autobiography*, p. 288.

or of mythology or of history," not, it is true, for purposes of didactic comment, but rather "to shape to a familiar and intelligible body something he had seen or experienced in the exaltation of his senses."[21]

All the Rhymers—except Yeats himself he implies—"silently obeyed a canon that had become powerful for all the arts since Whistler, in the confidence of his American *naïveté*, had told everybody that Japanese painting had no literary ideas." Yeats said that he filled his imagination with the "popular beliefs of Ireland," seeking "some symbolic language reaching far into the past . . .";[22] but he admits that his early poetry also suffered from his "refusal to permit it any share of an intellect which [he] considered impure."[23] The turning away from abstractions, from "moral zeal" and "irrelevant interests," was valid enough; but must one surrender the past only to "be alone amid the obscure impressions of the senses"? Was literature—or painting—"pure"? Turning the pages of Binyon's book on Eastern art Yeats discovered that Whistler had been wrong; that, in fact, the "literary element in painting, the moral element in poetry, are the means whereby the two arts are accepted into the social order and become a part of life and not things of the study and the exhibition."[24]

What Yeats recognized as the explicit limitation of the aesthetic doctrine of "pure" poetry (or painting) was its open denial of the past; for if a poetry was to rid itself of content, where were its roots, its lineage, its traditions?

> We... turned away from all ideas. We would not even permit ideas, so greatly had we come to distrust them, to leave their impressions upon our senses. Yet works of art are always begotten by previous works of art, and every masterpiece becomes the Abraham of a chosen people.

During this period Yeats notes a change of interest, in painting particularly, so that one focused on "the fall of drapery and the play of light without concerning [oneself] with the meaning, [with] the emotion of the figure itself." For the poet such "absorption in fragmentary sensuous beauty" was fatal: it deprived him of the power to conceive of scope and wholeness, to "mould vast material into a single image." Even the great long poems of the nineteenth century—Yeats lists *The Revolt of Islam*, *The Excursion*, *Gebir*, *Idylls of the King*, *The Ring and the Book*—"are remembered for some occasional

[21]*Literary Ideals in Ireland*, pp. 36–37.
[22]"Art and Ideas," *Essays*, p. 433.
[23]*Autobiography*, p. 116.
[24]*Ibid.*, p. 298.

passage, some moment which gains little from context." Until recently (the date of the essay "Art and Ideas," we recall, is 1913), Yeats complains, even those poems which did manage to convey a lyric "impression of a single idea" seemed "accidental," so much had everyone still been under the spell of Swinburne's verses, "arranged in any order, like shot poured out of a bag." Never must we surrender the "flow of flesh under the impulse of passionate thought," but ideas were one means of recapturing the great unifying images of the past, "architectural unity,"[25] what Arnold had called "*Architectonicè*," "that power of execution, which creates, forms, and constitutes: not the profoundness of single thoughts [Yeats called these "detachable ideas"], not the richness of imagery, not the abundance of illustration."[26] This clearly was what reawakened in Yeats the "old emotion" as he stood looking at the paintings of Millais and Rossetti: they were evocative beyond mere sensuousness; they suggested what he now wished to get back into all art—"vast worlds moulded by their own weight like drops of water."[27]

What is of special interest is Yeats's diagnosis of the "dissociation of sensibility" with an emphasis, in the present context, exactly opposite to that of Hulme and Eliot. A separation of thought and feeling, yes; but not with thought in the ascendant to destroy unity, rather with sensuous feeling triumphing over all else. Spenser's Acrasian islands showed the first separation of "certain qualities of beauty, certain forms of sensuous loveliness . . . from all the general purposes of life, as they . . . would not be again . . . till Keats wrote his *Endymion*." The paradox which had escaped the Rhymers, though Yeats suspected it, was that disembodied "images and regions of the mind . . . grow in beauty as they grow in sterility." Arnold, Browning, and Tennyson, in spite of their impurities, had "moral values that were not aesthetic values"—though Yeats did not endorse the separation. But Coleridge and Rossetti "made what Arnold has called that 'morbid effort,' that search for 'perfection of thought and feeling, and to unite this to perfection of form'. . . ." While Yeats sympathized with this effort, and recognized the martyrdom and consequent suffering it brought upon so many he had known himself, he wished now to escape from its dangers. In his dedication to Ashe King of his revisions of his early poetry, he wrote: "I tried after the publication of 'The

25"Art and Ideas," *Essays*, pp. 437–440.

26Matthew Arnold, *The Complete Prose Works of Matthew Arnold*, ed. R. H. Super (Ann Arbor, Michigan, 1960), I, 9.

27"Art and Ideas," *Essays*, p. 440.

Wanderings of Oisin' to write of nothing but emotion, and in the simplest language, and now I have had to go through it all, cutting out or altering passages that are sentimental from lack of thought."[28] In some respects, the "organicist" doctrine of art was at bottom, however paradoxically, not a living but a lifeless theory, and no one had better diagnosed it than Pater in his essay on Coleridge:

> In this late age we are become so familiarised with the greater works of art as to be little sensitive of the act of creation in them: they do not impress us as a new presence in the world. Only sometimes ... we are actual witnesses of the moulding of an unforeseen type by some new principle of association; and to that phenomenon Coleridge wisely recalls our attention. What makes his view a one-sided one is, that in it the artist has become almost a mechanical agent: instead of the most luminous and self-possessed phase of consciousness, the associative act in art or poetry is made to look like some blindly organic process of assimilation. The work of art is likened to a living organism. That expresses truly the sense of a self-delighting, independent life which the finished work of art gives us: it hardly figures the process by which such work was produced.... The philosophic critic ... will value, even in works of imagination, seemingly the most intuitive, the power of the understanding in them, their logical process of construction, the spectacle of a supreme intellectual dexterity which they afford.[29]

Neither Pater nor Yeats would ever relinquish their veneration for form; in this sense they were both organicists; but each was possessed of an historical consciousness that made "intellectual" not a term to fear but to require. Pater noted that "The works of the highest Greek sculpture are indeed *intellectualised* ... to the utmost degree"; in fact the figures "seem actually to conceive thoughts" (Yeats's "thinking body" comes to mind), though of course such "intellectualised" objects "are still sensuous and material, addressing themselves, in the first instance, not to the purely reflective faculty, but to the eye...." Yeats would have agreed: "Whatever method one adopts, one must always be certain that the work of art, as a whole, is masculine and intellectual, in its sound as in its form"; "drama that has no intellectual tradition behind it" is "demoralising"—the word "tradition" here being quite as important as "intellectual."[30] What was ultimately

[28]*Autobiography*, p. 188; Dedication to *Early Poems and Stories* (1925), in *Variorum Edition*, p. 854.

[29]Walter Pater, *Appreciations* (London, 1918), pp. 80–81.

[30]Pater, *Greek Studies*, p. 197; *The Irish Dramatic Movement*, in *Plays and Controversies*, pp. 47, 52.

wanted was something that defined intellect as an inherent element of tradition, not a "detachable idea" but an integrated and associative thought deeply embedded in history itself. Yeats said he found such unity in the *Comédie Humaine*, "in those passages . . . that suddenly startle us with a wisdom deeper than intellect. . . ."[31] Still, "intellect" and "intellectual" need further defining; in the process of that definition, we must come to terms now with Yeats's developing conceptions of symbolism.

The change of heart about Whistler is of more than passing interest: whereas in 1897 Yeats would include Whistler among the symbolists (fragmentary or whole), by 1913 he had developed rather more severe notions about *symboliste* indefiniteness. That Yeats should be writing an essay called "Art and Ideas" in 1913, and re-discovering in that essay the beauties of Pre-Raphaelitism, is a rather interesting fact, in view of the undisputed evidence that in that very year Imagism had certainly reached its peak. One need not repeat the familiar doctrines of that movement here, but Pre-Raphaelitism was not one of its chief rages. Yet it is true that the Imagists, too, were rather intent on getting away from *symboliste* indefiniteness; but instead of substituting for vagueness a certain dryness and hardness, Yeats wanted richness. His was to be a different way. Whistler now seems cursed by the modern "point of view"; Blake's insistence on the " 'hard and wiry line of rectitude and certainty' "[32] could no longer be ignored—Yeats had quoted those words in 1897. Whistler's weakness was that he had failed to place his symbols in the "procession" precisely because he was "critical": "We are but critics, or but half create." ("Ego Dominus Tuus").

Since we have raised the matter of Imagism and *symbolisme* it is proper to make at least one distinction which divided Yeats from both movements: Yeats conceived of the symbol or the image as "heraldic" or, as Pater was fond of saying, "hieratic." The indefiniteness of symbol and image was not in its inherent obscurity, its fundamental shadowiness, or its personal associative powers; indefiniteness was, like multitude, the expansiveness of symbol and image, and such expansiveness was inherent in the symbol's own history which was—perhaps paradoxically—a very concrete and specific matter. From such a point of view, neither symbol nor image could be considered autonomous, "uncommitted . . . having, in fact . . . *a life of its own* . . . independent of the author's intellectual intention . . . ,"

[31] "Louis Lambert," *Essays and Introductions*, p. 446.
[32] "Blake," *Essays*, p. 148.

to quote from Kermode's *Romantic Image.*[33] Indeed, symbol (or image) was only autonomous by being attached to a lineage, in the same manner that an aristocratic family would conceive of its offspring's independence as consisting in the degree to which they were able to carry on the family traditions—an analogy that might not have displeased Yeats. A poet could not help being aware of "intellectual intention" in creating such images and symbols. True enough, the issue of "personal utterance" and "egoism" was again involved and Yeats was always perhaps unduly frightened by the spectre of too personal a vision. Yet surely he recognized how involved the artist must be to place his symbols in the "procession"—particularly the modern artist, who was now the sole possessor of that procession.

Yeats's distinction between emotional and intellectual symbols is difficult to disentangle, and it is tempting to think that he was pushing for emotional symbols and registering a disaffection with intellectual ones. However, the issue is not so simple. "Besides emotional symbols, symbols that evoke emotions alone . . . there are intellectual symbols, symbols that evoke ideas alone, *or* [italics mine] ideas mingled with emotions. . . ." Strictly speaking, there are, then, three—not two—kinds of symbols which Yeats distinguishes in his essay "The Symbolism of Poetry": those which evoke pure emotion, or pure ideas, or both emotions and ideas. Aside from the "very definite traditions of mysticism and the less definite criticism of certain modern poets," the intellectual symbols—those purely intellectual or those both in-

[33]Kermode, pp. 55–56. Kermode also quotes part of a sentence from "The Symbolism of Poetry" (1900): "'. . . you cannot give a body to something that moves beyond the senses, unless your words are as subtle, as complex, as full of mysterious life, as the body of a flower or of a woman.'" In contending that "this remark contains, in germ, Yeats's whole aesthetic" (p. 51), Kermode casts his lot with a Yeats committed to a certain type of *symbolisme.* I should not say that "germ" is the proper word, if this implies a subsequent realization of that germ, yielding a final position. Yeats rather explicitly told George Russell (A. E.) in a letter in 1903 (*Letters,* p. 402) that he had rejected parts of the volume published that year—*Ideas of Good and Evil*—in which the essay on symbolism was included. I believe that the fragment of a sentence Kermode quotes is part of that "one half the orange" which, along with essays like "Moods" and "The Autumn of the Body," Yeats later discarded for firmer ground. He came to recognize rather early that vagueness and indefiniteness could be a severe limitation (or, if you wish, too great a freedom) for any poet about to embark on a dramatic career. All poetic language must have its share of subtlety, complexity, and mystery, but Yeats began to shape a language that would have its checks against obscurity or too much softness—hence, the increasing stress on "masculinity." In his letter to Russell, he writes: "I think I mistook for a permanent phase of the world what was only a preparation. The close of the last century was full of a strange desire to get out of form, to get to some kind of disembodied beauty, and now it seems to me the contrary impulse has come." It had certainly come for Yeats.

tellectual and emotional—"alone are called symbols." Now "symbols, associated with ideas that are more than fragments of the shadows thrown upon the intellect by the emotions they evoke, are the playthings of the allegorist . . . and soon pass away." That is, if symbols are evocative of and associated with ideas that dominate—"are more than fragments"—and so give back to the intellect ideas larger than the emotions evoked initially, then we have idea-dominated allegory. (Yeats goes on to illustrate this in subsequent sentences.) Ideas, then, should be no more than "fragments" returned to the intellect by the emotional evocativeness of the symbol chosen. But this does *not* render the intellect inoperative; on the contrary, "It is the intellect that decides where the reader shall ponder over the procession of the symbols, and if the symbols are merely emotional, he gazes from amid the accidents and destinies of the world; but if the symbols are intellectual too, he becomes himself a part of pure intellect, and he is himself mingled with the procession."[34] The emotional-intellectual symbol is therefore the preferable kind because it unites the reader —as it must the poet who uses it—to his symbol, unites his self-consciousness to the "procession" or, as Yeats called it in "Magic," to the Great Memory.

To turn to "Magic" is, I think, a legitimate digression; the essay is dated 1901, the year following the essay on the symbolism of poetry, but it is safe to assume that the two pieces are nearly contemporaneous. In "Magic" Yeats states his three famous beliefs:

> (1) That the borders of our mind are ever shifting, and that many minds can flow into one another . . . and create or reveal a single mind, a single energy.
> (2) That the borders of our memories are as shifting, and that our memories are a part of one great memory, the memory of Nature herself.
> (3) That this great mind and great memory can be evoked by symbols.

For present purposes, the second and third beliefs have the greatest relevance. Individual memories are saved from an egoistic or egocentric "point of view" when they become part of the "great memory" —something achievable, Yeats felt, only by the best poets. He had tried, he confesses in "Magic," to make distinctions between "inherent symbols and arbitrary symbols," symbols arising out of a received tradition or seemingly invented arbitrarily by the poet; but the dis-

[34]"The Symbolism of Poetry," *Essays*, pp. 197–198.

tinction, he says, came "to mean little or nothing."[35] (It is worth noting in passing, however, that in "Prometheus Unbound," 1932, Yeats returned to the distinction, calling Shelley's symbols "arbitrary" and saying of him: "his system of thought was constructed by his logical faculty . . . not a symbolical revelation received."[36]) Ultimately what the poet did with his symbols determined their power. "Whether their power has arisen out of themselves, or whether it has an arbitrary origin, matters little, for they act . . . because the great memory associates them with certain events and moods and persons."[37]

To return to the essay on Symbolism:

> If I watch a rushy pool in the moonlight, my emotion at its beauty is mixed with memories of the man that I have seen ploughing by its margin, or of the lovers I saw there a night ago....

This, then, is the "emotional symbol" and what Yeats would call at one time the "arbitrary" symbol, for it depends primarily on personal associations.

> ...but if I look at the moon herself and remember any of her ancient names and meanings, I move among divine people, and things that have shaken off our mortality, the tower of ivory, the queen of waters, the shining stag among enchanted woods....[38]

And here is the "intellectual symbol" evoking "ideas mingled with emotion," joining the reader to the "procession," making him respond to a symbol that is "inherent" (as distinct from "arbitrary"). Note that Yeats says, "if I *look* at the moon herself," not if I *think* of her: looking precedes thinking; the symbol is its own starting point, not the end but the beginning of the process.

Whether in practice Yeats was a Symbolist poet (in the Blakean sense) or a *symboliste* poet has been in dispute ever since Edmund Wilson confidently placed Yeats among the latter in *Axel's Castle*. The question is not likely to be decided to everyone's satisfaction. It has often been argued that Yeats was not a *symboliste* poet because he got his doctrines second hand from Arthur Symons and could read French only slowly and with great difficulty. This is a pretty thin argument; apply it more generally, and you deprive Yeats of an understanding of all foreign literatures, since he was a poor reader of any language except his own. All the evidence indicates that Yeats's understanding

35"Magic," *ibid.*, pp. 33, 60.
36"Prometheus Unbound," *Essays and Introductions*, p. 421.
37"Magic," *Essays*, p. 60.
38"The Symbolism of Poetry," *ibid.*, pp. 198–199.

of *symbolisme* was neither shallow nor haphazard; if he departed from these doctrines he did not do so out of ignorance of what he was departing from and his own goals were very clearly set. A tentative distinction between Yeats's conception of symbol and that of the *symbolistes* is possible, though I would be careful to point out that the distinction does not hold either for all of Yeats's poetry or for all of the poetry of *symbolisme*—luckily, I would add, since no great poets fit intellectual distinctions rigidly. Yet I do think it is possible to say that for the *symboliste* poet, let us say Baudelaire, the symbol is the end product, not the starting point. So Baudelaire's Paris (like Eliot's London) is his starting point, and often a very realistically rendered one; it is only gradually that the city itself becomes the City, and the City in turn something else—a hospital full of sick people, a hell, a house of prostitution. Baudelaire is interested primarily in his symbol, not that which goes into its making; the world is used to evoke the symbol. Yeats, I think, came to work in the opposite direction: he would use the symbol to evoke the world, and his interest, ultimately, was less in the symbol than in the things evoked. Hence, of course, his great desire to achieve "multitude." For Yeats the symbol became a true metaphor which evoked the world in terms of itself, and I have already quoted in the preceding chapter the notion of "correspondences" which Yeats outlined to his father and which differs considerably from Baudelaire's *correspondances*. It is clear from the excerpts quoted above that the symbol—say, the moon or the rushy pool—does not always evoke a multitude that is realistic or worldly, using those words in their simplest meaning: one thinks either of personal associations or of ancient mythological and folklore traditions. But in either case the mind expands from the symbol, whether it be rushy pool or moon, and that symbol is, in both cases, a "real" object.

The best example that comes to mind from Yeats's poems is Sato's sword, and the use Yeats makes of it in "A Dialogue of Self and Soul":

> The consecrated blade upon my knees
> Is Sato's ancient blade, still as it was,
> Still razor-keen, still like a looking-glass
> Unspotted by the centuries;
> That flowering, silken, old embroidery, torn
> From some court-lady's dress and round
> The wooden scabbard bound and wound,
> Can, tattered, still protect, faded adorn.

Yeats says that the sword and the embroidery are his "emblems" of day set against the emblem of night, the tower, another real object since it is his own tower he is writing about. So both sword and tower are real objects from which Yeats begins; and he begins with these objects already established as his symbols. The objective, therefore, is not to make the real sword or the real tower into symbols, but to let the symbols work upon the imagination so as to evoke "love and war"—the five hundred years which is the life of the blade itself, the woman from whom, perhaps in some violent struggle, the embroidery was torn, the tumultuous and multitudinous associations that are both history in the abstract and the symbol's own history (of which I spoke earlier). T. Sturge Moore designed the bookplate for Yeats's volume *The Tower,* and in a letter of instructions from Yeats, in 1927, there is a passage relevant to our present discussion: "I need not make any suggestions, except that the Tower should not be too unlike the real object, or rather that it should suggest the real object. I like to think of that building as a permanent symbol of my work plainly visible to the passer-by." Indeed, as early as 1908 (in a Note to *The Wind among the Reeds* in the *Collected Works*), Yeats had confessed the weakness of an over-indulgence in symbols for their own sake; these in turn required "lengthy notes" to clarify what he felt to be a "reckless obscurity." But into these notes he had, he admits, put "more wilful phantasy than I now think admirable. . . ." He would from now on stay closer to "the real object."[39]

When Rimbaud takes a "blade" as his symbol in "Honte" he works the matter quite differently from the manner in which Yeats treated his "consecrated blade":

> Tant que la lame n'aura
> Pas coupé cette cervelle,
> Ce paquet blanc, vert et gras,
> A vapeur jamais nouvelle...

Rimbaud's blade is an unspecified object, real only in the sense that it is an object taken from the real world. Like Yeats, Rimbaud begins with the object, but the "symbolic" quality of the blade becomes clear only as the poem progresses, and as we get farther away from its concrete associations and closer to what Rimbaud wants us to associate with it:

> (Ah! Lui, devrait couper son
> Nez, sa lèvre, ses oreilles,

[39]*W. B. Yeats and T. Surge Moore, Their Correspondence,* ed. Ursula Bridge, p. 114; *Variorum Edition,* p. 800.

Son ventre! et faire abandon
De ses jambes! ô merveille!)

Mais, non; vrai, je crois que tant
Que pour sa tête la lame,
Que les cailloux pour son flanc,
Que pour ses boyaux la flamme...

Rimbaud's blade is not quite the same as Baudelaire's Paris, since Baudelaire was a greater master of rendering the realistic detail before moving on to its symbolic implications. But both Rimbaud and Baudelaire desire effects that terminate in the symbol; Yeats the effects that are generated by it—toward associations that cannot properly be called symbolic any more, except as we call love, war, violence, courtly ladies, "symbolic" abstractions, poetic short-cuts, allusions.

One might go on making comparisons; for instance, one could take Yeats's symbol of the swan in "The Wild Swans at Coole" and set it against Baudelaire's use of the swan in "Le Cygne" and arrive at a similar distinction; but further comparisons would lead us too far afield from the present subject. I have suggested the difference in treatment, not because I think it operates unfailingly, but because it contains an essential truth worth stating: while *symbolisme* moved toward a coalescing symbol, Yeats moved away from an exfoliating one.

In theory, Yeats makes his distinctions quite clear. Shakespeare, he thinks, in "The Symbolism of Poetry," was "content" to give us emotional symbols "that he may come the nearer to our sympathy," and in response to them, "one is mixed with the whole spectacle of the world"; Dante, on the other hand, moves us so that we become "mixed into the shadow of God or of a goddess." Because his symbols are impersonal, the *symboliste* poet is closer to Dante than to Shakespeare, though he lacks Dante's consciousness of his own use of such symbols. Yeats shrewdly takes Gérard de Nerval's account of how in his madness he saw " 'vaguely drifting into form, plastic images of antiquity' " as an example of the modern symbolist. "In an earlier time," de Nerval would still have been one with the "multitude" revealing "those processions of symbols that men bow to before altars, and woo with incense and offerings," instead of exclaiming that what he saw " 'seemed to represent symbols of which [he] only seized the idea with difficulty.' " In short, de Nerval as a modern poet—though the Great Memory is never absent—is cut off from the "procession" of symbols, from the symbol's history. Hence, "being of our time," he has like all modern symbolists been "preoccupied with intellectual symbols"—that is, if we have followed Yeats's argument—with symbols that the poet recreates out of what he may think are "arbitrary" impulses; though, if he is good enough, he will make his symbols re-enter the Great Memory from whence they really came. This amounts to the modern poet's anticipatory defence against the charge of having created a private symbolism—a charge that has been frequently made against Yeats and others. Provided the symbol is "in the hands of him who has the secret," it can never be merely "arbitrary" or private —so Yeats believed in "Magic," an essay which closes with a question: "And surely . . . we must cry out that imagination is always seeking to remake the world according to the impulses and the patterns in that great Mind, and that great Memory?"[40] To *remake*: the artist is no mere mirror of the "procession," for he must continually remake what has been undone, restore what has been forgotten, reaffirm what has been discarded. This, if you wish, is the religion of the artist, his sacred mission.

That modern preoccupation with intellectual symbols, evoking "ideas mingled with emotion," promises a new "sacred book": so at least Yeats hoped at the close of his essay on "The Symbolism of Poetry." But he cautions that the arts must "overcome the slow dying of men's hearts that we call the progress of the world"—the increasing tendency to forget and unlearn the Great Memory or procession. The arts must once again learn to "lay their hands upon men's heart-strings." How—it is a question—can the arts achieve this "without becoming the garment of religion as in old times?" At least Shakespeare could still achieve some form of unity,

> [his] mind and the mind of his audience being interested in emotion and intellect at their moment of union and at their greatest intensity—he could only write his best when he wrote of those who controlled the mechanism of life. Had they been controlled by it, intellect and emotion entangled by intricacy and detail could never have mounted to that union which . . . is a conflagration of the whole being.[41]

Though he used emotional symbols, Shakespeare had not forgotten their intellectual history, and so his symbols would evoke emotions and ideas as well; the modern symbolist, using intellectual symbols, has become unconscious of that history and must refurbish his memory, make its borders dissolve and join with the Great Memory

[40]"The Symbolism of Poetry," *Essays*, pp. 199–200; "Magic," *ibid.*, pp. 63, 60.

[41]"The Symbolism of Poetry," *ibid.*, p. 200; *The Irish Dramatic Movement*, in *Plays and Controversies*, p. 20.

—and become conscious of the process. It seems curious that Yeats should call the modern symbolist's symbols intellectual, for we might expect him to say precisely the opposite: the modern symbolist, arbitrarily creating symbols out of personal responses, creates emotional effects, the effects of the senses. But Yeats was not confusing matters; he considered modern symbols intellectual for two reasons: they were created by intellectual effort no matter whether in madness, in trance, or in dream, for, as the example of de Nerval demonstrated, the poet barely recognized what arose out of his own mind. The intellectual effort consists both of having to create under abnormal conditions, induced voluntarily or the result of the artist's fate in our time, and of having then to grope back toward recognition. Secondly, modern symbols were intellectual because they depended ultimately upon a tradition—so at least Yeats thought in 1900—which had simply been forgotten; they resembled more the ancient names of the moon than the personal human associations of the rushy pool, but a poet like de Nerval, while he may use the moon, has forgotten her names. One must admit that Yeats was perhaps too optimistic in his appraisals and could not yet foresee all the dangers of Mallarmé's final obscurity, Rimbaud's vengeance upon poetry; but the issue he raised was central not only for himself but for his time. If, finally, he felt the need to write *A Vision* in order to back up the metaphors of his poetry with a "System," it is to his credit that he undertook the great task: it would do its service as a constant reminder of the Great Memory and the procession.

In any case, the artist must evacuate his work both of *disembodied* feeling and of *disembodied* intellect: the first would reduce art to mere pattern or shadow; the second to mere subject-matter. Both tended to occupy too much space and deprived multitude of the necessary motion, the sweep, that would bring the desired effect: a sense of reaching out and a sense of reaching back to the "old beliefs." "Shall we," Yeats asks in his 1913 essay, "Art and Ideas," once again "live amid the thoughts that can go with us by steam-boat and railway as once upon horse-back, or camel-back, rediscovering, by our re-integration of the mind, our more profound Pre-Raphaelitism, the old abounding, nonchalant reverie?" He wants no more ephemeral art, no art whose effects are so temporary that when we leave it we forget it; the more "profound Pre-Raphaelitism" showed him that an art still preoccupied with the "permanent" can achieve that lingering effect, arouse old emotions, cling to the memory.[42]

[42]"Art and Ideas," *Essays*, p. 441.

To achieve multitude, then, Yeats had first to discover as precisely as he could what he meant by "symbol"; and it is clear that symbol came to mean something more than an indefinite and suggestive image. A symbol would need to be first within a "received" tradition (or "procession") and then evoke worlds beyond the individual who invoked it. Poet and reader both must dissolve personal memories and re-enter the Great Memory toward which their personal memories would be pulled by the inherent force, the gravitational pull, in the magnet-like symbol itself. Thus in "The Second Coming" or in "Leda and the Swan" the poet could write of future or past events, not impersonally, but with the kind of prophetic or historic authority that remained as individual as parts of the Bible. Intensity would come of its own accord when all associations met at the centre, when borders dissolved, memories merged, and all became one—became what Yeats was to call "one vivid image." In his collection of "discoveries," Yeats had recognized that what had appeared at first to be a fulfillment was but a momentary promise, a way toward final goals but not yet the goal itself. Symbolism, to have any proper life in a world where it would be taken seriously, must take root in a time of belief, a common faith that would join not only artist and audience but artist and subject:

All symbolic art should arise out of a real belief, and that it cannot do so in this age proves that this age is a road and not a resting-place for the imaginative arts. I can only understand others by myself, and I am certain that there are many who are not moved as they would be by that solitary light burning in the tower of Prince Athanais [*sic*], because it has not entered into men's prayers nor lighted any through the sacred dark of religious contemplation.[43]

By 1916, Yeats was convinced that the tide was turning and that he must help to turn it; "pattern," he charged, was now being over-

[43]*Discoveries*, in *ibid.*, pp. 364–365. The quotation is from "Religious Belief Necessary to Religious Art," 1907: see Introduction, n. 8. This chapter of *Discoveries* was originally entitled "Religious Belief Necessary to Symbolic Art," and was so printed in *Discoveries*, 1907, and in *Collected Works*, 1908. In *The Cutting of an Agate* (1912) the title was altered from ". . . Symbolic Art" to ". . . Religious Art" and has remained so in all subsequent reprintings. It is interesting to speculate why this change was made (assuming it is a change and not an error that has simply remained undetected). One reason may well be that between 1908 and 1912 Yeats shifted away from an emphasis on the "symbolic" and moved toward a closer alliance of the term "symbolic" with "religious." Such an explanation seems supported by my discussion of "Art and Ideas" (1913) and by the preceding account of Yeats's changing attitudes toward symbolism in art.

emphasized at the expense of everything else.[44] Three years earlier he had once again noticed how the Pre-Raphaelites had found a way of achieving a rich art, but he would now be willing to attain such richness by sparser means. He was cleaning the slate that he had begun to clear of what he wanted to discard as early as 1901, when Sarah Bernhardt showed him a way.

III

Painting and sculpture, and their effects upon acting and staging, were perhaps the most important experiences in shaping Yeats's early aesthetic. He learned more, one suspects, from his solitary walks in the British Museum, his hours spent in the London and Dublin National Galleries and the Tate, his attentive ear bent toward the conversations of his father's artist-friends, and his visits to the theatre, than from any subsequent reading. Somehow in the theatre all the arts seemed to merge for him, and he was able to perceive how methods could be successfully transplanted from one art to another. His reaction to Sarah Bernhardt's *Phèdre* was intense and one can see the mind at work balancing elements like a juggler. The date is 1901:

> Sara[h] Bernhardt would keep her hands clasped over . . . her right breast for some time, and then move them to the other side . . . and then, after another long stillness, she would unclasp them and hold one out . . . not lowering them till she had exhausted all the gestures of uplifted hands. Through one long scene De Max . . . never lifted his hand above his elbow, and it was only when the emotion came to its climax that he raised it to his breast. Beyond them stood a crowd of white-robed men who never moved at all, and the whole scene had the nobility of Greek sculpture, and an extraordinary reality and intensity.[45]

The description of Miss Bernhardt's slow movements broken up by

[44]*Letters*, p. 607. I have tried, particularly in the present chapter, to keep separate the words symbolism and *symbolisme*, symbolist and *symboliste*. The former words apply, generally speaking, to poets such as Dante, Shelley, or Blake, poets whose work Yeats considered to be "symbolic" because it was unified by a self-consistent "system" of symbols. The French words, therefore, refer to the specific French school of poetry identified by the term *symbolisme*. It has been impossible to keep to this distinction rigidly, but I have attempted to adhere to it wherever my own argument, or Yeats's, seemed to warrant it.

Aside from Wilson's *Axel's Castle* and Kermode's study, the most interesting discussions of Yeats and Symbolism are in C. M. Bowra's *The Heritage of Symbolism* and in Northrop Frye's essay, "Yeats and the Language of Symbolism," *UTQ*, XVII (October, 1947), 1–17. The question has been raised most recently by Sr. Melchiori in *The Whole Mystery of Art*.

[45]*The Irish Dramatic Movement*, in *Plays and Controversies*, p. 21.

moments of "long stillness" and thus achieving intensity—all this anticipates the language of 1916 and 1938. Such oscillation between passion and repose might be maintained in several ways, but the final aim was always intensity which, Yeats learned very early, need not be achieved by an equivalent demonstration of activity, though it required the *effect* of a reverberating gesture—not mere dramatic intrusion—to produce it. Indeed, Miss Bernhardt's effect came as much from her withholding as from her giving, the giving being just sufficient to reveal the potential of power inherent in it.

Mrs. Patrick Campbell, the actress, received the same compliment as Sarah Bernhardt, though it was also a more personal comment. The same year he wrote with such admiration about the performance of *Phèdre,* he told Mrs. Campbell in a letter (*Letters,* p. 360):

> Your acting seemed to me to have the perfect precision and delicacy and simplicity of every art at its best. It made me feel the unity of the arts in a new way. I said to myself, this is exactly what I am trying to do in [my] writing, to express myself without waste, without emphasis. To be impassioned and yet to have a perfect self-possession, to have a precision so absolute that the slightest inflection of voice, the slightest rhythm of sound or emotion plucks the heart-strings.

Implicit passion and explicit discipline: it was precisely what he urged upon Dorothy Wellesley decades later in the famous injunction: "down Hysterica passio." The "slightest" motion must suggest the greatest passion: that was one way.

In the theatre, the dramatist had traditionally avoided the effects of contrivance or self-conscious pattern by creating illusions of haphazard reality, by attempting to imitate the rhythms of life which were, after all, accidental. Obviously Yeats could not accept that solution, for he was unwilling to compromise art for illusions designed essentially to deny it; besides he wanted above all "form." One of his earliest solutions was to suggest the possibility of a reciter, a minstrel-like actor creating allusion; that was a second way. "His art is nearer to pattern than that of the player [i.e., actor]. It is always allusion, never illusion; for what he tells of . . . is always distant. . . ."[46] Without crowding either the work or the spectator, allusion of language and the creation of distance on the stage enabled the artist to create multitude with a minimum of visible means. Yeats always stressed that language provided the literary artist with powers unique among the arts: the tonal strength of words, even when detached from mean-

[46]*Ibid.*, p. 181.

ing, produces echoes that carry beyond the boundaries of pattern. One of Blake's three "primary commands" had been "to desire always abundance and exuberance."[47]

Such rich abundance, whether in painting, poetry, or drama, must never be attempted quantitatively; the very nature of art, Yeats argued, was antithetical to an actual articulation of fullness. Artists who withhold gain a "lofty and severe quality," style and dignity.[48] To tell all would be to overwhelm through sheer immensity what ought to have been left to suggestion, allusion, and distance. And "Emotion of Multitude" demonstrated how drama had achieved this. It is typical of Yeats to find precedent for his idea not in the likeliest sources—the French *symbolistes*, Maeterlinck, the subtle lyricists, Keats or Shelley—but primarily in Shakespeare. Strengthened by traditional support, the theory of allusiveness gained in a corresponding hardness and masculinity of temper, for who could accuse Shakespeare of being vague? Moreover, Shakespeare provided the example of drama which might be translated to the art of poetry.

When still a boy Yeats had been subjected to his father's declamation of passionate speeches from Shakespeare, but when he re-read the plays at the turn of the century his ears were sensitive to different tones. Although he sees *Richard II* as essentially a play divided by the old and the new, the medieval Richard and the modern Bolingbroke, it is not the open conflict which gives the play its sad poignancy. It is rather Shakespeare's ability to "watch the procession of the world with that untroubled sympathy for men as they are" which is "the substance of tragic irony" in the play.[49] Like the procession of symbols in Dante or Blake, this "procession of the world" envelops Shakespeare's world with the psychological depth—perhaps reach is a more accurate word—which constitutes multitude. Among moderns, Synge, equally capable of exuberance and extravagance, has had this extraordinary talent for creating processions; it was consistently the quality which Yeats most admired in him, this and his dispassionate morality, an "untroubled sympathy" like Shakespeare's. Through their expansiveness the greatest artists give us always experiences of the imagination from which we had hitherto been barred. Dispensing with all attempts to attain strict verisimilitude, Sophocles and Shakespeare both "heighten the expression of life"; it is *their* plays which evoke a sense of familiarity from the audience, not Ibsen's, which

[47]"Blake," *Essays*, pp. 148, 151, 152.
[48]*Discoveries*, in *ibid.*, p. 337.
[49]"At Stratford-on-Avon," *ibid.*, p. 130.

depend so amply on more naturalistic effects.[50] When art delights us with the familiar it is, contrary to belief, most art, since "art, in its highest moments, is not a deliberate creation, but the creation of intense feeling, of pure life. . . ."[51] But what Shakespeare had conceived in the dramatic form could not be repeated.

From the start Yeats felt the burden of a moribund Shakespearean convention: the five-act blank verse drama. Yet Shakespeare provided an ethos. Full of the multiplicity of passions, the plays never depreciated in intensity; and the capacity for a far-reaching reverie in, say, Hamlet never degenerated into a listless immobility, a shadowy vagueness, or an overburdened allegory. While Yeats never intended to imitate Shakespeare's form, the unity of effect in the plays offered him a model, though such intensity was not easy to reach outside the grandeur of blank verse. Yet aside from style, Shakespeare and Synge seemed each to have found a common way of reconciling the two directions that always confronted Yeats: a bursting, joyous exfoliation of passion and an isolated, disciplined emotion. All see-saw movements of this kind gain stability when they find sanction in a dialectic, and in 1902 Yeats discovered an astonishingly useful dialectic in Nietzsche.

Dionysian and Apollonian were equated with the "two movements" of the soul: "one to transcend forms, and the other to create forms." Weary of the Dionysian transcending force, Yeats calls upon the restorative Apollo; dominant in his mind now is the will to create, to think only "thought that leads straight to action."[52]

Apparently Shakespeare had invigorated his imagination more or less permanently, for Dionysus was never again to play the dominant role in his creative drives; the "marriage" he had always pursued had at last been consecrated. Upon the "bride-bed" of art he placed sun and moon, in "mystical embrace." With its strong gravitational pull, the lunar was the source of all folk art, made "out of the common impulse," not through conscious arrangement. Dominated by the moon, art "thirsts to escape out of bounds," and it is this longing which makes folk art melancholy. Unchecked, sadness turns upon itself: "Such poetry . . . desires an infinity of wonder or emotion, for where there is no individual mind there is no measurer-out, no marker-in of limits." But in the greatest art

> there is the influence of the sun too, and the sun brings . . . not merely discipline but joy; for its discipline is not of the kind the multitudes impose

[50]*The Irish Dramatic Movement*, in *Plays and Controversies*, p. 157.
[51]*Ibid.*, p. 102. [52]*Letters*, p. 403.

upon us by their weight and pressure, but the expression of the individual soul turning itself into a pure fire and imposing its own pattern. . . . When we have drunk the cold cup of the moon's intoxication, we thirst for something beyond ourselves, and the mind flows outward to a natural immensity; but if we have drunk from the hot cup of the sun, our own fulness awakens . . .; the songs and stories . . . from either influence are a part, neither less than the other, of . . . the bride-bed of poetry.[53]

The distinction is between inner and outer multitude, between disciplined and undisciplined passion. Through its tidal influence, the moon occasions an "outward" flowing, "natural immensity"; in contrast, the sun brings the soul to perfection of pure fire and awakens a "fulness" within us. Clearly a marriage of outward flow and inner "fulness," cold and hot, would achieve an equilibrium between the spaciousness of multitude and the containment of intensity.

With increasing insistence, Yeats stressed that, partly through this marriage of sun and moon, it was possible to breathe into art a vastness of life without realistic simulations of grandeur—a multitude of characters, conflicts, situations. In drama, he asks, "is not the greatest play not the play that gives the sensation of an external reality but the play in which there is the greatest abundance of life itself, of the reality that is in our minds?"[54] After the turn of the century, the language of Yeats's prose bursts with exultant metaphors of depth and width, full of cries for "great open spaces" or "the soul rejoicing in itself" in the exalted idiom of spaciousness. Using his special talents to create a simple, powerful, and resonant language, Synge is "rammed with life" and compares with Homer, the Bible, and Villon.[55] Even at the close of the century in his essays on symbolism, Yeats identified the great liberating force of the symbol as being inherent in its singleness which, through intense focus, achieves the effect of a multitudinous life. In painting, as in literature, the particular objects call forth emotions equivalent to their intrinsic measurement, unless there is a "loosening" of the "bonds" that circumscribe and limit them. Such bonds are necessarily realistic encumbrances: the details that identify, locate, and describe particulars, "the bonds of motives and their actions, causes and their effects. . . ." Once freed from restrictive fetters, the object "will change under your eyes, and become a symbol of an infinite emotion," capable of moving beyond

[53]"Lady Gregory's *Gods and Fighting Men*," *Collected Works*, VIII, 163–165. See also Thomas Parkinson, "The Sun and the Moon in Yeats's Early Poetry," *MP*, L (1952), 50–58.

[54]*The Irish Dramatic Movement*, in *Plays and Controversies*, p. 120.

[55]"J. M. Synge and the Ireland of his Time," *Essays*, p. 415.

the ordinary and the accidental into the realm of the "perfected emotion." What accounts for Blake's or Wagner's spaciousness is the grandeur and wholeness of their symbolic patterns; fragmentary symbolists, still embodying symbols with "infinite emotion," fail to achieve the widening circles that give full-bodied symbols their embracing powers. In the same way, the "systematic mystic" falls short of being the best of artists because he goes too far in the opposite direction: "his imagination is too great to be bounded by a picture or a song . . . [;] only imperfection in a mirror of perfection, or perfection in a mirror of imperfection, delight our frailty."[56]

Multiplicity, then, must be bounded, quite literally framed like a painting, limited and checked, though the very process of enclosing encourages a reaching beyond, a heightening of tension, especially if the objects of art are universally symbolic. Both a too fragmented and a too inclusive imagination disturb the equilibrium. Because the universal symbol reaches perfection, the perfectly imagined pleases, but again only if incompletely expressed—in "the mirror of imperfection"; and, in corollary fashion, the partially conceived (Keats's fragmented symbols) wrought to artistic perfection and completion as in some perfect lyric still delights. If the symbol is itself perfect, the form must not be; should the symbol be only partial, it may reach perfection in form. Either way it is governed by the marriage of sun and moon. At the same time that symbols enrich the imagination, stir it to overflowing, they dictate the measure of shoring up necessary to preserve the work of art as art.

In his unsparing criticism of both realism and abstraction, Yeats fired against Wilde as much as against Shaw and George Moore. All three he considered "abstract, isolated minds, without a memory or a landscape";[57] all were lacking in that capacity to draw on the common passions that radiate from strong and simple works. None of them had experienced that mystical sensation of recognizing a corresponding inner feeling in an outer reality, an affinity that startles us with the hint that our own private memories belong to an inclusive memory, a collective unconscious that preserves and reinvigorates the world.[58] It is precisely this conjunction of the single memory with the greater which makes for the "emotion of multitude," and, as we saw, the essay on "Magic" had foreshadowed this idea from a different perspective.

[56]"Symbolism in Painting," *ibid.*, pp. 183–185.

[57]*The King of the Great Clock Tower*, 1934; commentary on "A Parnellite at Parnell's Funeral"; see *Variorum Edition*, p. 834.

[58]"The Philosophy of Shelley's Poetry," *Essays*, p. 96.

Schiller had remarked that the Greek chorus functioned both as a barrier against reality and as a force containing the dramatic world: it shut out and shut in. Following this closely, Yeats finds the "emotion of multitude" of Greek tragedy in the chorus, in its symbolic representation of a world outside the actual dramatic event, commenting and judging with a superior knowledge. When such an emotion is lacking, as in French classical drama it often is, imagination has given way to rhetoric, and for Yeats the magic has gone out of the play. But Shakespeare achieved the most magnificent effects of multitudinous life through his sub-plots, which invariably copy the central action. *Lear* is "less . . . the history of one man and his sorrows than . . . the history of a whole evil time"; Lear and Gloucester obviously shadow each other, "and the mind goes on imagining other shadows, shadow beyond shadow till it has pictured the world." Of course, *Hamlet* is the classic example, where each character is a shadow of another, though in most plays the sub-plot operates as "the main plot working itself out in more ordinary men and women, and so doubly calling up before us the image of multitude." With such symbols as the wild duck Ibsen has achieved similar effects (even more economically, though Yeats makes no note of this), and Maeterlinck, too, with his "vague symbols that set the mind wandering from idea to idea, emotion to emotion." Each successful attempt to attain multitude is a breaking of limitations—beyond the subject through form; a broadening that depicts "the rich, far-wandering, many-imaged life of the half-seen world" beyond the "little limited life of the fable."[59]

It cannot be too much stressed that by "emotion of multitude" Yeats never meant a multitude of emotions. Multitude was no mere summary of diversified emotions or events, no quantitative measure at all. Through the choice of the proper symbols, art attained a qualitative richness which, on the stage for instance, would be more successful proportionate to the economy of physical props. A stage filled with fifty characters against a realistic set and again with half as many different emotions was necessarily less suited to evoke the emotion of multitude than a Noh play dominated by three characters on an almost bare stage. The point is obvious: art that possesses multitude numerically is incapable of suggesting it as an emotion, for when all emotions are given names and places, are identified concretely, we have allegory of a kind that requires no imaginative act on the part of the audience. Therefore the strength of the emotion of multitude was inherent in the language it required: when a

[59]"Emotion of Multitude," *ibid.*, pp. 266–267.

dramatist can rely on his props to provide equivalents for the feelings and states of mind and conflicts he has built into his drama, the language he uses will necessarily be a reduced one—reduced to a conceptual and quantitative level. If a character looking out of a window toward a view unseen by any of the audience exclaims: "I see a thousand stars, like flashing fish, caught in this great net of sky," the metaphor and simile may be acceptable on faith. But if the stage is so set up—as nowadays it often is—that the view from the window is visible to the audience, the character could not offer this language, nor really could he speak in metaphor at all, since metaphor, no matter how precise, is allusive while the stage with props is illusive. Metaphor lets us imagine: stage props imagine for us. Since the character could not say, "I see twenty-three stars . . . ," he would most likely say nothing at all about the sky, but, rather, turn to the immediate scene, the room in which he stands perhaps, whose objects are less liable to occasion a need for metaphor since both character and audience can count off and identify what is clearly before them. Yeats knew what he was about when he said that drama had lost its respect for the "sovereignty" of language.

In his plays Yeats practised what he preached. *The Resurrection* (1931) is typical:

THE GREEK: Something I can see through the window. There, where I am pointing. There, at the end of the street. [*They stand together looking out over the heads of the audience.*]

THE HEBREW: I cannot see anything. . . .

THE GREEK: Though the music has stopped, some men are still dancing, and some of the dancers have gashed themselves with knives. . . . A little further off a man and woman are coupling in the middle of the street. . . . The crowd has parted to make way for a singer. It is a girl. No, not a girl; a boy from the theatre. . . . He is dressed as a girl, but his finger-nails are gilded and his wig is made of gilded cords. He looks like a statue out of some temple. I remember something of the kind in Alexandria. . . .

And Cuchulain's battle with the sea is envisioned by the Fool who describes it to the Blind Man, who can see nothing:

BLIND MAN. What is he doing now?

FOOL. Oh! he is fighting the waves!

BLIND MAN. He sees King Conchubar's crown on every one of them.

FOOL. There, he has struck at a big one! He has struck the crown off it; he has made the foam fly. There again, another big one!

BLIND MAN. Where are the kings? What are the kings doing?

FOOL. They are shouting and running down to the shore, and the people are running out of the houses. They are all running.

BLIND MAN. You say they are running out of the houses? . . .

FOOL. There, he is down! He is up again. He is going out in the deep water. There is a big wave. It has gone over him. I cannot see him now. . . .

(*On Baile's Strand*, 1904)

Wherever possible Yeats opposed an art which relied on cumulative effects, though he always desired the suggestion of "nonchalance." Wilde's *Salomé* was a failure mainly because he had "thought he was writing beautifully when he had collected beautiful things and thrown them together in a heap." Having no visible discipline of a structured, rising action, the play remained static; it lacked the *élan vital* essential to all art.[60] Often enough, the abstraction Yeats hated tended, like realistic props, merely to crowd and make indistinct the scene of play, or poem, or painting. During the year of his essay on multitude, he worked with renewed purpose to rid his poetry of "womanish introspection," to file down the elaborateness of pattern and so to make the poetry distinctive "with a pure energy of the spirit," an art pungent with "athletic joy."[61] In suggesting instead only the allusive multitude, Yeats was aware of the dangers of losing himself in *hodos chameliontos*; he had tried to explain his life by saying: "It is not so much that I choose too many elements, as that the possible unities themselves seem without number. . . ."[62] Greater still was the danger of mistaking the allusive for the illusive, in the realist's sense; or to have the allusive turning away, passionless, from life, creating a distance from the concrete too long and too wide. Without the palpable response of the audience to the life in the work, art would be dead; the old masters triumphed in that knowledge. Looking at two paintings of Venice, Yeats comments that "Neither . . . could move us at all, if our thought did not rush out to the edges of our flesh, and it is so with all good art. . . ." Too much loyalty to discipline might easily sow the seeds of disloyalty to the other half of the dialectic, the passion of life; and once more pattern would become, as in the Cubist paintings, frozen and devoid of rhythm: "Art bids us touch and taste and hear and see the world, and shrinks from what Blake calls mathematic form. . . ."[63]

To avoid the frigidity of form without substance as well as the quicksand of substance without form, the artist must insist on maintaining the transitional relationships that keep him close to

[60] *W. B. Yeats and T. Sturge Moore, Their Correspondence*, ed. Ursula Bridge, pp. 8–9.

[61] *Letters*, pp. 434–435.

[62] *Autobiography*, p. 226.

[63] *Discoveries*, in *Essays*, p. 362.

his work. Like a puppeteer he holds all the strings, no matter how multitudinous they become; and like Fielding in the middle of *Tom Jones* he delights in that power. All contemplation must be directed toward the object, not away from it, whether the object is image or symbol; for when the artist dreams without purpose or vigilance, when he turns his back forgetfully on his own created scene, he is engulfed by the material flux and surrenders all claim to the perfection of art. This is at least one theme of "Byzantium." To withstand the tide there must be order:

> All art is sensuous, but when a man puts only his contemplative nature and his more vague desires into his art, the sensuous images through which it speaks become broken, fleeting, uncertain . . . unsubstantial and fantastic. . . . If we are to sojourn [in the purely sensuous world] . . . that world must grow consistent with itself, emotion must be related to emotion by a system of ordered images, as in the *Divine Comedy*. It must grow to be symbolic . . . achieve a distinct separated life where many related objects at once distinguish and arouse its energies in their fullness.[64]

After he had unofficially forsaken the Abbey Theatre and had already behind him the first of his Noh plays, Yeats repeated his desire for an evocative art, once again distinguishing it from the purely conceptual (as well as the merely vaporous). The distinction was between the evocative and the declarative: "I desire," he wrote (in "A People's Theatre" [1919]), "a mysterious art, always reminding and half-reminding . . . of dearly loved things, doing its work by suggestion, not by direct statement. . . ." Far from conceiving of "suggestion" in disembodied intellectual (or mystical) terms, Yeats underscored the aesthetic elements of such art: "a complexity of rhythm, colour, gesture, not space-pervading like the intellect but a memory and a prophecy."

Some conception of a collective unconscious operates in this emphasis on poetry as "any flower that brings a memory of emotion"; but the metaphor of the flower suggests also the exfoliation image, the opening up, the growing and spreading of the rose petals, just as that emblem is shown decorating the covers of some of Yeats's early volumes of poetry. Out of the growing-spreading image comes the image of ever widening circles: "Tragic emotions . . . need scenic illusion [not to be confused with realistic props], a long preparation, a gradual heightening of emotion. . . ." While art echoes and surges out it sheds itself of the external world—not life: "The arts are at their greatest when they seek for a life growing always more scornful

[64]*Ibid.*, pp. 363–364.

of everything that is not itself and passing into its own fullness . . . as all that is created out of the passing mode of society slips from it. . . ."

In the *Convito* Dante had defined beauty as proportion, as the perfectly proportioned human body; for Yeats this meant a "unity of being, the subordination of all parts to the whole . . . and not . . . the unity of things in the world. . . ."[65] No more basic a distinction could be made: true art sought unity within itself, that is, by an ordering of the whole to which the parts contribute in *subordinate* fashion—else pattern would again subdue rhythm, the detail the whole design. Instead of mirroring and trying to balance the objective things of reality—filling the work wholly and faithfully with the rhythms of life in the hope that such rhythms would make a pattern—the artist cut through "the passing mode of society" to reach a deeper reality at the circumference of form. What he cuts through is space, and the process of forging a path creates in turn the echo or resonance Yeats desired.

This concept of the poetic echo works thematically and structurally in countless poems by Yeats himself. Even in so lyric a poem as "The Wild Swans at Coole" the elements of the widening circles, widening from some centre often seen as rock or stone or a single colour, are there. The water "Mirrors a still sky" but yet itself is "brimming," and "among the stones" are the swans: nine-and-fifty of them, a number so large that their profusion of white must ultimately fuse into a single image. Indeed, the poet cannot count them all, for suddenly they "mount / And scatter wheeling in great broken rings / Upon their clamorous wings." From the illusion of stillness in the water rises the whirling movement of the ascending swans, and it leads the poet to the heart of his theme: "Passion or conquest, wander where they will, / Attend upon them still"—always, yet, and in stillness, all three meanings of "still"are implicit. At the end of the poem the swans "drift on the still water" in their mystery and beauty, somehow immortal amidst the poet's mortality, for—paradoxically—it is his death that will take them from his sight when he "awake[s] some day /To find they have flown away."

So in "Easter 1916" all the heroes of the uprising have been transformed, all changed "utterly," though their hearts, adamant with a single purpose, remain "Enchanted to a stone" in the midst of the "living stream." Though life brims, like the swans, and "Minute by minute" the landscape is metamorphosed with the rhythms of life,

[65]*The Irish Dramatic Movement*, in *Plays and Controversies*, pp. 213, 208, 179, 123, 207.

"The stone's in the midst of all," radiating through its stillness all the life around it.[66]

Most obviously the widening circles shape the entire structure of "The Second Coming," the echo travelling so far beyond control that control is lost:

> Turning and turning in the widening gyre
> The falcon cannot hear the falconer;
> Things fall apart; the centre cannot hold;
> Mere anarchy is loosed upon the world,
> The blood-dimmed tide is loosed, and everywhere
> The ceremony of innocence is drowned.

Daring though the order of images is, it succeeds: from the spatial conception of the widening circle in the context of the sky Yeats forces us, in the fifth and sixth lines, to think suddenly of water: the tide is surging, the innocence is drowned, the sky mirrors the water in some inverse way in these opening six lines. In this way the concept of growing dimensions is reinforced doubly: Yeats has structured pictorially the interpenetrating gyres that form the philosophical metaphor for the poem.

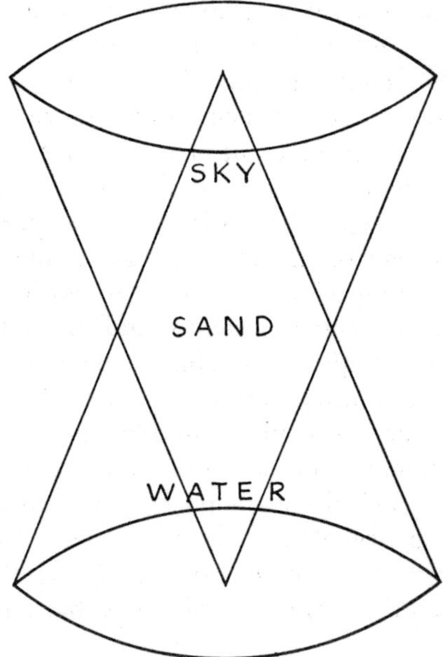

[66]I cannot agree with Unterecker's interpretation of the stone as a "dead stone" (p. 161), not while the stone is still seen in positive terms as the intensity around which revolves the life which owes its movement to the centre. In the second section,

In the second section of the poem the sand is envisioned as forbidding space, like Marvell's "Deserts of vast eternity," in the midst of which appears the beast gazing "blank and pitiless as the sun," a spherical stare that blends with the vastness of the desert itself. The beast moves, though slowly, while "all about it / Reel shadows of the indignant desert birds," circling much as the falcon had at the beginning of the poem. From the sky "darkness drops" and encases the scene, making the beholder conscious of its immediacy, of the "stony sleep" that has been deceptively lulled by a "rocking cradle" in its midst. Finally the spatial vastness is pinned down temporally by the "hour" that has "come round at last." The word "round" completes—and not accidentally—the metaphor of the cycle.

"A Prayer for My Daughter" follows "The Second Coming" chronologically, and for the first two stanzas Yeats follows somewhat the same method of infusing his poem with spaciousness. As the storm howls the poet sees, in telescoped images, the cradle of his child, Lady Gregory's wood, "one bare hill," and the wind itself beyond the shores of Ireland, "Bred on the Atlantic." He wishes us to see the wind as a "sea-wind," because the sea is on his mind, the tide and its "murderous" ability to swallow up all in its wake. The wind screams "upon the tower, /And under the arches of the bridge, and . . . / In the elms above the flooded stream." And in his "reverie" there comes a vision of the "future years" dancing to a "frenzied drum"— dancing perhaps round it, having come out of the sea. As a critic has recently noted, the wind joins the laurel tree and the horn of plenty to complete the triad of images that dominates the poem.[67] The cornucopia, an image of profusion, Yeats sets against the overflowing "haystack- and roof-levelling wind" from the sea. As for the tree, it is, of course, a metaphor of rooted existence, and his daughter—so invokes the prayer—should remain immutable while round her the future blows and dances its sinister storms.

Yeats's aim was not, of course, entirely novel; from one point of view it was no different from the various attempts of aesthetic philosophers before him—particularly among English critics—to search out a northwest passage between particular and general. Efforts to make the best of both worlds sometimes engendered major quarrels, among which that between Blake and Reynolds is perhaps the most notorious.

Yeats changes the image by saying that the hearts, formerly enchanted *to a stone* may, through "Too long a sacrifice," *become* stone. Here the stone can indeed become dead.

[67]Unterecker's analysis (pp. 166–168) is excellent.

On the one hand stood Reynolds, with his "grand style" and all its attendant sins: the "abstract," the "ideal," the "general"; on the other side stood Blake, championing the linear and concrete, the particular and the symbolic. Conceived as a form of allegory, the "grand style" did not offer the procession of symbols that Blake or Yeats imagined necessary to art. The lines of Blake moved consciously from the abstract to the concrete; not the "concrete universal" of Johnson and Reynolds, but the universal in concretely symbolic terms; not the world seen in its likeness at the highest level of abstraction, the aesthetic cosmopolitanism of neo-classicism, but the world seen in its likeness at the highest level of concreteness. It was the fearful symmetry at war with allegory, full of an insatiable need to generalize, an almost indecent tendency to sprawl over the canvas with a kind of massive assurance, like the nudes of Rubens. This was monstrous not multitudinous. If he chooses well, Yeats was to say, the artist needed, now and again, only a single image to achieve the sense of "far-off multitudinous things."

But the choice of such an image or symbol was no mere capricious act: the artist had to choose and place image and symbol at the proper place, both in time and in space. And it was through such a placing that multitude could become intense. For methods we turn again, as Yeats did, to the plastic arts, for sculpture offers the best introduction to an examination of the Noh theory as Yeats was to develop it to suit his own needs: symbol, allusion, multitude—all terminating in the "single image."

IV

The issue which opens Lessing's *Laocoön* centres in fact on the choice of a proper moment for achieving a specific desired effect. The argument begins with a discussion of the motive for the half-open mouth of the Laocoon figure which Winckelmann insisted was neither shriek nor cry but an "oppressed and weary sigh," accentuating the victim's stoical endurance and "great soul," as he and his sons are in the death embrace of the serpents. Lessing countered that the Greeks never found it necessary to subdue passion in order to attain dignity of spirit, that the Greek temper did not evade expressions of grief and suffering on philosophic grounds. He found the explanation for Laocoon's half-open mouth in aesthetic terms: possessing as his chief aim the creation of beauty, the sculptor, Lessing argued, "was obliged . . . to abate, to lower . . . [the shriek], to tone down cries to sighing...." The difference between Winckelmann and Lessing was, then, not in interpreting the half-open mouth as sigh rather than shriek, but in ascribing motives for it. And it is by way of this difference that Lessing reached his main hypothesis. Granted that the artist is an imitator of life, he is no mere recorder; the plastic artist must choose some moment in time and space at which to begin: he must select a "fruitful" moment, the "one single moment." Such a "fruitful" moment must never be the "supreme moment," for it would leave nothing unsaid, nothing for the spectator's imagination: "When...Laocoön sighs, the imagination can hear him shriek; but if he shrieks, then she cannot mount a step higher...."[68] Wagner had obviously been mindful of this concept when he suggested that the artist isolate a "supreme moment of action" in which all "motives ...are to be condensed and absorbed into one";[69] and Yeats had been searching for the intensity of the moment whose supremacy would be suggested, not stated. Such a moment would leave, as it were, a good deal of space which an echo could traverse, a potential in which intensity had room to expand.

The sweeping nature of Yeats's imagination, coming of age in a century when artists were not notably inclined to limit their scope, put him on guard at once against the pressing "thirst for unbounded emotion."[70] The problem was not to diminish the emotion but to find the means of articulating it. To check the tremulous upheavals of great joy or grief, the artist arrests the moment to attain a temporary stillness, both hushing and intense; and that intensity would again be a kind of motion beyond arrest. Like the half-open mouth of Laocoon, the disembodied moment of the artist's choice must suggest the energy (without defining it) in which it is embodied, must suggest what it does not directly express. With Wyndham Lewis, Yeats despised the mere "deification of the moment"—he was, to that extent, anti-Bergsonian—for he considered it a propitiatory act that weakened lesser souls and turned the world into "fruit-salad."[71] Emptied of all but its own stationary existence, art would lack the essential rhythm, without which, like the Cubist paintings, it would turn into mere abstraction—the pictures of allegory with defined limitations. Yeats was pleased to find support in the philosophers, particularly in Whitehead, who denied the existence of objects in "'localized space'" and

[68]G. E. Lessing, *Laocoön*, ed. William Steel (London, 1950), pp. 6, 13–14.
[69]Symons, "The Ideas of Richard Wagner," *Studies in Seven Arts*, p. 171.
[70]"The Celtic Element in Literature," *Essays*, p. 227.
[71]*Letters*, p. 782.

thought in terms that resembled Yeats's cones and gyres. Always turning, the gyres never permitted cessation or fixation: the two moving gyres "represent the conflict...of plane and line, by two movements, which circle about a centre because a movement outward on the plane is checked by and in turn checks a movement onward upon the line...."[72] As when a pebble is thrown into the water, there were ever-widening circles from a focal centre.

Convinced that "reality is timeless," Yeats considered the most fundamental, "the most obvious," of antinomies to be that between past and present.[73] But past and present were not, as sometimes in the early Eliot, opposed either to shore up ruins or to make the present pay the price of a damaging comparison. Yeats went about his conception more philosophically: the past represented for him both the burden and the exhilaration of bearing up under the strain of accumulated vastness; the present demanded from the artist that most difficult of transmutations, or transvaluations: to make the past, mere dream, a living present.

Any conception of a living present must be based on a metaphysical conviction that reality—life—is fluid, that the living being modifies and is in turn modified by reality. Such a view would harmonize with the aesthetic conceptions of multitude and intensity, for the outward and inward movements in a work of art corresponded with that free reaching forward and backward in time characteristic of a conception of reality as fluid and in part created by the individual. Yeats's immediate source for this metaphysic was Bergson, whom he read carefully and, it seems, sympathetically. In *Creative Evolution* —the title already announces the thesis—Bergson compared art and life, both being essentially fluid: "Each... [moment] is a kind of creation. And just as the talent of the painter is formed or deformed—modified—under the very influence of the works he produces, so each of our states, at the moment of its issue, modifies our personality, being indeed the new form that we are just assuming." For Bergson, then, life was process: "we are creating ourselves continually"; for the conscious man existence was synonymous with change. Bergson also emphasized the limitation of sense perceptions, a position which Yeats had already approved in Berkeley. The human eye, said Bergson, misses the essential "intention" of life, and the artist is one type of man who seeks to regain the significance of that intention in his

[72]Notes on "The Second Coming" in *Michael Robartes and the Dancer,* 1921; *Variorum Edition,* p. 824.
[73]*Letters,* p. 784.

work. He achieves this by "placing himself back within the object by a kind of sympathy, in breaking down, by an effort of intuition, the barrier that space puts up between him and his model."[74] This effort of sympathy and intuition corresponds very closely to Yeats's early and tentative notion of the "moods" and to his conception of how the poet's perceptions of a fluid reality allow him to unify discord, to dissolve the boundaries of memory, as he said in "Magic," in order to attain a blending of perceiver and object outside the bounds of causality, time, and space.

Surely part of "Among School Children" is about this process, and certain stanzas of the poem appear to objectify it both in theme and in technique.

I

I walk through the long schoolroom questioning;
A kind old nun in a white hood replies;
The children learn to cipher and to sing,
To study reading-books and histories,
To cut and sew, be neat in everything
In the best modern way—the children's eyes
In momentary wonder stare upon
A sixty-year-old smiling public man.

II

I dream of a Ledaean body, bent
Above a sinking fire, a tale that she
Told of a harsh reproof, or trivial event
That changed some childish day to tragedy—
Told, and it seemed that our two natures blent
Into a sphere from youthful sympathy,
Or else, to alter Plato's parable,
Into the yolk and white of the one shell.

[74]Henri Bergson, *Creative Evolution*, tr. Arthur Mitchell (New York, 1911), pp. 7, 177. I am indebted to Professor Thomas Parkinson of the University of California (Berkeley) for generously passing on to me the information that Yeats had read *Creative Evolution* with great care, especially the first one hundred pages; the margins of his copy appear to be free of ironic commentary, a pastime Yeats indulged in when he read philosophers, particularly Russell. Professor Parkinson also tells me that *Matter and Memory* was read with care as well as Whitehead's *Science and the Modern World*; Yeats's copy of the latter again is free of ironic comment.

This poses somewhat of a problem, for Yeats approvingly read Wyndham Lewis's *Time and Western Man* when it appeared in 1927. Lewis's two chief targets in that polemical book are Bergson and Whitehead. I do not think Yeats changed his mind. He found in Lewis a certain manly expression and a rigorous and assertive quality which attracted him; the exact nature of his philosophic agreement remains obscure,

III

And thinking of that fit of grief or rage
I look upon one child or t'other there
And wonder if she stood so at that age–
For even daughters of the swan can share
Something of every paddler's heritage–
And had that colour upon cheek or hair,
And thereupon my heart is driven wild:
She stands before me as a living child.

IV

Her present image floats into the mind–
Did Quattrocento finger fashion it
Hollow of cheek as though it drank the wind
And took a mess of shadows for its meat?
And I though never of Ledaean kind
Had pretty plumage once–enough of that,
Better to smile on all that smile, and show
There is a comfortable kind of old scarecrow.

Many readers have commented on the brisk opening stanza: the poet seems to stride in and see, in a quick succession of glances, the whole scene: the nun in white, the children at their many activities, and their staring eyes. In fact it is perhaps those staring eyes that transfix the poet and move him into his reverie, his dream of a Ledaean body, Maud Gonne, and the images of spheres and eggs that emerge naturally from those of the children's eyes. "I walk"; "I dream": the opening words of the first two stanzas are clearly meant to distinguish between the poet's active and passive states, his motion and emotion. The memory of the trivial event is a dream-tableau, with a sense of dissolving and merging focused on the blending of the two natures, the sphere, the yolk and white of the egg. "And thinking": the third stanza begins with an activity still mental, but the poet is reflecting rationally, not dreaming: the past begins to come to life under the aspect of the present, for already he is looking again at the children in the classroom, wondering, creating his parallel between Maud Gonne, the child, and the children consciously, deliberately. Even for Yeats, used to the unusual experience, this phenomenon of trans-

but anyone familiar with *Time and Western Man* will discover there too many things Yeats could not possibly have found acceptable. Also Yeats's previous remarks about Lewis's cubist paintings and some of his novels–*Tarr*, for example–were not complimentary. At any rate the Yeats-Bergson-Whitehead, Lewis-Bergson-Whitehead, and Yeats-Lewis relationships need further exploring.

lating the living image into the dream and vice versa becomes, for a moment, too much; his heart is "driven wild," motion drives emotion. And the colon in the penultimate line calls attention to itself dramatically for the breakthrough that has occurred, as, suddenly, Maud Gonne stands before him "as a living child." This high pitch is subdued in the stanza following, for the instant of union between life and image is already gone. She is an "image" after all, and "floats" to mind, where, not satisfied with the conception of some finished portrait, Yeats muses on its creation, animates the image as he thinks of the "Quattrocento finger" that fashioned it, that hollowed out the cheeks. As he sinks again deeper into his own dream he attempts to link himself through the memory of his own "pretty plumage" to the Ledaean body but, like Hamlet, he checks himself: "enough of that"—he is dangerously close to becoming transfixed by his own dream, by the floating image that began the stanza. It is better, he argues, to concede to the present, to those who smile. Past image cannot deny present life, no matter what its powers are. And so the stanza, until now liquid and soft with the shifting images of dream (floating image, Ledaean body, pretty plumage, even smile) ends abruptly, and half-humorously, in the static, lifeless—but present—image of the scarecrow. The antinomy of past and present remains, for the moment, fruitfully unresolved. But reality *is* "timeless": the surging waves of memories which subtly double themselves through the historical allusions—the reach toward distance—achieve a momentary sense of multitude radiating from the central reality of the poet's presence in the schoolroom; and, inevitably, it is back to the single image of his presence that he returns.

The whole process of ranging over the perceptions of one's memories, selecting here or there some dominant moment which for a time appropriates the whole consciousness, owed something to Yeats's sensibilities and intuitions, partially acquired, one supposes, through his early and brief training as a painter. Shape, form, and colour all had a way of flooding his imagination which, when it seized on any one of them, was able to bring it into dominant focus. He describes in detail the effects of such an experience:

I opened my eyes and looked at some red ornament on the mantlepiece, and at once the room was full of harmonies of red, but when a blue china figure caught my eye the harmonies became blue upon the instant . . . the reds were . . . there . . . but they were no longer important or harmonious; and why had the blues so unimportant but a moment ago become exciting and delightful? . . . it struck me that I was seeing like a painter, and that in the course of the evening every one there would change through every kind of artistic perception.[75]

So, by analogy, he would choose from the scenes of life special passions, fix his eyes upon some "fruitful moment" to highlight poem or play. Other passions would be there, but they would not be "important or harmonious": the ruling passion would draw, like a magnet, everything to its gathering tension. In the absorption of what surrounds it, the single powerful image gained in sovereignty and there was no danger in having to compete with any neighbours. Unlike the realist Yeats would not mix all colours to achieve an illusion of a faithful description of reality; the effect came from merging, not profusion:

All sounds, all colours, all forms . . . evoke indefinable and yet precise emotions, or . . . call down among us certain disembodied powers . . . we call emotions; and when sound, and colour, and form are in a musical relation . . . to one another, they become as it were one sound, one colour, one form, and evoke an emotion that is made out of their distinct evocations and yet is one emotion. The same relation exists between all portions of every work of art. . . .[76]

In the proper scheme, the multiple units of art merge into a unity by way of their patterned relationships; this is quite different from a conscious motive to isolate, with obsessive attention, a single subject, as Yeats accused Wyndham Lewis of having "isolated" sex in *Tarr*. Just as overcrowding with detail diminishes effectiveness by sacrificing depth for breadth, so the isolation of subject-matter suffers the same consequences of limitation by sacrificing echo for the immediate and short-lived power of pure concentration. What was wanted was fusion: the one emerging from the many, or the many merging into the one.

That a controlled multiplicity would play back the effects of isolated and intense moments, Yeats had already glimpsed in his essay of 1903. But his introduction to the Noh plays convinced him that this was the art he had been in search of for so long. A drama of "the greatest passions," clothed in tradition, full of allusion and distance, the Noh plays became—for the moment—the synthesis of all his previous aesthetic theorizing. For some time after 1900 he had been insisting that poetry must rid itself of the "energetic rhythms, as of a man running," which betray a hurried, utilitarian will intent

[75]*Discoveries*, in *Essays*, p. 349.
[76]"The Symbolism of Poetry," *ibid.*, pp. 192–193.

only on action, creative or destructive. In place of such harried rhythms he would have "wavering, meditative, organic rhythms," which issued from an imagination "done with time," and one that "only wishes to gaze upon some reality, some beauty." And in order to give shape to the supra-sensory (that beyond the shapes of material reality), language must be subtle and complex.[77]

Without the meditative rhythm Yeats describes, poems would be in danger of the diminution that would divorce them from the grander effects toward which he had always striven. At the end of the nineties, in "The Autumn of the Body," Yeats tells us that Arthur Symons had predicted that symbolism would usher in an age of "poetry of essences, separated one from another in little and intense poems." Yeats agrees that such poetry was now inevitable but, even then, he reserves for the future something beyond "disembodied ecstasy," long poems which "we will not cease to write," but write "more and more."[78] The prophecy was not literally accurate; the "length" of the poem, Yeats discovered, could be suggested, so that the "short" poem could have "long" power. Choosing cluster symbols of infinite variety, the traditional symbolist (Botticelli, Blake, Shelley) would fare better than the "poet of essences and pure ideas," who "must seek in the half-lights that glimmer from symbol to symbol . . . all that the epic and dramatic poet finds of mystery and shadow in the accidental circumstances of life."[79]

But Symons had also described Eleonora Duse's face as a "mask for the tragic passion," changing from "moment to moment." Fluidity provided the essential technique for her effects: "The outline of the face is motionless, set hard, clenched into immobility; but within that motionless outline every nerve seems awake, expression after expression sweeps over it. . . ."[80] Thus her disembodied ecstasy never isolated stillness without suggesting the contrary turbulence of passion latently, but always palpably, present. This was precisely the kind of intensity Yeats aimed at achieving.

"All art," Yeats wrote in 1902, "is . . . a monotony in external things for the sake of an interior variety, a sacrifice of gross effects to subtle effects, an asceticism of the imagination."[81] The *interior* variety reemphasizes the need to protect art against the external bulk, the need of containment. As early as 1900 Yeats had written that the

[77]*Ibid.*, pp. 201–202.
[78]"The Autumn of the Body," *ibid.*, p. 238.
[79]"The Philosophy of Shelley's Poetry," *ibid.*, p. 107.
[80]"Eleonora Duse," Symons, *Studies in Seven Arts*, p. 220.
[81]"Speaking to the Psaltery," *Essays*, p. 21.

lyric operates first by engaging a single emotion which then "gathers others about it and melts into their being in the making of some great epic."[82] The whole process again resembles his perceptions of the reds and blues. Moving from singleness the emotions of art draw to themselves others and achieve a momentary illusion of vastness; the vastness itself, however, soon coagulates to form merely another singleness, a mixture of many emotions that equal some dominant passion. Perhaps the technique is best illustrated from one of Yeats's own poems; for the sake of its familiarity and suitability, I take "Sailing to Byzantium."

Each stanza of the poem begins with a singleness that has the potential of depth; the depth is then explored in all its multifariousness; and the stanza ends with a confluence of plurality to make another, and a new, singular. In the first stanza the "country" is immediately bared in all its detail in the following lines: "The salmon-falls, the mackerel-crowded seas, / Fish, flesh, or fowl. . . ." But the stanza concludes with the "monuments of unageing intellect," the sum of the antithetical emotions aroused by the "country" in the opening line. Beginning with the "aged man," the second stanza continues to describe him and ends with the image of Byzantium as the destination where the ageing man's "tattered" body and unschooled soul will both be remade. Following is the image of the mosaic, which begins the third stanza, with its "sages standing in God's holy fire," who during the course of the stanza are given the powers that will at the end of it enable the poet to be transported "Into the artifice of eternity"—certainly an image that abstracts the nature of the holy sages. In the final stanza the entire poem is, in a way, recapitulated: the image of a projected soul out of nature is expanded to what it wishes to be (and in great detail) until the last line where, to return to Yeats's quotation, all the emotions are gathered and melt "in the making of some great epic" emotion. For "what is past, or passing, or to come" is the essential nature of the epic sweep.

Beginning with the *Four Plays for Dancers* Yeats's later plays are often intensely lyrical and passionate moments, carefully controlled and focused emotions which are skilfully embedded in a stylized and ritual form. And the Cuchulain plays certainly add up to some kind of epic effect. A heightening of life, the achievement of a transfixing intensity, can be attained only through non-realistic effects. Novels like Tolstoy's *War and Peace* gather a measure of momentum by

[82]"The Symbolism of Poetry," *ibid.*, p. 194.

sheer addition, by an architectural growth of detail, not the architectonic balance of structure of *The Divine Comedy*; though there are peaks and valleys and climactic moments, the whole of *War and Peace* is built solidly on cumulative lines. Perhaps it was this that once made Yeats remark that although *War and Peace* was the best thing he had ever read he could not remember much of it. To remain sharply aware of a work, to think outward from some centre, one must be drawn irresistibly to some single effect. In rather Platonic terms, Yeats suggested a relationship between the disorganized mass of emotions ("the crude circumstance of the world") and the emotions that the isolated artist feels "in moments of poetical contemplation." If we do not accept the visible world as the final reality, then "we must believe that the gross is the shadow of the subtle"; that through "multiplying mirrors" the profusely populated world of circumstance merely reflects the ideal, which is always single because it is perfect.[83] Elsewhere Yeats had put it more eloquently: "The imaginative writer shows us the world as a painter does his picture, reversed in a looking-glass that we may see it, not as it seems to eyes habit has made dull, but as we were Adam and this the first morning...."[84]

One temporary solution was to write one-act plays; after his dissatisfaction with his long prose play, *Where There is Nothing*, Yeats recommended the one-acter with enthusiasm, and cautioned Lady Gregory that even three-act plays have "to seem only one action."[85] From the start he had felt convinced that unity was the artist's prime and final goal. Moreover before the Noh plays, he had marked out the efficacy of the "intensity of personal life" in arousing a natural man's emotions. Deep satisfaction is one of the rewards of being witness to "the strength, the essential moment" of someone's life, his display of "personal energy." However stylized in form, the Noh plays of Japan were full of deeply human passions, not "states of mind, lyrical moments, intellectual essences"—the abstractions of two decades earlier which had nearly cut Yeats off from human compassion. While one might isolate emotions, passions, and "character[s] ... by the deed," one could never isolate oneself from life and still less from oneself. And it is *self* which gives broad power to any original single emotion, for creator and created must, at some point, fuse: it was impossible "to separate an emotion ... from the image that calls it

[83]*Ibid.*, pp. 194–195.
[84]"J. M. Synge and the Ireland of his Time," *ibid.*, p. 420.
[85]*Letters*, p. 427.

up and gives it expression,"[86] so long as that image came from the personal energy not the abstract intellect.

The aesthetic principles in "Certain Noble Plays of Japan" (1916) are not, then, a radical shift. Growing out of Yeats's increasing disappointment with the realistic-comic trends of the Abbey Theatre, the essay follows logically (and even synthesizes) the various aesthetic dialectics proposed thus far. What the model of the Noh plays provided that no European theatre had yet achieved was a certain quality of high symbolism entirely traditional and, in addition, a self-contained tension between tumultuous passion and lyrical quietude. Primarily this was accomplished by a necessary distance reminiscent perhaps of the Greek chorus: "All . . . art remains at a distance and this distance once chosen must be firmly held against a pushing world." Encroached upon by the circumstantial world art would again be confused with life. Yet, while there should be distance *between* the work and life, such distance ought not to exist *within* the work: indeed, the aesthetic elements that operate *inside* the work successfully barricade it against external invasion by closing ranks and sealing possible points of vulnerability. Thus, "Verse, ritual, music, and dance in association with action require that gesture, costume, facial expression, stage arrangement must help in keeping the door." Truly imaginative art does not merely "frame" but posits its "figures, images, symbols" to "enable us to pass for a few moments into a deep of the mind that had hitherto been too subtle for our habitation. As a deep of the mind can only be approached through what is most human, most delicate, we should distrust bodily distance, mechanism, and loud noise."

European art, the essay continues, has been fickle, moving under the "illusion of change and progress" and always abandoning the "stylistic" for new modes of realism. Such changeability never plagued the early Greek or Japanese artists; the latter had always realized that the styles which once pleased the best minds can never diminish in vitality or lose their reference. In Japan the artist has always chosen "the style according to the subject." Untempted by the illusions of realism, the "august formality" of the stylized art of Greece, Egypt, and Japan "implies traditional measurements, a philosophic defence" against life: the measurement has helped to hold the distance. Were we still ancient Greeks ("and so but half-European"), we would never have tolerated the "progress" of natural scenery or the death of the soliloquy because it was "unnatural" for the modern temper.

One of the chief innovations Yeats borrowed from the Noh was the

[86] *Discoveries*, in *Essays*, pp. 328–329, 335, 354.

mask, which would de-emphasize an actor's individual face and reduce the chances of eccentric facial expressions peculiar to some personal interpretation of a role. Quite literally the mask masked the "curiosity" and "alert attention" of a face which, deprived of these strenuous characteristics, would become nobler—and more quiet, for the mask will always be "stilling the movement of the features." Everything from the poetry of a Noh play to its scenery should be highly "artificial," radically removed from representational illusions. Philosophically conceived, the Noh drama is heavily weighted toward *being* rather than *becoming*. By and large Shakespeare's method was cumulative development of plot and character over five acts; and Maeterlinck's "static" drama moved nonetheless, since length and dialogue, subject and scenery still belonged—on the whole—to the older conventions. Of course the Noh plays were not motionless; their movement came, as already suggested, from all the fluidity embodied in mask and gesture. Pure being, Yeats thought, might belong to the dead alone; and perhaps it is that knowledge, he suggested, which "makes us gaze with so much emotion upon the face of the Sphinx or of Buddha."[87] But such states were primarily for the saint, not the artist, for whom all discipline was, in the end, as Yeats said elsewhere, a constraining act on passion—"the passion of the verse comes from . . . holding down. . . . All depends on the completeness of the holding down. . . ."[88]

In addition to mask and gesture, the Noh plays offered a formal dance. The attraction, at the turn of the century, to the human form, to dance and pantomimic gesture, has recently been explored thoroughly in Kermode's *Romantic Image*. Yeats was part of a group of artists who responded sympathetically to Loie Fuller's symbolic whirling, to what Kermode calls the ". . . Image . . . all movement, yet with a kind of stillness," but it is difficult to imagine that Yeats saw the dance chiefly in terms of this reawakening affinity with an organicist conception of Image. For one thing, his interest in the dance seems very clearly to hearken back to ancient ritual:

> O body swayed to music, O brightening glance,
> How can we know the dancer from the dance?

From Synge's *Aran Islands* Yeats quoted a passage which, if not a source, is at least closer to this final couplet than Loie Fuller: "'In a moment I swept away in a whirlwind of notes. My breath and my

[87]"Certain Noble Plays of Japan," *ibid.*, pp. 277–280.
[88]*Letters on Poetry from W. B. Yeats to Dorothy Wellesley*, p. 94.

thoughts and every impulse of my body became a form of the dance, till I could not distinguish between the instrument or the rhythm and my own person or consciousness.' "[89] The loss of conscious ego in a whirlwind of body, music, and rhythm has the most ancient associations with ritual—religious, heroic, dramatic. As a *leit-motiv,* the human form acts as a kind of "rhythm of metaphor"; Yeats himself admitted the Noh dramatists seemed less interested in the human form than "in the rhythm to which it moves, and the triumph of [the dancer's] . . . art is to express the rhythm in its intensity."[90] When Yeats refers to Loie Fuller in "Nineteen-Hundred and Nineteen," he does so by drawing the wider analogy between the Chinese dancers and the Platonic Year, both whirling in, with amoral abandon, right and wrong, good and evil, past and future. Inherently the dance is, of course, parallel to the whirling gyres and to the Heraclitean flux of "Byzantium," checked by the smithies of artistic discipline, subdued and shaped into artifacts of perfection. In essence, like the *danse macabre*, the dance in Yeats synthesizes an allegory: the pulse of life and the stillness of death stop time with the momentary hesitation of great intensity. Expressly, the whole experiment of the Noh plays was, as Yeats said in his note to *At the Hawk's Well,* to achieve the heroic and the grotesque which, scrupulously distanced from life, "would seem images of those profound emotions that exist only in solitude and in silence."[91] Through mask and dance he might join passion, extravagance, and stillness, as once he had looked, with Synge, for ecstasy, austerity, and asceticism.

Aesthetically the dance also resembled the general structure which balanced fluidity (dancer) with unity (dance). A painter who realizes that his painting must possess an essential unity from the initial sketch realizes too that "a work of art must remain fluid to the finish." If it lacks unity the sketch can never be completed, for it can grow only in "richness of detail," not in primary, formal cohesiveness.[92] Yeats ascribed his father's difficulties as a portrait painter precisely to his failure to comprehend the urgency of initial unity. "Instead of finishing a picture one square inch at a time, he kept all fluid, every detail dependent upon every other"; and fluidity without the initial vision of structure led him to "final confusion." In relating the problem to himself Yeats went further. While folk art derives some of its charm

89"J. M. Synge and the Ireland of his Time," *Essays*, p. 412.

90"Certain Noble Plays of Japan," *ibid.*, p. 285.

91"Note on the First Performance of *At the Hawk's Well,*" *Plays and Controversies*, p. 419.

92"Louis Lambert," *Essays and Introductions*, p. 443.

and mystery through an apparent and actual unrelated, piecemeal construction, when the artist attempts to remake such material—to turn the puppet play into *Faust*—he "must . . . try, fail perhaps, to impose his own limits."[93] Goethe had said that all greatness derives ultimately from limitation, and only a perception of unity can prevent fluidity from overflowing and blurring all semblance of structure. Balzac, Yeats felt, never fell victim to profusion or confusion. Confident of his vision, he set about his grand work like "those painters who set patches of pure colour side by side, knowing that they will combine in the eye into the glitter of a wave, into the sober brown of a grass seed."[94] The isolated colours combine to form a "glitter," a multiple of related colours, and then the whole turns to a single image, the wave.

It is precisely as the "single image" that the Noh was an answer to Yeats's quest for a form which would embrace, within carefully bounded limits, a single unfolding story capable of achieving a single effect. As Pound had written, at the root of Noh was "allusion" and its "unity" was "in emotion." Pound was thinking of his own interest in *imagisme* when he compared Noh to the effects of Imagistic poetry as he and others had worked them out several years earlier. Noh has "what we may call Unity of Image. At least, the better plays are all built into the intensification of a single Image . . . ," and it is Pound's footnote to this which is of interest: "This intensification of the Image, this manner of construction, is very interesting to me personally, as an Imagiste, for we Imagistes knew nothing of these plays when we set out in our own manner. These plays are also an answer to a question that has several times been put to me: 'Could one do a long Imagiste poem, or even a long poem in *vers libre*?'" The answer, of course, was yes—and Pound tried it; Yeats, perhaps wisely, did not. Yet both Pound and Yeats were impressed by the singleness of effect in the Noh, which Pound likened to Greek drama. "The [Noh] plays are at their best," he writes, ". . . an image; that is to say, their unity lies in the image—they are built up about it as the Greek plays are built up about a single moral conviction."[95]

However, we should make a clear distinction between Pound's *imagiste* conception of the "single image" and what Yeats was to call, as we will presently see, the "one vivid image." Pound's doctrines were complicated by his various interests in such movements as vorti-

[93] *Autobiography*, pp. 264–265.

[94] "Louis Lambert," *Essays and Introductions*, p. 445.

[95] Ezra Pound, "The Classical Stage of Japan," *The Drama*, 18 (May, 1915), 201, 224, 232.

cism, but essentially he offers a clear definition of "single image" when he describes the composition of his famous two-line poem "In a Station of the Metro." After giving us an account of the occasion for the poem, he goes on to outline his difficulties in finding the equivalent language to express the intense feelings he has experienced. Quite suddenly, after the first futile attempts, came a "language in colour." This discovery of the painter's techniques encouraged him to predict playfully that, were he a painter, he "might found a new school of 'non-representative' painting"; but even the "language of colour" failed him at first: a thirty-line poem was destroyed because it was not thought worthy. A whole year will pass before Pound finally writes the two-line poem we now have. From this experience Pound concluded: "The 'one image poem' is a form of super-position, that is to say, it is one idea set on top of another." For Pound, then, the "single" or "one" image was almost entirely a means of economizing and also a way of eliminating or minimizing idea or content. Moreover, he was almost defensive about separating image from symbol, and he insisted that the image does not necessarily need to have a place in any traditional framework: "If it [the image] have an age-old traditional meaning . . . that is not our affair. It is our affair to render the *image* as we have perceived or conceived it."[96] Yeats not only demanded that his "one image" be of the "procession," but also insisted that it be used not as a mere economizer but as a jewel foiled to dramatic advantage by lesser words.

When Yeats began to revise his earlier poems radically, this theory of single image was most clearly stated, having now the added advantage of practical example:

> In later years, through much knowledge of the stage, through the exfoliation of my own style, I learnt that occasional prosaic words gave the impression of an active man speaking. In dream poetry, in *Kubla Khan* . . . every line, every word, can carry its unanalysable, rich associations; but if we dramatise some . . . singer or speaker we remember that he is moved by one thing at a time, certain words must be dull and numb. Here and there in correcting my early poems I have introduced such numbness and dullness, turned . . . "the curd-pale moon" into the "brilliant moon," that all might seem . . . remembered with indifference, except some one vivid image.[97]

[96]Ezra Pound, *Gaudier-Brzeska: A Memoir* (New York: New Directions, 1960), pp. 87, 89, 86.

[97]*Autobiography*, p. 263. For discussions of Yeats's revisions directly relevant to the paragraphs which follow, see Rudolf Stamm, " 'The Sorrow of Love,' a Poem by W. B. Yeats Revised by Himself," *ES*, XXIX (June 1948), 78–87; Louis MacNeice, *The Poetry of W. B. Yeats* (Oxford, 1941), pp. 69–72; Thomas Parkinson, *W. B. Yeats, Self-Critic*, pp. 165–172.

This passage may best be discussed in terms of a simple analogy. A single heavy beat on a kettle-drum produces a far more powerful resonance than twenty pairs of drumsticks hitting little snare drums simultaneously. For one thing the kettle-drum is larger, and the rich reverberation comes precisely from the additional emptiness inside the drum, the larger space—compared to the snare drum—in which sound may travel. Translated into aesthetic terms Yeats wanted an art powerful in source and echo with what Rilke called "spaces" between words. Moreover, to achieve the deepest resonance, the widest repercussion, the kettle-drum must be struck on its sensitive middle—the hero, the single "vivid image," the isolated emotion. And the sound is then carried outward to the walls of the drum—the chorus, the symbolic multitude—which again play it back to the middle. The exchange equals dramatic intensity.

"The Sorrow of Love," the poem Yeats discusses in the passage cited, serves admirably as an example. Although the revisions of this poem have often been noted, another view of them—in terms of the theory outlined above—is still possible. Following are two versions of the poem, one from 1895 and the version found in all texts subsequent to the 1933 edition of *Collected Poems*.

1895	(1925) 1933
The quarrel of the sparrows in the eaves,	The brawling of a sparrow in the eaves,
The full round moon and the star-laden sky,	The brilliant moon and all the milky sky,
And the loud song of the ever-singing leaves,	And all that famous harmony of leaves,
Had hid away earth's old and weary cry.	Had blotted out man's image and his cry.
And then you came with those red mournful lips,	A girl arose that had red mournful lips
And with you came the whole of the world's tears,	And seemed the greatness of the world in tears,
And all the sorrows of her labouring ships,	Doomed like Odysseus and the labouring ships
And all the burden of her myriad years.	And proud as Priam murdered with his peers;
And now the sparrows warring in the eaves,	Arose, and on the instant clamorous eaves,

The curd-pale moon, the white stars in the sky,
And the loud chaunting of the unquiet leaves,
Are shaken with earth's old and weary cry.

A climbing moon upon an empty sky,
And all that lamentation of the leaves,
Could but compose man's image and his cry.

In the first stanza of the early version the sparrows are plural and the moon full; the second line with its "laden" virtually loads the opening lines with plurality. Also, in the following two lines the song of the leaves hides the cry of the whole earth. In the revision a single sparrow brawls; the moon is brilliant against a single-colour sky—milky, and the leaves blot out (a more active metaphor certainly than hide) not the whole earth but man's cry, with its suggestion of singleness and dying echo, the multitudinous arising out of the particular. Clearly the revision makes singular, both grammatically and evocatively, the plural of the earlier version.

The second stanza of the early version collapses from an overburdening metaphysical conceit: the coming of "her" brings the whole of the world's tears, nearly drowning the whole poem; and it seems the ships in the next line merely float in the flood of the preceding line. With their rather weak "sorrows" ("burden" again weighs the line down) and the abstract "myriad" the last two lines give the entire stanza an explicit all-inclusiveness. Through revision the "you" becomes in some way more particularized as a girl, and she but "seemed" to embody the whole world's tears, Yeats attempting to make the metaphor more reasonable. The allusions to Odysseus and Priam not only suggest, with choric objectivity, the wider context for the poem, but make the ships organic, justify their presence, give them gesture in addition to picture.

Continuing this pattern of the first version, the third stanza murmurs somewhat indistinctly of sparrows, chaunting leaves, and a weary cry; there is a blurring. When he revises Yeats attempts to transform all this softened effect into a single idea and image, precisely as he said he did: by removing most of the "poetic" language in order to foil some single effect. Dramatically, the girl arises, picking up in continuous action from the second stanza; and suddenly, "on the instant," the clamouring leaves, the moon against an empty sky (the empty space of the kettle-drum), and all lamentation become, in one sense of the word "composed," "man's image and his cry." Not only is the poem finally composed into unity but, in the other sense of the word, it is hushed and quieted; the tumult is reduced to a stillness.

By "dullness" and "numbness" in terms of word and image Yeats meant the stark, single, and strong in relation to the richer tonality that surrounds it; even the prosaic, the "ugly little surprising things" of Synge, were permissible. The "indifference" he hoped would encircle a nucleus word or image that could be measured only in relation to that image.

An abundance of riches destroys the fundamental requirement of art—a measured effect of distance: "there are scenes in [Synge's] *The Well of the Saints* which seem to me over-rich in words because the realistic action does not permit that stilling and slowing which turns the imagination in upon itself."[98] When he experimented with setting his *Deirdre* to music by Florence Farr, Yeats attempted to find "the exact distance from ordinary speech necessary in the first two lyrics, which must prolong the mood of the dialogue while being a rest from its passions."[99] Spatial distance between dominant words achieved the unique relatedness and tension which the Byzantine painters had controlled so masterfully by establishing significant "caesurae" between their figures; these "had to be placed at some distance apart in order that they might be brought opposite each other by the curving of the ground. The resulting distances and empty spaces are filled with a tension, an air of expectancy . . . more dramatic . . . than violent action and gesticulation, or a closely knit [dense] grouping. . . ."[100]

In microcosm, Yeats's second Byzantine poem, "Byzantium," illustrates the poetic theory that binds the essay on multitude with that on the Noh drama thirteen years later. The whole poem is an illustration of reverberating drums; the gong of the Cathedral works literally to evacuate the "scene" of the poem of all flux-like, daylight multiples, in order to clear space for the mummy-guide who is to control the rest of the poem. In the final magnificent stanza, the echoes again become clearly audible: the push, the persistence of the sea, forces itself continually on the "marmorean stillness" of the marbles with an "overflowing turbulent energy."

Although "Byzantium" may not be a poem solely about the creation of a work of art, as F. A. C. Wilson has cautioned convincingly,[101] it is a poem that reflects the aesthetic dialectic of turbulence and stillness which see-saws throughout Yeats's discussions of art. Already in his essay on Blake, Yeats had noted Blake's insistence that colour de-

[98]"An Introduction for my Plays," *Essays and Introductions*, p. 529.

[99]"The Music for Use in the Performance of These Plays," *Plays in Prose and Verse*, p. 442.

[100]Otto Demus, *Byzantine Mosaic Decoration* (London, 1948), p. 10.

[101]*W. B. Yeats and Tradition*, p. 15.

pended not on its position in the picture but upon "'where the light and dark are put, and all depends upon the form or outline'—meaning . . . that a colour gets its brilliance or its depth from being in light or in shadow." If we substitute image (or sometimes symbol) for colour, and intensity and multitude for light and shadow respectively, the theory applies to poetry as well. Surrounding images of multitude and intensity is the outline that structures the whole arrangement. By "outline" Blake had not meant "the bounding-line dividing a form from its background . . . but the line that divides it from surrounding space.[102] That space is created in "Byzantium" by the resonant gong from the dome of St. Sophia. The whole beginning of the poem works out the double movement of expansion and contraction: as the "unpurged images of day recede," as the streets are emptied and the resonance of night recedes as well, the emptiness is filled by the gong. The arching dome, rendered in the metaphor of a starlit and moonlit sky, rejects the "complexities" of life. In the second section comes the "image, man or shade," the shadowy form that now stands singly amidst both the silence and the empty darkness, like the stark single image that the poet had intended it to be. In the form of a dance the shade begins to unwind the winding path to the place where the golden bird sits, and it is probable that the unwinding movement was intended to be conceived of as an upward and outward spiralling movement, since the bird certainly sits on the highest bough ("starlit") of the highest tree.

The first two sections of "Byzantium" strongly echo Dante, *Purgatorio*, VIII, ll. 1–12, though it is true that Dante's tone is more elegaic, less sombre than Yeats's. However, both poets, it should be remembered, are in purgatory:

> It was now the hour that turns homeward the longing
> of those at sea, and softens their hearts
> on the day when they have said good-by to their friends,
> and which pierces the new pilgrim's heart
> with love, when he hears the distant bells
> which seem to mourn for the dying day.
> I stopped listening and began
> to watch one of the spirits
> who, risen, with signs, asked for quiet.
> He clasped and lifted both his hands,
> fixing his gaze on the east, as if saying to God,
> "For nothing else do I care."

102"Blake," *Essays*, p. 148.

Te lucis ante came so devoutly from his lips
  and with such sweet notes
  that I was unconscious of all else,
and then the others, sweetly and devoutly,
  followed through the entire hymn,
  keeping their eyes fixed on the revolving stars.[103]

Though the elements are here and there very different the spirit of Yeats's poem and Dante's excerpt remains very close: in Dante, as in Yeats, it is the homeward hour for those at sea, only in Yeats, of course, home is death. The ringing bells parallel the gong, as the day is dying, and for each poet appears the spirit or shade. Like Yeats's shade, who with "A mouth that has no . . . breath" summons the poet to be breathless as well, Dante's spirit asks for quiet. When the spirit, joined by the choir, sings the evensong, the resemblance to "Byzantium" seems to lessen, but we should note the equivalent song of Yeats's golden bird, which like the cock of Hades faces its God "east" and, caring only for Him, disdains all else. Finally, the chorus fix their eyes on the revolving stars, a fixity within motion that certainly again suggests the end of Yeats's poem.

After the visit to the golden bird, the scene of "Byzantium" shifts to the Emperor's pavement and the unconsumed and unconsumable flame. (We have actually moved from the street up to the dome, and still further up to the star-lit bough before descending again to the pavement.) All the images in this section are developed in terms of stasis and flux, for the flame itself remains unchanged while the spirits are purged by it, as the "complexities of fury leave." Also, as the "blood-begotten spirits" die they do so by unfolding, as it were, into a dance which, however, is also a "trance," so that the movement of the dance is caught and held in the stillness of trance, just as in old paintings the whirling rings of Saturn are usually represented as solid rings. Surging in against the shore, the tide in the final section is broken by the order of the smithies, and again we have the image of stillness which moves (or vice versa), because the "Marbles of the dancing floor" change their patterns as the waves apparently spill over them:

[103]I have used the prose translation of H. R. Huse, *The Divine Comedy* (New York, 1959). The opening two or three lines of "Byzantium" also echo Sappho, whom, in turn, Eliot echoes in "The Fire Sermon" of *The Waste Land*, l. 220 ff.

After completing this chapter, I discovered the following item: F. N. Lees, "Yeats's 'Byzantium,' Dante, and Shelley," *Notes & Queries* (July, 1957), pp. 312–313. Lees finds a number of similarities between "Byzantium" and Dante's *Purgatorio*, especially in cantos VII, XXV, XXVII. He does not mention canto VIII.

this is the process of breaking the waves and it gives the sea (life), not the marbles, the ability to create afresh always new images. Through the intensity of this final image—surely one of the most sustained in Yeats's poetry—surges, in the last line, the emotion of multitude after all: the sea not only has the last word (literally) but it is a sea of turbulence, torn asunder by dolphins and echoing with the resonance of the gong. Nowhere in Yeats's poetry do emotion of multitude and still intensity fuse more effectively.[104]

It was coincidence that at the reception when he was awarded the Nobel Prize in 1923, Yeats fully captured in prose the astringent qualities he was to put into his poetry from *The Tower* (1928) through the last poems and plays. Particularly happy was it that the occasion of his remarks was not a study of unageing monuments but a living woman, the Princess at the Swedish court: ". . . the face of the Princess Margaretha [is] full of subtle beauty, emotional and precise, and impassive with a still intensity suggesting that final consummate strength which rounds the spiral of a shell."[105] It is no accident that Yeats chose a spherical object for his metaphor, and moreover an object of concentric whorls. Here, then, was the perfect metaphor to describe "still intensity"—the shell, with its murmurs of "far-off multitudinous things" and its hard, spiralling rings that ended in a consummation at the centre. Such "still intensity" was indeed an echo of silence, and this is no mere paradox, for silence has its echoes. Arthur Symons was not contradicting himself when, two pages apart, he described Eleonora Duse in these terms:

with her there can be no . . . arresting moment of repose; but an endless flowing onward of emotion, like tide flowing after tide, moulding and effacing continually.

Her greatest moments are the moments of most intense quietness . . . and the very expression of emotion, with her, is all a restraint, the quieting down of a tumult until only the pained reflection of it glimmers out of her eyes. . . .[106]

[104]F. A. C. Wilson has described some of the arguments developed in this chapter in his discussion of Yeats's dramatic techniques: ". . . what Yeats primarily requires of the theatre is less katharsis than what he calls 'stillness'; a single moment of emotional equipoise to which all the 'passionate intensity' of the action will tend . . . ; one might define it as an awareness of stasis, a moment when the mind passes through profound emotion into a condition of absolute calm" (*W. B. Yeats and Tradition*, p. 37). I have tried to emphasize that the stasis is never an end in itself, never a permanent condition.

[105]*Autobiography*, p. 328.

[106]Symons, "Eleonora Duse," *Studies in Seven Arts*, pp. 220, 222.

Finally all art reflects, Yeats sees, not an "eddy of momentary breath," but "passion." In order to perceive the passion purely, enough of it must, in the "fruitful moment," be isolated: "a passion can only be contemplated when separated by itself . . . and aroused into a perfect intensity by opposition with some other passion. . . ."[107] When two intense passions confront each other in dialectic conflict, the artist has entered the tragic dimension.

[107]*The Irish Dramatic Movement*, in *Plays and Controversies*, p. 105.

5 ❀ PASSIONATE REVERIE: The Tragic Correlative

. . . what is passion but the straining of man's being against some obstacle that obstructs its unity? "A People's Theatre" (1919) in *Plays and Controversies*

. . . I came to understand that . . . reverie, this twilight between sleep and waking . . . this perilous path as on the edge of a sword, is the condition of tragic pleasure, and to understand why it is so rare and so brief. *Plays for an Irish Theatre* (1911)

It is Apollo who tranquillizes the individual by drawing boundary lines. . . . But lest the Apollonian tendency freeze all form into Egyptian rigidity . . . the Dionysiac flood tide periodically destroys all the little circles in which the Apollonian will would confine Hellenism. Nietzsche, *The Birth of Tragedy*

Yeats undoubtedly had a good sense of humour, though he recoiled from the comic spirit; but, fearing it, he understood it very well. The threats in comedy were irony and parody, both of which he detected in Wilde and Beardsley, distorting and undercutting the integrity of their art. "I was in despair," he writes in the *Autobiography*, "at the new breath of comedy that had begun to wither the beauty that I loved, just when that beauty seemed to have united itself to mystery."[1] And though he responded enthusiastically to Cervantes and Rabelais, Synge and Villon, and cultivated an expert's interest in naughty ballads, it was gusto—another form of passion—which really attracted him, not the comic perceptions of life. The ecstatic moment was, after all, the highest achievement of literary art, and ecstasy was possible only in tragedy. But between the quiet dignity of Greek tragedy and the salty flavour of one of Synge's "reckless" comedies lay the whole spectrum of literary modes. Great combiner that he was, Yeats built into his vision of tragedy—and often into his poems—a tension between comic and tragic (he once called it a "quarrel"), between

[1] *Autobiography*, p. 200.

the desire to adapt comic gusto, vitality without strain, and the necessity of allowing for the resonant ecstasy of tragedy, passionate and energetic with struggle. This, ultimately, became the dialectic balance between passion and reverie.

Passion for Yeats was a motif rather than a term; though he used the word in several different ways, it held a sacredness in his vocabulary second to none. In a letter to Joseph Hone, dated 1932, Yeats wrote: "There was something not himself that Swift served. He called it 'freedom' but never defined it and thus has passion. Passion is to me the essential. I was educated upon Balzac and Shakespeare and cannot go beyond them. That passion is his [Swift's] charm."[2] Passion then depends, at least in one instance, on an undefined commitment to something beyond the self, the gesture of dedication, like Hamlet's, to the time out of joint. But passion was more than the civilized impulse to serve; it was also, at the opposite end, the power of primitive energy: "All folk literature has indeed a passion whose like is not in modern literature and music and art, except where it has come by some straight or crooked way out of ancient times."[3] And both these meanings share with a third the quality of scope beyond an individualized emotion: "great passions ... not in nature ... 'ideas' that 'lie burningly on the divine hand,' as Browning calls them," or, as Poe had said, "'the beauty that is beyond the grave.'"[4]

Passion, then, seems to suggest several associations, both aesthetic and thematic: it is a primordial feeling, surging from the ancestral and ancient soil, the memory of myth and mythology; it is the liberating gesture of heroic sacrifice; it is finally also the intellectually wrought ideals of man himself, those principles for which he struggles and dies. Such a combination of associations is characteristic of Yeats and of a special significance in understanding the working of his mind, the way he would seize on the most seemingly disparate elements to force a hard-earned unity. For consider how these elements give him all that any art could embrace: the great moving assertions of folk literature (the sort of "passion" that Lawrence carried to embarrassing extremes); the opposite of this, too, the individual expression of a free and noble nature, the private not the mythic emotion; and finally the passion which links the civilized and social impulse to an Absolute, the passionate "ideas" which are neither natural nor personal but supernal—ideals fashioned by man's

[2]*Letters*, p. 791.
[3]"The Celtic Element in Literature," *Essays*, pp. 221–222.
[4]"John Eglinton and Spiritual Art," *Literary Ideals in Ireland*, p. 35.

mind in the image of his God. Passion was truly the emblem of tragedy: "Tragedy is passion alone...."

But passion alone is not tragedy; again Swift is the example: "passion enobled [*sic*] by intensity, by endurance, by wisdom."[5] Both endurance and wisdom suggest something of the readiness and ripeness, the achieved patience strengthened by knowledge, which rest amidst the passionate intensity that binds all tragic art. On most occasions Yeats used the word "reverie" (he often equated it with wisdom) to describe this counterpoise of philosophical contemplation to the action of the tragic hero. In the tension between the desire to fulfil action and the contemplation of the desire itself, Yeats located the centre of the tragic conflict. Contemplation was not, of course, mere thought; the greatest works "excel in their action, their visibility." Odysseus, Don Quixote, Hamlet, Lear, Faust—each is the hero of some visible action, carried forward by men whose capacity for reverie (contemplation) is equal to their passion for action. It is primarily this "visibility" of action which distinguishes "ancient art" from that of the "circulating libraries," which "is urban [art and] belongs not to the small ancient town ... but to the great modern town where meditation is impossible, where action is a mechanical routine ... where 'individuality' or intellectual coherence is the sole distinction left."[6] Nietzsche had blamed Socratic rationalism for achieving the same results: control (through rational means) and extreme individualization (carried into tragedy via Euripides), both of which denied the Dionysian surge, what Yeats was to call the "flood" of tragedy.

Influenced no doubt in part by Nietzsche's attack on Euripides' emphasis on character, Yeats himself developed a distinction—well known to his readers—between Character and Personality. John Butler Yeats wrote to the poet in 1910: "your splendid sentence 'character is the ash of personality' has my full assent."[7] In essence, Personality was the core of a man, unindividual to the point where it shared with the core of mankind; untypical, too, shorn of locality and public masks. Individual eccentricities, the typed person existing in "accidental circumstance," "some one place, some one moment of time"—all this belonged to the making of Character.[8]

[5]*Letters*, p. 776.

[6]*On the Boiler*, pp. 33–34.

[7]*J. B. Yeats: Letters*, p. 128. Yeats's distinction between Character and Personality has been explained by several critics; it is to put his remarks into my own context that I repeat them here. Yeats's interest in Personality owes something, of course, to the ritualistic reverence which a number of the chief figures in the nineties (e.g., Wilde and Lionel Johnson) bestowed upon it.

[8]"The Theater of Beauty," *Harper's Weekly*, LV (November 11, 1911), 11.

Yeats rejected, in "The Tragic Theatre," the premise that "the dramatic moment is always the contest of character with character." Such a character-dialectic was merely an extension of the Hegelian dialectic, in which not characters but moral forces are in perpetual opposition. By discarding the conflict of both character and moral forces, Yeats had to substitute not so much the conflict of passions as their strategic pattern. A tragic play became a virtual choreography of passions which move the action of the drama functionally to its crisis. In the greatest tragedies, character was always subordinated to "lyric feeling" and passion, which set it apart from comedy: "Suddenly it strikes us that character is continuously present in comedy alone, and that... [in the] tragedy . . . of Corneille . . . Racine . . . Greece and Rome . . . its place is taken by passions and motives, one person being jealous, another full of love or remorse or pride or anger." Yeats finds ample support especially in Shakespeare, for even in the tragedies, "it is in the moments of comedy that character is defined, in Hamlet's gaiety. . . ." Conversely, it is precisely "amid the great moments . . . [that] all is lyricism, unmixed passion, 'the integrity of fire.'" Since Shakespeare, Yeats thinks, was always "a writer of tragi-comedy," there is everywhere a balance: character seldom becomes completely defined to the exclusion of passion; the passions can never entirely sustain the play without touches of character.

Contrary to popular opinion, it is not, Yeats further argues, the tragic Personality which gives us the sense of recognizing a man known to us in worldly terms; we do *not* "when the tragic reverie is at its height... say, 'How well that man is realised, I should have known him were I to meet him in the street,' for it is always ourselves that we see upon the stage. . . ."[9] The self that we see is a primary ego, not the secondary ego that distinguishes us in the world.

By 1909 Yeats had made a clear distinction: "Tragedy . . . rejecting character... gets form from motives, from the wandering [reverie] of passion; while comedy is the clash of character." As it had for Coleridge, *Romeo and Juliet* provided an apt illustration: "Juliet has personality, her Nurse has character. I look upon personality as the individual form of our passions. . . ."[10]

Yeats did not come to these definitions through purely theoretical speculation; the experience with the Abbey Theatre provided an example. He had begun his dramatic ventures with a rather vague notion of an heroic revival; he was against the play of manners, of

[9] "The Tragic Theatre," *Essays*, pp. 296–297.
[10] *Autobiography*, p. 286; *Letters*, p. 548.

drawing-rooms, of the middle class; but he appeared to be for nearly everything else, mostly because he failed to define his position in the early years of the movement. Then as the Abbey pressed relentlessly toward a realistic-comic and social drama, he found his own view, through its very isolation, focused more sharply. While he did not reject the new Abbey art, he now defined it and placed it, for the time being, outside the larger scope he was envisioning for himself. "Certainly," he wrote, "it is . . . objectivity, this making of all from sympathy, from observation, never from passion, from lonely dreaming, that has made [the Abbey] players . . . great comedians, for comedy is passionless."[11]

In fact the discovery that comedy was passionless came to him as he watched one of Lady Gregory's plays, in which a man displayed a fear of death—"the subject of the play in all its forms"; and still it all seemed finally comic, " 'a game, all like a child's game.' " What gave him that impression was the feeling that the man in the play "was really never in fear of death—he was [therefore] passionless." The point needs to be stressed: the real fear of death, as Yeats recognized, is necessary for any man who does not wish to go gentle into that good night; and Dylan Thomas must have known Yeats well enough to write in that fine poem that a man must "rage against the dying of the light." Passion and heroism are part of rage, as rage is part of fear —real fear. The children of comedy may display a fear of death but they do not really feel it: they have not strength enough to fear or fear enough to generate strength. And it is this weakness Yeats began to see everywhere as he looked at the passionless world.[12]

II

Yeats did not limit his definitions of tragedy and comedy to the theatre; in time, everything passionless became an antithesis to the higher art and symptomatic of modern man's chief disease: an over-indulgence in the characteristically individual. For example, at Coole one summer, wandering about the rooms and corridors of Lady Gregory's expansive house, he observes certain pictures:

> . . . I pass a wall covered with Augustus John's etchings and drawings. I notice a woman with strongly marked shoulder-blades and a big nose, and a pencil drawing called "Epithalamium" . . . [in which] an ungainly,

[11] *The Irish Dramatic Movement*, in *Plays and Controversies*, pp. 205–206.
[12] "The Theater of Beauty," p. 11.

ill-grown boy holds out his arms to a tall woman with thin shoulders and a large stomach.... There is not one [of John's subjects]... that has not been broken by labour or wasted by sedentary life.

Only half-facetiously Yeats, in this passage in the *Autobiography*, recommends to the characters of these drawings the rigours of gymnastics; their bodies are deprived of strength and real energy. Augustus John, he remarks, "is not interested in the social need... for greater health, but in character, in the revolt from all that makes one man like another." Reading like a National Socialist "Strength through Joy" poster, the beginning of this sentence is disconcertingly misleading; Yeats is more involved in drawing lines between the old and the new art than in championing healthy bodies. Immensely attracted as he was to the half-anonymous art of Egypt and Byzantium, he took every opportunity to point out how the older art sacrifices individuality and difference for an effect of sameness that gains in intensity and evocativeness what it surrenders in eccentric detail. It had passion. As typified in John's drawings, modern art seems wholly committed to individual differences, to character, and through it ideal form becomes impossible. "The old art," Yeats felt, "if carried to its logical conclusion, would have led to the creation of one single type of man ... gathering up by a kind of deification a capacity for all energy and all passion, into a Krishna, a Christ, a Dionysus"; the "new art can create innumberable personalities, but in each of these the capacity for passion has been sacrificed to some habit of body or of mind." That Phidian or Byzantine art had been carried to such a "logical conclusion" seems evident from what Yeats had to say about them at various times.

Despite the threat of monotony Yeats was willing to chance an emphasis on passion to protect art against the even greater dangers which he saw in modern examples of it—an art unstamped by traditions or conventions, making out of its subjects individual "character studies." Fundamentally, the figures of modern art were unable to feel passion. The big-shouldered woman in John's drawing "has ... a nature too keen, too clever for any passion, with the cleverness of people who cannot rest...," as in "The Statues" Hamlet is "thin from eating flies." Restlessness precludes contemplation or reverie; the stillness necessary to passion is all wasted in *nervous* energy, outward rather than inward movement. Also, in the other drawing by John, "that young lad with his arms spread out will sink back into disillusionment and exhaustion after the brief pleasure of a passion which is in part curiosity." Like the temporary flames of the "tragic generation," who, after all, invented the self-consuming passion without "endurance" or "wisdom," these figures are flickers only:

Some limiting environment or idiosyncrasy is displayed; man is studied as an individual fact, and not as that energy which seems measureless and hates all that is not itself. It is a powerful but prosaic art, celebrating the "fall into division" not the "resurrection into unity." Did not even Balzac, who looked at the world so often with similar eyes, find it necessary to deny character to his great ladies and young lovers that he might give them passion?

What is particularly evident in the older paintings (and almost wholly absent in the new, which Yeats dates approximately with Van Eyck) is "the expression of desire." In his room at Coole Yeats used to observe the old masters: Botticelli, Giorgione, Mantegna. Even the martyrs and saints in these paintings "must show the capacity for all they have renounced."[13]

Chiefly because in comedy one assumed "a personal mask," a character, it was "joyous," a term which Yeats used rather inconsistently. The shifting of masks, the simulation of comic action, produced an energy both free and joyous. Tragedy, on the other hand, derived from the soul: "It has not joy . . . but ecstasy, which is from the contemplation of things vaster than the individual...." In this context, the relationship between Yeats's conception of tragedy, which he began to formulate about 1909–1910, and his previous aesthetic principles becomes clearer:

The masks of tragedy contain neither character nor personal energy. They are allied to decoration and to the abstract figures of Egyptian temples. Before the mind can look out of their eyes the active will perishes, hence their sorrowful calm. Joy is of the will which labours.... The soul knows its changes of state alone, and... the motives of tragedy are not related to action but to changes of state.... Yet is not ecstasy some fulfilment of the soul in itself, some slow or sudden expansion of it like an overflowing well? Is not this what is meant by beauty?[14]

Tragedy suits Yeats's notions of austere beauty and disciplined multitude; but the barriers of social convention which delineate so neatly the world of comedy are swept away in the tragic flood: "tragedy must always be a drowning and breaking of the dykes that separate man from man...."

Yeats did not forsake comedy; on the contrary, at various times

[13] *Autobiography*, pp. 304–305.
[14] *Ibid.*, p. 286.

he saw within himself a real "quarrel" between the comedian and the tragedian (though what he feared most was not simply comedy but the ironic surrender to parody, the peculiar temptation of the modern artist). When we are young, Yeats claims, we do not much care for comedy; it is either too flippant or too ordinary for the serious imagination, passionate and suffused with innocence. As a young man, Yeats intensely disliked some of the "comedy" in certain of the French Impressionist painters, and for years, he recounts, he was wholly indifferent to Manet's "Olympia" (Plate VI), though, of course, for reasons different from those that provoked the Paris art critics to revile the same painting. In the commonness of the scene—the reclining nude, the negro maid who bears flowers wrapped in paper—he sensed something repellent or unworthy. Yeats quotes, and agrees with, Congreve's definition of comedy and humour: a representation of the "external and superficial," "a 'singular and unavoidable way of doing anything peculiar to one man only... distinguished from all other men....'" When, however, in middle life Yeats has occasion to react to Manet again—this time to the equally famous "Eva Gonzales" (Plate VI)—he is impressed with the sense of particularity that he had slighted in the "Olympia." This portrait of a woman looking momentarily away from the vase of flowers she herself is painting, in the relaxed posture of amusement, strikes Yeats as extraordinary in its supremely conceived sense of character. "'How perfectly,'" he is now able to say to himself, "'that woman is realised as distinct from all other women that have lived or shall live.' . . ."[15]

The shift in attitude is important, not only because it carries Yeats to an ultimate reconciliation with comedy but also because it explains what Yeats began to recognize as a valid feature of art. In the circumstantial and accidental nature of comedy, he now saw what at times relieves and delights by lifting us out of that sense of merged identification which on occasion overwhelms and becomes burdensome. For tragedy always makes us feel "'That man is myself'" rather than "'How like that man is to himself.'"[16] Objective distance comes as a distinct relief, as in comic art we are able to dissociate ourselves from the doings on the stage; tragedy permits no such respite: the passions of the actors appropriate us, or we surrender to them—either way we become involved and deeply committed. But in contemplating

[15]"The Tragic Theatre," *Essays*, pp. 298–299. But in the Introduction to *The Oxford Book of Modern Verse*, Yeats still speaks of Manet as giving him "incomplete pleasure" (p. xxii).

[16]"The Theater of Beauty," p. 11.

the circumstantial and accidental, the ego remains sufficiently untouched to delight in recognizing the *otherness* of itself, the outscape rather than the inscape of the soul. And that which outscape hides is in itself delightful to contemplate, especially for a poet who now took more and more to thinking in terms of masks. Tragedy unveiled precisely because it first veiled the outer and characteristic aspects of Self; comedy masqueraded by letting us be ourselves. That is why Yeats identified comedy with a child's game. Of course, comedy could never be the highest art, and poetry remains the province of tragedy; but the comic and the real are also art.

At the close of his central essay, "The Tragic Theatre" (1910), Yeats divided "poetic" from "real" art in terms that often resemble the neo-Platonic shadings of late neo-classical aesthetics, particularly the middle ground developed in the *Discourses* and elsewhere by Sir Joshua Reynolds. In 1910 such doctrines were out of fashion, and this accounts for some of their novelty. Undoubtedly Yeats had read—and approved—Blake's attacks on Reynolds, and Yeats's remarks reveal no conscious affinities with Reynolds's; but they are close enough to the central doctrine of neo-classical aesthetics, the balancing of particular and general, to warrant comparison, if only for the sake of a paradoxical kinship that yet serves to widen the context of Yeats's remarks. What Reynolds called the "grand style" depended on the artist's continually distinguishing between the incidental or the accidental in nature, and striving consciously for ideal form. But this represented only one side—the ideal; Reynolds insisted that no greater judgment was needed than when the artist steered his perilous course "between general ideas and individuality. . . . An individual model, copied with scrupulous exactness, makes a mean style," but "proceeding solely from idea, has a tendency to make the painter degenerate into a mannerist."[17] In his conception Yeats is not far removed from this definition of an equilibrium; because of its manifest abstractness, he had condemned realistic drama as manneristic art, lacking as it did wisdom, reverie, and passion, all qualities of the Yeatsian "high art." For Reynolds the general consisted in what all particulars have in common, though somewhere the individual always needs to be asserted: "a judicious detail will sometimes give the force of truth to the work . . .";[18] while Yeats remarked that "Some little irrelevance of line, some promise of character to come, may indeed

[17]*The Literary Works of Sir Joshua Reynolds*, ed. Henry William Beechey (London, 1855), II, 132, 322.

[18]*Sir Joshua Reynolds' Discourses*, ed. Helen Zimmern (London, 1879), p. 181.

put us at our ease": no art, however ideal, can completely ignore the real. What was sublime for Reynolds was tragic for Yeats. The comparison is easily made. First Yeats:

...in mainly tragic art one distinguishes devices to exclude or lessen character, to diminish the power of...daily mood.... If the real world is not altogether rejected, it is but touched here and there, and into the places we have left empty we summon rhythm, balance, pattern, images that remind us of vast passions, the vagueness of past times...and if we are painters, we shall express personal emotion through ideal form...or we shall leave out some element of reality as in Byzantine painting, where there is no mass, nothing in relief....[19]

And Reynolds, annotating Du Fresnoy's *De Arte Graphica*:

There is an absolute necessity for the Painter to generalise his notions; to paint particulars is not to paint nature, it is only to paint circumstances. When the Artist has conceived in his imagination the image of perfect beauty, or the abstract idea of forms, he may be said to be admitted into the great Council of Nature....[20]

Viewed broadly, the theory of tragedy appears to be an extension of Yeats's earlier concern with the illusion of multitude and the intense isolation of emotions. Full of "sadness and gravity," the faces of the old masters had "a certain emptiness . . . as of a mind that waited the supreme crisis." Extreme intensity embodied in fatalistic strength, in the full recognition of the tragic inevitability of life, was made impossible in the new art where energy was always carried to completion, not held back. While modern art (Yeats used the appellation loosely) "sings, laughs, chatters or looks its busy thoughts," tragic art "moves us by setting us to reverie, by alluring us almost to the intensity of trance," like the single focused image. Eventually, "The persons upon the stage...greaten till they are humanity itself." With its echoes of things beyond (not removed from) the individual, tragic art is "an art of the flood," bringing always "new images to the dreams of

[19]"The Tragic Theatre," *Essays*, pp. 300–301. It should be remembered that many writers in the nineties—whom Yeats knew—were at war with realism. Compare Yeats's remarks above with this from Wilde's *The Decay of Lying*: "The whole history [of the decorative arts] in Europe is the record of the struggle between Orientalism, with its frank rejection of imitation . . . and our own imitative spirit. Wherever the former has been paramount, as in Byzantium . . . we have had beautiful and imaginative work. . . . But wherever we have returned to Life and Nature, our work has always become vulgar, common and uninteresting"; "One touch of Nature may make the whole world kin, but two touches of Nature will destroy any work of Art."

[20]Reynolds, *Works*, II, 300.

youth"; it is the art of Shakespeare "when he shows us Hamlet broken away from life by the passionate hesitations of his reverie." Such also is the nature of poetic art. Real art belongs—and rightfully so—to character which, being of the real world, can best express itself through an illusion of it.[21]

Tragic and comic parallel the movements of the soul, which is "always moving outward into the objective world [comedy] or inward into itself [tragedy]."[22] All his life, it would seem, this double movement resembled in Yeats's creative efforts some quarrel between two worlds. He did not really attempt tragedy until *On Baile's Strand*, begun in 1901 but often revised and not acted at the Abbey until 1904. Still working without any real theory, Yeats found the writing of this play a problematic and difficult task. Curiously enough, he worked on his Cuchulain tragedy at a time when *The Shadowy Waters* was still being revised, and he did not fail to comment on the difference between the two plays. In 1904 he wrote to Frank Fay that he considered *The Shadowy Waters* to be "an exception"; he now felt prepared to go beyond the "remote" and "impersonal" mystique which had governed that play. When all was said and done he could see it now merely as "picture," as "more a ritual than a human story... deliberately without human characters." *On Baile's Strand* was intended to be "the other side of the halfpenny." In very detailed terms, he explained to Fay how he was setting about to *make* the play tragic. In itself the theme was fairly stock bardic material: a father duels with his son and slays him, with recognition coming too late to prevent the tragedy. Put into dramatic terms this incident from the Celtic hero's life needed movement and motive: "epic and folk literature can ignore time as drama cannot...." The son declines any affection for his father; he does not know him. Such rejection could be made tragic, Yeats felt, only "by suggesting in Cuchullain's character . . . something a little proud, barren and restless. . . . He is a little hard, and leaves the people about him a little repelled...." Lacking this motive for the son, the play would not have had "any deep tragedy." There is no lack of passion in the hero; in fact it is foiled by the "reason" of the old king Conchubar—a reason "that is blind because it... is cold." Whatever tragic joy there is in the play comes not merely from the struggle for supremacy between the passionate Cuchulain and the temperate old king but from their

21"The Tragic Theâtre," *Essays*, pp. 300–303.

22Notes on "The Second Coming" in *Michael Robartes and the Dancer* (1921); see *Variorum Edition*, p. 824.

contrasting effects on the whole play: "Are they not the cold moon and the hot sun?"[23] Creating motives to accentuate certain qualities of Cuchulain's character was a concession to individualizing him, to making him, in some unique way, a "character," without slipping into actual comedy, or even tragi-comedy. *On Baile's Strand* remains a grim play.

The confusion between tragic and comic is most apparent in *The Player Queen*. Early in 1909, when Yeats was deep in his thoughts on tragedy, he wrote his father (*Letters*, p. 524): "I find that my talent as a stage manager is in the invention of comic business, in fact I am coming to the conclusion that I am really essentially a writer of comedy, but very personal comedy." Even when comedy is considered in its broadest sense, the statement remains curious; Yeats had written nothing independently (a few short comic plays were helped along by Lady Gregory) that could remotely be called comic. Clearly, *The Player Queen*, which some months later he described as "my most stirring thing," was creating confusion. It is certain that the play had been planned and begun as a tragedy. After some periodic revisions during several summer holidays at Coole, he suddenly realized that every man attempts to be his own opposite, and so he "banished the ghost and turned what [he] had meant for tragedy into a farce. . . ."[24] Obviously to turn tragedy into farce was to dip too sharply; in a letter of 1914 he reverted to calling the play a "wild comedy, almost a farce, with a tragic background—a study of a fantastic woman." Assuredly the play is not tragic, and its "tragic background" is never more than that: a vague sense of disaster enveloping the real queen who is helplessly supplanted by the player queen herself. In the true sense of "character," the play is not comedy either, for the character which allows the pretender to become real queen ultimately becomes higher than itself by virtue of her success alone. Moreover the mask-symbolism tends to play down the characteristic and typical. No one, however, can quarrel with the description of the play as "fantastic"; bordering often on a mere episodic arrangement, *The Player Queen* almost fits Yeats's definition of farce. It is lacking in any deep reverie on life, contemplative wisdom, single passions intensely highlighted for wider effects. And, despite the Prime Minister's

[23]*Letters*, pp. 424–425.

[24]Introduction to *The Resurrection*, in *Wheels and Butterflies*, p. 93. But *The Player Queen* proved useful in suggesting how the assumption of the absurd mask might lead to a kind of tragi-comedy congenial to Yeats. For a defence and interpretation of the play see William Becker, "The Mask Mocked; or, Farce and the Dialectic of Self," *SR*, LXI (1953), 82–108.

homely language, there are few sharply drawn outlines of a real, objective world. The play remains an unmixed compound, neither tragedy nor comedy (and not quite tragi-comedy either) but an unresolved quarrel between the two: the real queen is the unreal persona (Personality), while the imposter is a Character from the real world who must transcend it in order to succeed. Yeats explained his theme in a sentence: "[it] is that the world being illusion, one must be deluded in some way if one is to triumph in it."[25]

If *The Player Queen* is a montage of genres and intentions, its wildness and recklessness, its spirit of bitter-sweet farce, were unquestionably influenced by Synge. "The Tragic Theatre" (1910) opens with a reference to Synge's *Deirdre of the Sorrows*, moments of which Yeats considers the "noblest tragedy"—a play purified of the usual Syngean wildness until perfection of tragic form is inescapable. Deirdre's cry, " 'Is it not a hard thing that we should miss the safety of the grave and we trampling its edge?' " provides for Yeats a supreme instance of that "reverie of passion"—the phrase is explicitly paradoxical—which he himself had long sought to achieve. Passionate reverie "mounts and mounts till grief itself has carried [Deirdre] beyond grief into pure contemplation," into Schopenhauer's will-less state of suspended desire. At this juncture there is tragic joy (or ecstasy and gaiety as Yeats will later say), for the hero, liberated beyond grief, is elevated out of the circumstantial into the immutable, out of the real into the ideal. As he listened to the play Yeats felt that the players themselves "ascended into that tragic ecstasy which is the best that art—perhaps that life—can give."[26]

Especially in Synge's language did Yeats find the special capacity for reverie, the wandering thought which, never random, always led to specific goals, though it was a language no longer actuated by conscious (and limiting) will: "it perfectly fits the drifting emotion, the dreaminess, the vague yet measureless desire.... It blurs definition, clear edges," the rigid boundaries of a realistic world, "everything that comes from the will." Even "joy" was essentially a Syngean quality, an "astringent joy and hardness that was in all he did." Without fears of claiming too much, it may be asserted with some confidence that the terms Yeats applied to Synge's art in a number of places fitted, at every turn, his own aesthetic (if not always his art). Synge had a way of writing "simply, so naturally"; it was an "impersonal" art, with little "hatred and... scorn"; he possessed an

[25]*Letters*, pp. 588, 534.
[26]"The Tragic Theatre," *Essays*, pp. 294–296.

"ecstatic contemplation of noble life"; and he wrought out of his self and anti-self an art replete with "passion and heroic beauty," "energy," "extravagance," "wisdom," "irony," and "tragic reality." Like the bird-symbol Yeats used in *Calvary*, Synge was the solitary, objective, "pure artist," a man "whose subjective lives . . . were over . . ." (*Autobiography*, p. 207). Above the trivial and temporary, as Yeats rather too self-critically felt himself not to be, Synge's dignity as an artist was embodied in a silence that was not brooding, contemptuous, or cunning: "He loves all that has edge . . . all that heightens the emotions by contest, all that stings into life the sense of tragedy," and, he might have added, all that stings into tragedy the sense of life.

Because Synge was full of "passion," he was the perfect tragedian of poetic reverie, alternatively defined as "the speech of the soul with itself"; and he belonged to the oldest and the best of traditions, finding space for his reverie through technique, through "some device that checks the rapidity of dialogue." Greek and French drama had maintained a fairly "even speed of dialogue" by excluding all "common life"; Shakespeare, however, already has a "troubled" verse. Opening his plays to the life of common reality, Shakespeare managed to get his reverie "by an often encumbering Euphuism"; or he would make his plot casual and loose enough to "give his characters the leisure to look at life from without." Even Maeterlinck, in spite of his "static" plots, attained some effects of wandering thought by juxtaposing the contemplative with the external needs toward movement of some kind, and then by checking action with "a language slow and heavy with dreams." Synge himself

> found the check . . . in an elaboration of the dialects of Kerry and Aran. The cadence is long and meditative, as benefits the thought of men . . . alone . . . each man speaking in turn and for some little time. . . . Their thought . . . is as though the present were held at arm's length. It is the reverse of rhetoric . . . so little abstract. . . .

Reverie, then, was not day dreaming, not a flight of fancy from unbearable realities, but a confrontation of the higher—and perhaps momentarily even unbearable—realities, the tragic truths of life. Functioning somewhat like the chorus, reverie brought ultimate wisdom, rooted in the experience of this world and the prophetic insight into the next. Using Irish dialect "for [a] noble purpose," Synge retained both "imaginative richness and . . . the sting and tang of reality." One finds in Synge, as one finds in the earliest poetry, "some beautiful or bitter reverie . . . mingle[d] . . . so subtly with reality, that it is a day's work to disentangle it. . . ."[27]

That Yeats was attracted to Richard II comes as no surprise, a man of reverie and dream, though no simple dreamer; a man who could utter the profoundest wisdom about life and yet lacked the practical wisdom to be an efficient king. Extravagant and impulsive Richard is a hero of both masks and passions. As Yeats asked Dorothy Wellesley, in a letter, "Did Shakespeare in *Richard II* discover poetic reverie?"[28] In Richard, Yeats saw the "defeat that awaits all . . . Artist or Saint, who find themselves where men ask of them a rough energy and have nothing to give but some contemplative virtue. . . ." Although there was a danger of turning sentimental, this was the line the Yeatsian tragic hero followed; what ennobled him finally was his passion, his ability to roam imaginatively, thereby turning wise in the very act of surrender to the practical world. All of Shakespeare was for Yeats an elaborate parable, a single "Myth," which "describes a wise man who was blind from very wisdom, and an empty man who thrust him from his place, and saw all that could be seen from very emptiness." Although Hamlet, for instance, was unwilling to sacrifice his disturbed visions of the "great issues" for the "trivial game of life," Fortinbras, the practical man, has a different strength, as has the practical Bolingbroke who supplants Richard.[29]

Blindness brings wisdom, emptiness brings sight; it is an ancient interpretation of an ancient paradox: the relative strength of illumination generated by the lamp and the mirror. What is inner can be seen only when man is blind to the outer, when the outer no longer interferes; what is outer can be seen only when man is blind to the inner, when the inner no longer reminds him of things he wishes to forget. We may put it still another way: the tragic hero gains in wisdom in

[27]I have selected only a few phrases from the three key essays on Synge: "Preface to the First Edition of 'The Well of the Saints,'" "Preface to the First Edition of John M. Synge's Poems and Translations," and "J. M. Synge and the Ireland of his Time." See *Essays*, pp. 369–424.

Sr. Melchiori's book on Yeats (which appeared after my own was written) called my attention to a work by one of his colleagues: Agostino Lombardo, *La poesia inglese, dall'estetismo al simbolismo* (Rome, 1950). Sr. Lombardo has a relevant chapter on Yeats (pp. 249–288) which I have been unable to make full use of here; but it is worth noting his agreement that Synge was a major influence in guiding Yeats toward a more "astringent" and less sentimental art: "Certamente l'influsso di Synge deve aver avuto importanza notevole nel determinare il nuovo orientamento yeatsiano . . ." (p. 287).

[28]*Letters*, p. 899.

[29]"At Stratford-on-Avon," *Essays*, pp. 129–131.

proportion as he sloughs off knowledge, the knowledge of the practical world; while the practical man—who must, to remain practical, retain his sight of the outer—gains in perception and knowledge of the outer world as he surrenders his inner sight, his wisdom, and thus becomes "empty." Since reverie brings wisdom, the practical man cannot afford to indulge in it; consciousness is not the same as self-consciousness. But, though the tragic hero gives up consciousness (of the outer) to suffer the consequences of self-consciousness, there are rewards. The lamp lights a small but a passionate centre; the mirror but reflects one's whole self-image: "Knowledge increases unreality," as Yeats was to write in "The Statues." But knowledge which he called deeper than intellect is the blinding, visionary ecstasy—the flash of lightning, the moment of release when blindness brings the solace of wisdom: and that is also the moment of tragic joy.

III

Yeats has sometimes been misunderstood in his use of the word "joy" to describe the tragic emotion,[30] partly because he was himself inconsistent. Although he realized its ordinary connotations and on occasion recruited such terms as "gaiety" and "ecstasy," the implica-

[30]See Irving Suss, "Yeatsian Drama and the Dying Hero," *SAQ*, LIV (1955), 369–380. When he was deeply under the spell of Nietzsche, Yeats did sometimes use "joy" to evoke a pure, Zarathustran Destructive Laughter (e.g., in *Where There is Nothing*). But the rejoicing "tragic joy" of a later poem, "The Gyres," is a subtler version, more akin to the gaiety discussed in my subsequent analysis of "Lapis Lazuli." The notion that tragedy can be joyous is by no means unique with Yeats. Several colleagues have called passages to my attention which seem very close in intention to Yeats's theory of "tragic joy." Professor Arthur M. Eastman notes that Havelock Ellis wrote of life in Shakespearean tragedy as "always a pageant . . . a tragi-comedy, but [it] has in it always, even in *Lear*, an atmosphere of enlarging and exhilarating gaiety" (*Impressions and Comments* [Boston and New York, 1914], p. 94); and Professor Mark Spilka has pointed out a passage in Lawrence: "Lear was essentially happy, even in his greatest misery" (*Selected Literary Criticism*, ed. Anthony Beal [London, 1955], p. 123). Yeats, of course, was to single out Hamlet and Lear as "gay" in "Lapis Lazuli" (see below), and there is perhaps something interesting behind the selection of *Lear*—certainly one of Shakespeare's most terrifying tragedies—as having gaiety. It seems that Ellis, Lawrence, and Yeats were thinking along the same lines: the greater the dread the greater the potential for ultimate gaiety—beyond dread. Several critics have written perceptively on Yeats and tragedy: T. R. Henn, *The Harvest of Tragedy* (London, 1956); B. L. Reid, "Yeats and Tragedy,"*HR*, XI (1958), 391–410; Walter E. Houghton, "Yeats and Crazy Jane: The Hero in Old Age," *MP*, XL (May, 1943), 316–329; Una Ellis-Fermor, *The Irish Dramatic Movement* (London, 1939), pp. 65–66, 86–88. (Since writing this note, I discover that B. L. Reid has expanded his essay into a book: *William Butler Yeats: The Lyric of Tragedy* [University of Oklahoma Press, 1961]; the essay "Yeats and Tragedy" has now been incorporated into the book as the final chapter.)

tions of "joy" suggested something frigid and Celtic, an undue delight, with Wagnerian echoes, in heroic death. In one sense joy was what the hero experienced when he had partially renounced the reality preying on his soul; it was an emotion of relief: "The readiness is all." Certainly there is nothing irresponsible in the word joy, or in ecstasy; as early as the writing of *The Shadowy Waters* that latter word was joined to a balancing one: "I am trying to get into this play," Yeats wrote to Mrs. Clement Shorter, "a kind of grave ecstasy."[31] Even joy, however misleading, was not meant to convey some purely Dionysian frenzy, but strength, a defence against the more melancholy conceptions of tragedy that centred only on the pitiable with no one left to pity. Had Yeats been musical—which he was not—he might well have thought Schiller's ode to "Joy" (at least as Beethoven used it to climax his work) an appropriate parallel to his own special use of the word. "Let us have no emotions," he cautioned A. E., "however abstract, in which there is not an athletic joy." Upbraiding himself for his own sentimentality, his early "decadence" and "subjectiveness," he now demanded the "pure energy of the spirit . . . [and] will" in order to clear the "vapours which kill the spirit and the will, ecstasy and joy."

Gaiety, likewise, is a strong emotion which, even unconsciously, "leaps up before danger. . . ." When the messenger brings Hamlet Laertes' challenge Hamlet's mood confirms this special gaiety.[32] In two letters to Dorothy Wellesley, 1936 and 1938, Yeats again takes up the conception of joy. The first letter is a defence of his omission from *The Oxford Book of Modern Verse* of Wilfred Owen and the war poets: "We that are joyous," he writes, "need not be afraid to denounce. . . . Joy is the salvation of the soul." And a performance of *On Baile's Strand* occasions this remark: "'Cuchulain' seemed to me a heroic figure because he was creative joy separated from fear."[33] Cuchulain exemplifies the tragic art of "flood": in fighting the waves with his sword he penetrates beyond ecstasy into the joy of deliverance he himself creates.

For the most part Yeats's objections to much of modern literature were based on the isolation of a single weakness: its effeminate and ephemeral nature. Heroes are not victims; they must be impassioned not imprisoned, as he conceived the characters of Ibsen's *Ghosts* to be. All that traps men in circumstances deprives them of final triumph. Defeat is an ambiguous concept; the first tragedians had known how to salvage a victory from a visible downfall. Cynicism

[31] *Letters*, p. 322. [32] *Ibid.*, pp. 434–435, 733. [33] *Ibid.*, pp. 876, 913.

and stoicism are not what Yeats had in mind; "only when we are gay over a thing, and can play with it, do we show ourselves its master, and have minds clear enough for strength . . . strength shall laugh and wisdom mourn." Always when he thinks of tragedy Yeats recalls Shakespeare, whose heroes display—without contemptuous defiance—the victory in the teeth of accomplished failure: "when the last darkness has gathered about them, [they] speak out of an ecstasy that is one half the self-surrender of sorrow, and one half the last playing and mockery of the victorious sword, before the defeated world."[34] The mention of "mockery" ought not to mislead; the tragic context always includes passion and wisdom, and mockery in this sense is not mere bitterness. In the sharply satirical lines of Beardsley's art Yeats detected a different "spirit of mockery" out of which Beardsley created "a form of beauty where his powerful logical intellect eliminated every outline that suggested meditation or even satisfied passion."[35] And he was dismayed by this mockery, for it remained below to struggle against the circumstances which truly tragic mockery abandoned in the knowledge (wisdom) of assent to the futility of conflict on that level of existence.

When Yeats decides to use "ecstasy" in place of "joy" for one of his lectures in 1914, he explains his use of the term: "Ecstasy includes emotions like those of Synge's Deirdre after her lover's death which are the worst of sorrows to the ego. . . ."[36] Operating as the primum mobile of art, style—sharing in both poles of the emotional spectrum—becomes the means of identifying what a work of art achieves. Style, he says in "Poetry and Tradition,"

> is in the arrangement of events as in the words, and in that touch of extravagance, of irony, of surprise, which is set there after the desire of logic has been satisfied and all that is merely necessary established, and that leaves one, not in the circling necessity, but caught up into the freedom of self-delight.... If it be very conscious, very deliberate, as it may be in comedy... [which is] more personal than tragedy, we call it fantasy ... joy, because it must be always making and mastering, remains in the hands and in the tongue of the artist, but with his eyes he enters upon a submissive, sorrowful contemplation of the great irremediable things... a pure contemplation.

Entirely realistic tragedy must always fall short of these particular elements, since any movement beyond the personal immediately

[34]"Poetry and Tradition," *Essays*, pp. 312, 314.
[35]*Autobiography*, p. 200.
[36]*Letters*, p. 587.

makes such art somehow symbolic and impersonal. But although realism in drama meant limitations, Yeats saw it as having in the novel a distinctly different form. In the *Comédie Humaine*—all forty volumes of which he claimed to have read without ever finishing *Ulysses*—there is, for all of Balzac's studied detail, passion and abundance. Even the novel of "contemporary educated life is . . . a permanent form because having the power of psychological description it can follow the thought of a man who is looking into the grate."[37] Capable of reverie it might achieve ecstasy.

But the substitution of ecstasy for joy was not to remain consistent, ecstasy giving way later to "gaiety," which again touched close to joy. The distinction which Yeats was labouring to achieve was between a feeling of a high, almost mystical, attainment of suspended passion and a feeling of release. Both emotions were present at the end of the tragic struggle and both shaped the reassertion of enduring strength against the "sorrows" which the ego suffered in defeat. While joy seemed at times too contradictory as a tragic emotion, too "much of the will which labours"—and contemplation is beyond labour—ecstasy seemed perhaps too static to account for the whole of the tragic consummation; it suggested little of that fundamental power of assertion in the hero's final hour. Ecstasy, it seemed, preceded release. Although a clear choice among the three terms was never made, gaiety became a favoured term: it implied something more impersonal and austere than the felicity or "pleasurable element" sometimes associated with joy. Of course, neither joy nor gaiety denied ecstasy: the hero's ego, on the recoil from the world which wounded it, attained an ecstasy of "pure contemplation" of the "irremediable things" which the tragic contest had bared; from that contemplative fixity, gaiety would then release it. Deliverance therefore came not merely from the wisdom of contemplative reverie but from the gaiety of dissociation and the finding of true individual consciousness, a "timeless individuality" beyond the ego.[38] Such timelessness once achieved, the hero is prepared for ultimate wisdom; having transcended

[37]"Poetry and Tradition" and *Discoveries*, in *Essays*, pp. 314–315, 341.

[38]Introduction to "The Words upon the Window-Pane," *Wheels and Butterflies*, p. 32. Cf.: "The maid of honour whose tragedy [the people] sing must be lifted out of history with timeless pattern . . . must be carried beyond feeling into the aboriginal ice" ("A General Introduction for my Work," *Essays and Introductions*, p. 523).

" 'An aimless joy is a pure joy' " says Tom O'Roughley in the poem that bears his name. Yeats's conceptions of "joy" and "play," and the supporting idea of aimlessness, have precedent in the aesthetic theories of Kant and Schiller. It is likely that Yeats borrowed from Arnold's knowledge of Schiller. In the "Preface to the First Edition of *Poems*" (1853), Arnold quotes Schiller approvingly: " 'All art,' says

ego, he is ready for the final vision which permits him to transcend in turn even his own private tragedy and perceive in it, from a new perspective, its comic counterparts. Of course tragedy does not merely become comedy once viewed from a different point of vantage; but the hero's liberation from personal dread also absolves him from personal commitments, and such absolution places him in a position removed from time and ego, a position from which life becomes a kind of divine comedy.

IV

Tragedy always involves at least two sets of characters: the tragic heroes, who must leave the world, and those who remain behind. Yeats added a third: those who, having left the world, are sufficiently dissociated to bear witness to the "tragic scene," enactment of the struggle being already of the past. Chaucer's Troilus is such a figure. All three kinds of characters are "gay." In Yeats's late poem, "Lapis Lazuli," the word gay appears four times, in the first, second, third, and fifth section. Although the shades of meaning differ, they follow upon one another in a sequence, except for the first reference, which exposes the misuse of the word, the mistaken connotation the "hysterical women" give it, that gaiety is an irresponsible expression of frivolity. The next three references to gay parallel very closely the "three aspects" of "Matter" which Yeats described in detail in his "Introduction to 'The Holy Mountain'": *Tamas*, *Rajas*, and *Satva*.

All men have aimed at, found and lost;
Black out; Heaven blazing into the head:
Tragedy wrought to its uttermost.

Schiller, 'is dedicated to Joy . . .' "; we know that Yeats was familiar with this Preface (though not *when* he first read it), because he refers to it in the Introduction to *The Oxford Book of Modern Verse*. At any rate Schiller's important formulations on *Spieltrieb* (play instinct) and *Stofftrieb* (sense instinct) are often echoed in Yeats's writings on art, certainly more directly there than in Arnold's. Yet in Arnold's "Preface to *Merope*," there are again many comments on tragedy that resemble in spirit Yeats's tragic theory: the stress on the emotional quality of tragedy; the general approval of the Greek tragic spirit—the emphasis on action, on singleness of effect, on lyrical heightening. (See *The Complete Prose Works of Matthew Arnold*, ed. R. H. Super [Ann Arbor, Michigan, 1960], I, 2, 38–64.) The *Concordance* to Arnold's poetry lists more than a hundred entries for "joy."

Arnold also wrote: "Our word *gay*, it is said, is itself Celtic"; and, "The Celt's quick feeling for what is noble and distinguished gave his poetry style; his indomitable personality gave it pride and passion . . ." (*Complete Prose Works*, III, 343, 374). The citations are from *On the Study of Celtic Literature*. Yeats read Arnold's essay as a young man, commenting on it in his own essay, "The Celtic Element in Literature," dated 1897.

Tamas is "'darkness, frustration'"; the tragic heroes, Hamlet and Lear, are "gay" in the face of the darkness; theirs is the gaiety "transfiguring" the "dread" of the struggle. Those who remain to rebuild "Old civilisations put to the sword" are also gay, but theirs is the gaiety of engagement with time and history, the gaiety of the group. The tragic hero, singled out to "perform [his] tragic play," makes the moment in history, but his survivors make history over again, reshape the contours, until some single chosen man again takes to the tragic wars. It is the rhythm of history. So the second stage is "'... *Rajas*, activity, passion....'"

All things fall and are built again,
And those that build them again are gay.

In the final sense, gaiety belongs to the wise, who are no longer of this world, the transfigured souls of the tragic heroes, symbolized in "Lapis Lazuli" by the carved design of three Chinamen. This stage is "'... *Satva*, brightness, wisdom.'"[39] Everything in the final section of "Lapis Lazuli" contributes to the "brightness" of such wisdom: the "water-course or... avalanche," the "slope where it still snows," "mountain and the sky," and finally, of course, the "glittering" eyes of the Chinamen, which brighten "mid [the] many wrinkles" of the darkness, a testament of the victory over suffering. It is also proper that the Chinamen "stare," for the "brightness" and "wisdom" are radiant, still, and contemplative, like the faces of the old Madonnas which Yeats so much admired.

The tragic struggle is every man's, but every man has his own struggle:

Though Hamlet rambles and Lear rages,
And all the drop-scenes drop at once
Upon a hundred thousand stages,
It cannot grow by an inch or an ounce.

"It" clearly must refer to the "tragedy wrought to its uttermost." In Indian philosophy, there is an insistence that "everybody's road is different, everybody awaits his moment." And the uniqueness of each man's struggle and death is an argument against the hysterical women, whose hysteria is part of a social conscience that weeps quantitatively for the millions who suffer from war, famine, or disaster of some kind.

[39]"The Holy Mountain," *Essays and Introductions*, p. 461.

"Our moral indignation, our uniform law, perhaps even our public spirit, may come from the Christian conviction that the soul has but one life to find or lose salvation in. . . ."[40] In this most assertive poem, Yeats sets the individual tragic impulse against the "public spirit" of the body politic. Herein lies the quintessence of his tragic theory: the hero is never hysterical or self-righteous: these are the qualities of the "public spirit." Sometimes the Greeks would use their chorus for voicing that spirit; it balanced the tragic hero: "When Oedipus speaks out of the most vehement passions, he is conscious of the presence of the Chorus, men before whom he must keep up appearances . . . [men] who do not share his passion."[41] Hysteria is passion socialized; the tragic hero never submits to it.

In any final synthesis of Yeats's thought tragedy must also rank high as a way of life, a philosophically constructed mode of existence for the artist and the man. It is "through passion" that the artist becomes aware of his inner conflicts, his "buried selves" or masks. At first unknown to him, these other selves seem alien and intrusive, but the ensuing conflict makes art. In "supreme masters of tragedy, the whole contest is brought into the circle of their beauty." Whatever Dante suffered in life he did not evade in his art, however transmuted the experience became; it is all "mirrored in all the suffering of desire." Both halves of the man are so closely combined "that they seem to labour for their objects, and yet to desire whatever happens. . . ." Such art is not merely a "work of art" but the "re-creation of the man through that art."[42] In the search for his mask Dante enhanced and heightened the drama of his life and his art, where the quarrels of life might find resolution. Of course, though born out of conflict, art is no mere reflection of the life lived nor is it simply its opposite. The mask celebrates the subtle inner life on a level of articulation impossible outside of art. In *Per Amica Silentia Lunae* Yeats offered a philosophic explanation of a paradox: Dante, banished for lechery, beatified Beatrice; Shakespeare, living an apparently colourless life, created the most stirring passions; "busy" and "happy" William Morris wrote of "dim colour and pensive emotion"; and Walter Savage Landor "topped us all in calm nobility." It is in "disappointment" that the poet finds his mask; the hero finds it in "defeat": "The saint alone is not deceived. . . ." Schopenhauer, with whom Yeats was already familiar, had permitted the poet just enough

[40]"An Indian Monk," *ibid.*, p. 436.
[41]"J. M. Synge and the Ireland of his Time," *Essays*, p. 413.
[42]*Autobiography*, p. 165.

struggle and deception to make art possible. For the artist escape from the Will was partial; only the saint gained permanent release. A hero, Yeats argued, "loves the world till it breaks him." Only by complete renunciation of "Experience itself" does the saint accept "his mask as he finds it," a disavowal of life impossible for the poet to make. From some early reading Yeats recalled a fragment of a sentence: "'a hollow image of fulfilled desire,'" and decided that all "happy art" was "that hollow image." When, however, the "lineaments" of this art "express also the poverty or the exasperation that set its maker to the work, we call it tragic art." A similar point had already been made in "Ego Dominus Tuus"—the line that separates tragic from comic (or "happy") art is thin after all—when Hic insists on Keats's deliberate happiness, only to be answered by Ille (Yeats): "His art is happy, but who knows his mind?"

If self-conflict produces tragic art, the intensity of this conflict is in direct proportion to the strength of the combatants: "The more insatiable in all desire, the more resolute to refuse deception or an easy victory . . . the more violent and definite the antipathy." Passion, not originality, is the artist's business, for originality consciously searched for is an aim outside the artist's inner life: it will produce neither happy nor tragic art, for it will yield no sustaining power. Since man can only satisfy a limited number of passions in his everyday life on earth, we must make a "bargain," a "compromise," and when this precarious balance is upset we become subject to madness, delusions, the "hysterica passio" that must always be subjugated to ennoble passion:

> so when a starved or banished passion shows in a dream we . . . break the logic that had given it the capacity of action and throw it into chaos again. But the passions, when we know that they cannot find fulfilment, become vision; and a vision . . . prolongs its power by rhythm and pattern. . . .[43]

In this fashion life becomes art, passion is turned into tragedy, reverie into wisdom.

Ultimately the hero emerges triumphant out of the chaos of his *bellum intestinum* toward "his final joy."[44] Reconcilement then becomes possible in the "bridal chamber of joy," where all art marries, tragic and comic. In spite of its radically different direction, the comic spirit of the Abbey Theatre did not, at last, seem so distant

[43] *Per Amica Silentia Lunae*, in *Essays*, pp. 489–505.
[44] "Other Matters," *On the Boiler*, p. 35.

from Yeats's tragic visions. All the "extravagance, the joyous irony, the far-flying phantasy, the aristocratic gaiety, the resounding and rushing words of the comedy of the countryside, of the folk," had their kinship to the "elevation of poetry," were but the other half of the final unity. Yeats envisioned himself as the writer of the tragic tales which the characters of the comedies told "over the fire"; never, he confesses, could he view his own plays, which were sometimes performed together with a play by some leading Abbey playwright, without being struck by the rightness of the juxtaposition. Always he feels "that [his] tragedy heightens their comedy and tragi-comedy, and grows itself more moving and intelligible from being mixed into the circumstance of the world by the circumstantial art of comedy." Doubting, indeed, that he would ever have written in "so heady a mood" without the reassurance of balance, he delights to know that his tragic vision will be enriched by "a bushel of laughter [thrown] into the common basket."[45] It was an ingenious attempt to make his links with an art he admired but could not write, but it was also one way of resolving the "quarrel" between tragedian and comedian. But there was another way, for the tragic theory itself, at its apotheosis, suggested the laughter and the joy, the reassertion of life and will in the very act of surrendering them.

It is with this joy, or gaiety, that tragedy again touches comic gusto. And it is able to do so because it has never wholly surrenderd reality, has maintained its touch of Character to save Personality from abstraction and annihilation, and to prepare for this ultimate transcedence to the comic—in Yeats's special sense. While passion provides the intense centre, reverie serves to carry the echoes of intensity outward beyond the action of struggle toward the joyful capitulation to a world that breaks the hero. But only an art consecrated to the highest tragic flood can overreach itself into joy; that is what troubled Yeats in his walks at Coole when he saw Augustus John's portraits of character-bound people enslaved to environment, incapable of desire, and therefore incapable of passion. The hero's joy in the face of disaster can come only after the assertion of action (of which John's moribund subjects are again incapable); and the comedy that ensues is divine comedy: "The victim's joy among the holy flame, / God's laughter at the shattering world" (*The King's Threshold*). To find ultimate gaiety and joy the hero must assume his mask; like the poet he finds it in the "disappointment" and "defeat" which break him, though the passion that has become gusto

[45]Preface to *Poems, 1899–1905* (1906) in *Variorum Edition*, p. 850.

enables him to prevail. The supreme sacrifice, made in splendid loneliness, achieves also the salvation of splendid survival:

> The heroic act, as it descends through tradition, is an act done because a man is himself, because, being himself, he can ask nothing of other men but room amid remembered tragedies; a sacrifice of himself to himself, almost, so little may he bargain, of the moment to the moment.... So lonely is that ancient act, so great the pathos of its joy....[46]

"So lonely is that ancient act": yet when the hero surrenders himself to himself, his achievement has come full circle and the surrender binds itself, in closing the circle, to victory.

Out of all the struggles to make an art unified by its internal oppositions—whether earthiness and etherealness, multitude and intensity, motion and arrest—tragedy emerged at the pinnacle where a true equipoise might be achieved. At the end of his life Yeats wrote to Ethel Mannin: "All men with subjective natures move towards a possible ecstasy, all [men] with objective natures towards a possible wisdom": only in tragedy could the hero achieve passion and wisdom both, for tragedy was the enactment of equilibrium. Yeats's insistence that tragedy have passion as well as reverie was motivated metaphysically as well as aesthetically. It is true that in an often quoted passage from a letter to Dorothy Wellesley he denied that the East could "raise the heroic cry" because it "has its solutions always"; but the West is therefore not without solutions. The final "heroic cry in the midst of despair" is neither mere despair nor mere defiance: action converted through contemplation beyond itself delivers the hero to freedom and a gaiety that even the Chinamen in "Lapis Lazuli," though Eastern, can attain. Yet the struggle that chiefly concerned Yeats was Western: tragedy belongs to Europe and to Europe Yeats always returned. Its very literature offered the possibility of another marriage: "We desire an extravagant, if you will unreal, rhetorical romantic art," allied both to Racine and to Cervantes.[47] It was in the vigour of the "passionate reverie" of tragedy that Yeats hoped finally to find his antidotes against any undue softness that might still remain from the nineties, against what Pound has described as the "porcelain revery" of aestheticism (*Hugh Selwyn Mauberley*). Through the marriage of tragic and comic and through the correlative interplay of action and contemplation, tragedy achieved for him—as did the converging gyres—that Unity of Being in which passion softened into wisdom and reverie hardened into intensity.

[46]Introduction to *Fighting the Waves,* in *Wheels and Butterflies,* pp. 66–67.
[47]*Letters,* pp. 917, 837, 440.

6 ❋ THE SINGLE IMAGE: Beyond the Design

One image crossed the many-headed.... "The Statues"

Nations, races, and individual men are unified by an image.... *Autobiography*

... the content of freedom is revealed by two basic manifestations in Europe. . . . First, life in polarity: Europe itself has developed the counter-position for every position. Europe *is* Europe perhaps only because it is capable of becoming everything. Karl Jaspers, *The European Spirit*

If Yeats kept his eyes faithfully on the "eternal pursuit," the "endless battle for an object never achieved,"[1] he also looked with longing, and suspense, away from that Keatsian vision at the moment in time and space when subject and object merge to shape a single image. That was also the moment of self-annunciation. The fear of abstraction was, finally, a fear of engulfment of self, a fear so strong it was equalled only by the persistent fascination with—even the occasional need of—being engulfed. The metaphor of "a breaking wave intended to prove that all life rose and fell" Yeats rejected for *The Wanderings of Oisin*; but it accurately describes both the rhythm and the philosophic see-saw that governed his poetry from the beginning.[2] When the wave fell man descended toward engulfment; when it rose he moved out of it—temporarily perhaps, but he did rise.

The simultaneous need and fear of being absorbed, and thereby obliterated, by some higher force, empty and spacious, is a characteristically Western anxiety: the East needs no defences against the dissolution of self. To be apart and yet be free; to be alone and yet to be self-sufficient; to be alive under the certain aspect of death: these have been the great themes of Western literature. And since the Fall the heavens have been forbidding—if not forbidden—territory; in self-defence, man has often struggled from a position of weakness. He

[1]Introduction to *"The Resurrection,"* in *Wheels and Butterflies*, p. 91.
[2]*Ibid.*, p. 92.

has been put in his place, by religion as well as by science. Happiness to men like Yeats came only from the struggle itself. In despair man can dissociate himself from mortality; curse, like Job and Faustus, not life but *my* life, *my* birth. Or, unforgiven, he may, as does Yeats's Self in "A Dialogue of Self and Soul," "forgive [himself] the lot." In either case, however, the personal and individual cry rules over the consciousness of the act: self and ego become strongest when oppression seems bent on making them weak. Job and Faustus scream "Self!" with increasingly painful loudness as the great obliterating hand descends upon them. In the face of the All, which Western man prefers to call the One, the individual feels threatened by annihilation. Platonism was, from one point of view, a defence against eternity, for it calmed a man to feel the union of his body and soul, to know they could not be disjointed. It was a hard doctrine to consider the oneness we experience as humans as divisible, to know that on death the soul would be severed from body and thrust into space–up or down–divorced from the total consciousness of self that the European has always considered the prime gift of mortality. "'No voice breaks thro' the stillness of this world; / One deep, deep silence all!'" cries the soul in Tennyson's *The Palace of Art*, as she expresses a later and more intellectualized version of annihilation anxiety. Isolated, the soul is but "A spot of dull stagnation, without light / Or power of movement . . . / 'Mid onward-sloping motions infinite." Propped against the Ptolemaic system, the concept of infinity had been finite after all: Dante knew that the ninth sphere was the last.

Because infinity and eternity became overwhelming absolutes, Yeats could contemplate only a cycle, in which souls, reincarnated, keep returning. It was too much to lose one's soul forever–to the powers of light or dark. This is precisely why Soul loses the argument in Yeats's poem, for she offers the very permanence Self cannot accept. When Yeats declared his "faith" in "The Tower" it was in the soul, but in a soul that was self-created ("self-delighting, /Self-appeasing, self-affrighting . . ."):

> Death and life were not
> Till man made up the whole,
> Made lock, stock and barrel
> Out of his bitter soul,
> Aye, sun and moon and star, all,
> And further add to that
> That, being dead, we rise,
> Dream and so create
> Translunar Paradise.

Such a self-created universe was not without its God, "dreamt" as he might be by man himself. God and man shared in each other's existence: "Your words," cries the Greek who feels the beating heart of the phantom of Christ in *The Resurrection*, "are clear at last, O Heraclitus. God and man die each other's life, live each other's death." The rising out of death was as necessary as the sinking into it, but such a rising invested death with a meaning beyond absurdity by making of it one part of the see-saw antinomy, not a surrender to the void of a hereafter, the cessation of life. In *The Resurrection* the Greek says: "I cannot think all that self-surrender and self-abasement is Greek, despite the Greek name of its god. . . . Man, too, remains separate. He does not surrender his soul. He keeps his privacy."[3]

Marlowe's Faustus has been regarded rightly as the quintessential Renaissance man, and he embodies certainly what Yeats considered the full Renaissance Personality, the subjective man. But he is also the man who, at all costs, would "remain separate," would "not surrender his soul," would "keep his privacy."

II

Faustus' disaster is partly the result of his illusion that selling his soul while alive, and on earth, is a way of holding on to it, a way of preventing it from being engulfed by heaven. Throughout the play he tells us clearly that it is hell he disbelieves, *not* heaven. It is an irony that pays home in the end; but it also reveals the characteristics of what we have come to call "Faustian." The rationalized syllogism that leads to Faustus' rejection of divinity is underscored by the thought of "an everlasting death." What Faustus wishes is to give man eternal, everlasting life, or to raise the dead back into the living. Everlasting life against everlasting death; in Yeats's terms, the sword and the tower, "emblematical" of day and night. Faustus does not really want to be God; he wants to be more of a man than God permits. There is a distinction, for he desires not the incorporeality of angelic life but indefinite mortality. Within the conception of disembodiment, it is true that he rejects the immortality of the soul: it is immortal life he wants, eternal death he fears.

The struggle is over Faustus' soul, not over the total man, and Faustus is acutely aware of this synecdochic conflict from which true self-consciousness is eliminated while, external to him, good and bad angels argue over his fate. Hence, too, his fright. By refusing to believe

[3]*The Resurrection*, in *ibid.*, pp. 115, 108.

in the reality of hell, he hopes to keep his temporal bargain divorced from the spectre of the spatial void that hell is: it is another rationalization. Although he blames the inability to repent on his hardened heart, it is more the fear of surrender which finally blocks repentance: "self-surrender" and "self-abasement." "Yea, life and soul!" he cries out, "Oh, he stays my tongue! I would lift up my hands, but see, they hold them, they hold them!" It is relevant that Faustus views his spiritual paralysis in physical terms (Claudius, speaking for a later time, sees it in verbal terms): the physical orientation has governed his rise, just as now it will govern his fall.

Yeats called Faustus' final speech "mighty," a "last agony" which no doubt reverberated in his mind as it had in the minds of many other poets before him. In this final hour Faustus ironically seeks the obliteration he has feared: the spheres of heaven are asked to stop Time itself. The fixed mark of a Faustus suddenly finds himself, like Othello, the centre of a turning (and scornful) world—"The stars move still"[4]—making his consciousness of separateness all the more complete. Again he would leap up but is pulled down (again the physical metaphor). The last forty lines of his soliloquy are woven together by a series of annihilation images: he asks that mountains fall on him, that he be hidden from God, that he be dismembered, that the earth gape open to swallow him, that he be drawn up like a mist by the stars into the fabric of a cloud. In that terrible cry of anguish that God put some limit on the time he must suffer in hell is the fear of heaven now properly inverted. Faustus now knows that hell is where heaven is not. Were it only true that souls migrate as Pythagoras said! It would bring temporary ends to endlessness. Through the curse of himself and then his begetters, Faustus effects his total capitulation: it is not only consciousness of self that he abandons but uniqueness. In the final lines he pleads that his soul dissolve into "little water-drops, / And fall into the ocean—ne'er [to] be found." It is obliteration with a vengeance. And yet the final irony is that this obliteration is shaped to cheat God and Satan both of the soul: if not for me for no one.

The mistake that Faustus makes is that he misinterprets freedom (as, in Yeats's eyes, the Renaissance was wont to do) as physical consciousness limited to one fixed life. As a consequence he fails to see the unity of heaven and hell (as, say, Blake saw it). He is, of

[4]There is little reason to doubt that the Elizabethans used "still" in its double sense of yet and quietly; compare Bosola in Webster's *The Duchess of Malfi*: "Look you, the stars shine still."

course, also the victim of the times, of the steady movement toward the supremacy of intellect and thought, which come to supplant the view of warring contraries. That division creates a whole new direction after the waning of Greece: "instead of seeking noble antagonists, imagination moved towards divine man and the ridiculous devil."[5] Also, it is not Time that Faustus is obsessed with, but Space; he is not a victim of what Yeats called the "modern conception of a finite space always returning to itself to obsess one's thought...." Only a "like obsession with what somebody [Wyndham Lewis] has called the 'Time philosophy' of our day can have made Spengler identify the Faustian soul, which, as he points out . . . is always moving outwards, always seeking the unlimited, with Time."[6]

Through this expansive movement in a space which the Faustian man fears, the self achieves the very annihilation it originally seeks to avoid. Faustus cannot find a way of contracting, forming, returning to the self which his expansive ambitions have drawn outwards. By means of his separation from the limits of what reassures—the Icarus flight—the Faustian man separates belief from act, which is the final tragedy: Faustus refuses to serve what he believes in (heaven) or to believe what he serves (hell). He remains at the end a single tragic image who is caught in the great design.

III

Yeats's conception of the single image in relation to the vast design is the subject of a late poem, "The Statues" (1938), in which individual and design, artist and society, personal utterance and anonymity all find expression and resolution. "The Statues" is both a final poetic embodiment of the aesthetic and a philosophic analogue to Yeats's aesthetic-centred interpretation of history.

> Pythagoras planned it. Why did the people stare?
> His numbers, though they moved or seemed to move
> In marble or in bronze, lacked character.
> But boys and girls, pale from the imagined love
> Of solitary beds, knew what they were,
> That passion could bring character enough,
> And pressed at midnight in some public place
> Live lips upon a plummet-measured face.

[5] *A Vision*, pp. 272–273.
[6] *Ibid.*, pp. 259–260.

No! Greater than Pythagoras, for the men
That with a mallet or a chisel modelled these
Calculations that look but casual flesh, put down
All Asiatic vague immensities,
And not the banks of oars that swam upon
The many-headed foam at Salamis.
Europe put off that foam when Phidias
Gave women dreams and dreams their looking-glass.

One image crossed the many-headed, sat
Under the tropic shade, grew round and slow,
No Hamlet thin from eating flies, a fat
Dreamer of the Middle Ages. Empty eyeballs knew
That knowledge increases unreality, that
Mirror on mirror mirrored is all the show.
When gong and conch declare the hour to bless
Grimalkin crawls to Buddha's emptiness.

When Pearse summoned Cuchulain to his side,
What stalked through the Post Office? What intellect,
What calculation, number, measurement, replied?
We Irish, born into that ancient sect
But thrown upon this filthy modern tide
And by its formless spawning fury wrecked,
Climb to our proper dark, that we may trace
The lineaments of a plummet-measured face.

Joining Hellenic Greece with modern Ireland, Yeats sets forth in this poem a parallel of historical events in the poem, his intention being clearly to point toward the approaching world crisis seen in the mirror of the Greek defeat of the Persians at about the time that the Dorian and Ionian elements of Greek life met in fruitful confluence in the work of Phidias. Both the philosophic and aesthetic meanings which Yeats ascribes to this period of history were fully and brilliantly available in Pater's *Plato and Platonism* and *Greek Studies*. Whether Yeats knew these works closely is not crucial: the evidence of Pater's views merely corroborates the existence of an historical development which re-interpreted Hellenism by celebrating its achievements and crediting it with nothing short of having saved Europe from Asiatic engulfment. This is a view Yeats fully accepted, in "The Statues" and elsewhere; and Pater's contribution to it—direct or indirect—may help us to see that the Aesthetic Movement as Pater conceived it was, despite its Oriental trimmings, a European movement, a last philosophic defence of beauty and order against grotesque chaos, of individuality against multiplicity.

We shall profit, I think, if we regard the Aesthetic Movement in England as at least attempting to find, however unsystematically, a way of seeing art and ethics as co-operative enterprises. If Arnold sometimes leaned too far in the direction of ethics, Pater leaned too far in the direction of art; and Wilde quipped in paradoxes, which has (unfortunately) deprived his criticism of the serious ear which it sometimes deserves. So to call this haphazard effort to unite ethics and aesthetics "philosophic" might be going too far; but in Yeats, who was unique in having matriculated and graduated from the Aesthetic School, that unifying effort gained the quality and proportion deserving of that word "philosophic." In his basic views of the relation of art to social life and to culture Yeats resembles most closely Schiller who, himself not a very systematic philosopher, had assimilated his philosophy from Kant and applied it to art much as Yeats was to do in his later writings. Both Schiller and Yeats—as had Arnold and, to a lesser degree, Pater—insisted that art was a crucial function of man's self-expression, but that such expression was ultimately responsible to the larger context of history, culture, and *a* morality. Schiller's letters *On the Aesthetic Education of Man* consistently make a single point: man's aesthetic education is a prerequisite and a preparation for his moral education, since art leads man into the area of right action, sensitizing his moral feelings by first alerting, as it were, his aesthetic responses. Such a *causal* sequence—art first, morality second —paid homage to the primacy of art without denying its relationship to the rest of man's behaviour.

Schiller's *Spieltrieb* theory (the play instinct), to which I have already referred in the previous chapter, is the foundation of his letters and it is the fifteenth letter in particular which I find most relevant to "The Statues" and to Yeats's conceptions in and surrounding that poem. At the conclusion of this letter Schiller attempts to reconcile art and ethics, beauty and duty (*Pflicht*), arguing that the Greeks had achieved genuine freedom through such a reconciliation and offering as his example Greek sculpture:

> For, to declare it once and for all, Man plays only when he is in the full sense of the word a man, and *he is only wholly Man when he is playing*. This proposition . . . will assume great and deep significance when we have once reached the point of applying it to the twofold seriousness of duty and of destiny; it will . . . support the whole fabric of aesthetic art, and the still more difficult art of living. . . ; this statement . . . has long . . .

been alive and operative in Art, and in the feeling of the Greeks, its most distinguished exponents.... Guided by its truth, they caused not only the seriousness and the toil which furrow the cheeks of mortals, but also the futile pleasure that smooths the empty face, to vanish from the brows of the blessed gods, and they released these perpetually happy beings from the fetters of every aim, every duty, every care, and made idleness and indifference the enviable portion of divinity; merely a more human name for the freest and sublimest state of being. Not only the material sanction of natural laws, but also the spiritual sanction of moral laws, became lost in their higher conception of necessity, which embraced both worlds at once, and out of the unity of these two necessities they derived true freedom for the first time. Inspired by this spirit, they effaced from the features of their ideal, together with inclination, every trace of volition as well.... It is neither charm, nor is it dignity, that speaks to us from the superb countenance of a Juno Ludovici; it is neither of them, because it is both at once. While the womanly god demands our veneration, the godlike woman kindles our love; but while we allow ourselves to melt in the celestial loveliness, the celestial self-sufficiency holds us back in awe. The whole form reposes and dwells within itself, a completely closed creation, and—as though it were beyond space—without yielding, without resistance; there is no force to contend with force, no unprotected part where temporality might break in. Irresistibly seized and attracted by the one quality, and held at a distance by the other, we find ourselves at the same time in the condition of utter rest and extreme movement, and the result is that wonderful emotion for which reason has no conception and language no name.

This description of Greek sculpture demonstrates what at the beginning of the sixteenth letter Schiller calls "the most perfect possible union and equilibrium of reality and form," though he admits that such perfect union was to be found wholly only in the "idea," not in actuality.[7] In this qualification Schiller remains more rigidly Pla-

[7]Friedrich Schiller, *On the Aesthetic Education of Man*, tr. with an Introduction by Reginald Snell (London: Routledge & Kegan Paul, 1954), pp. 80–81. "Denn, um es endlich auf einmal herauszusagen, der Mensch spielt nur, wo er in voller Bedeutung des Worts Mensch ist, *und er ist nur da ganz Mensch, wo er spielt.* Dieser Satz . . . wird eine grosse und tiefe Bedeutung erhalten, wenn wir erst dahin gekommen sein werden, ihn auf den doppelten Ernst der Pflicht und des Schicksals anzuwenden; er wird . . . das ganze Gebäude der ästhetischen Kunst und der noch schwierigern Lebenskunst tragen . . .; dieser Satz . . . längst schon lebte und wirkte . . . in der Kunst und in dem Gefühle der Griechen, ihrer vornehmsten Meister. . . . Von der Wahrheit desselben geleitet, liessen sie sowohl den Ernst und die Arbeit, welche die Wangen der Sterblichen furchen, als die nichtige Lust, die das leere Angesicht glättet, aus der Stirne der seligen Götter verschwinden, gaben die ewig Zufriedenen von den Fesseln jedes Zweckes, jeder Pflicht, jeder Sorge frei und machten den Müssiggang und die Gleichgültigkeit zum beneideten Lose des

tonic than Yeats; for, in "The Statues," Yeats appears to assert the possibility of unifying reality and form as an historical fact, not an "idea." If I have read the poem correctly, he maintains that the form of art itself—the Phidian statues—creates the "reality" as much as reality may give rise to the form of art. We may say with Wilde that Life imitates Art or, as he says in the Preface to *The Picture of Dorian Gray*, "It is the spectator, and not life, that art really mirrors." As Yeats would have it, the Phidian statues mirror back their spectators (reality) whom, in a sense, they have also created. Sanction for such an optimistic view of the efficacious influence of art on culture may well have come to Yeats from his own scheme of history; but the philosophic quarrels centring on the tension between form (stasis) and reality (flux), and the attempted Platonic synthesis between stasis and flux, were outlined in detail by Pater in *Plato and Platonism*.

Pater's position in the first three essays of *Plato and Platonism* reflects the background of a philosophic equipoise between motion and rest which bears resemblances at every turn to the Yeatsian aesthetic that I have presented in the preceding chapters. According to Pater's first essay, "Plato and the Doctrine of Motion," Plato was influenced by three precursors: Heraclitus, Parmenides, and Pythagoras. Each contributed to Plato's philosophy, either by irritating Plato into attack or by serving to support a position to be further developed. Chief among the irritants was, of course, Heraclitus' theory of "eternal flux," which Plato felt bound to oppose with his "Doctrine of Rest." Pursued to its logical end, the Heraclitean position rendered knowledge relative, reality plastic, and Absolutes untenable. This stress on Becoming, rather than Being, paralleled, as Pater noted, the scientific-

Götterstandes: ein bloss menschlicherer Name für das freieste und erhabenste Sein. Sowohl der materielle der Naturgesetze als der geistige Zwang der Sittengestetze verlor sich in ihrem höhern Begriff von Notwendigkeit, der beide Welten zugleich umfasste, und aus der Einheit jener beiden Notwendigkeiten ging ihnen erst die wahre Freiheit hervor. Beseelt von diesem Geiste, löschten sie aus den Gesichtszügen ihres Ideals zugleich mit der Neigung auch alle Spuren des Willens aus. . . . Es ist weder Anmut, noch ist es Würde, was aus dem herrlichen Anlitz einer Juno Ludovisi zu uns spricht; es ist keines von beiden, weil es beides zugleich ist. Indem der weibliche Gott unsre Anbetung heischt, entzündet das gottgleiche Weib unsre Liebe; aber indem wir uns der himmlichen Holdseligkeit aufgelöst hingeben, schreckt die himmliche Selbstgenügsamkeit uns zurück. In sich selbst ruhet und wohnt die ganze Gestalt, eine völlig geschlossene Schöpfung, und als wenn sie jenseits des Raumes wäre, ohne Nachgeben, ohne Wiederstand; da ist keine Kraft, die mit Kräften kämpfte, keine Blösse, wo die Zeitlichkeit einbrechen könnte. Durch jenes unwiderstehlich ergriffen und angezogen, durch dieses in der Ferne gehalten, befinden wir uns zugleich in dem Zustand der höchsten Ruhe und der höchsten Bewegung, und es ensteht jene wunderbare Rührung, für welche der Verstand keinen Begriff und die Sprache keinen Namen hat."

philosophic movements of his own time: Darwin and Hegel. And Pater put the Doctrine of Motion to the test:

Mobility! We do not think that a necessarily undesirable condition of life. . . . 'Tis the dead things, we may remind ourselves, that after all are most entirely at rest, and [we] might reasonably hold that motion (vicious, fallacious, infectious motion, as Plato inclines to think) covers all that is best worth being.[8]

But motion, however desirable, was only half of the Greek ideal: Plato's Hellenism completed it, and Pater makes clear that the balance was desirable—motion checked by rest; rest animated by motion.

"Plato and the Doctrine of Rest" examines this Platonic check against the still dominantly Asiatic conception of flux. Here the role of Parmenides seems crucial, for it is he, according to Pater, who suggested to Plato the idea of an "unchangeable reality"—an idea which Yeats, through Bergson, had once rejected on philosophic grounds. But even Parmenides' Doctrine of Rest was based not on inherent stasis but on the paradoxical theory that "perpetual motion" in space becomes eventually "perpetual rest": the analogue to Yeats's aesthetic use of the dance.

Pater's treatment of Plato's abhorrence of motion is often hostile, even irreverent, for Pater's doctrines of art depended on the vitality of process—growth and change. Like Yeats he felt that Pure Being might lead to Pure Nothing, to death. To Parmenides' paradoxes, "'that what is, is not; [and] . . . that what is not, is,'" and "'that what is, is; and that what is not, is not,'" Pater ascribed a harmful influence: "the European mind . . . will never be quite sane again," because a too relentless quest for the One, the Absolute, is quixotic, a search for the "algebraic symbol for nothingness." Himself essentially a relativist, Pater felt such an uncritical dedication to a single deity to be a "mania," leading to the "self-annihilation" of "Old Indian dreams," to the "ecstasies of the pure spirit, leaving the body behind it," to a "literal negation of self"—in short, to "moral suicide."[9] Yeats never went so far: he would need to keep both impulses, self-realization and self-surrender, and maintain his grasp on reality with the "profane perfection" of his soul. "I think," he wrote in 1930, "that two conceptions, that of reality as a congeries of beings, that of reality as a single being, alternate in our emotion and in history, and must always remain something that human reason, because subject always to one or the other,

[8]Walter Pater, *Plato and Platonism* (London, 1922), p. 22.
[9]*Ibid.*, pp. 39–41.

cannot reconcile."[10] For Yeats, therefore, single and multiple reality, the One and the Many, were irreconcilable, except within the pattern of their alternating rhythms in man and the history he shapes. If Yeats moves forward from his position of 1930 it is only to see that the Many can become the One, that "congeries," assembled in the proper design, assume the shape of a "single being." On the other hand, Pater saw the whole movement in philosophy from Plato through Spinoza, Descartes, and Berkeley as a futile pursuit of Pure Being "attained by the suppression of all the rule and outline of one's own actual experience and thought"; and at such a price he disallowed it.[11]

During the nineteenth century, both philosophy and physical science supported, respectively, the doctrines of flux and rest; the old Greek *Streben* was revived—centrifugal and centripetal "tendencies" were once again in conflict. Like Pater, Yeats too sensed this conflict and it was, I think, from the very start, his desire to combine the two halves, to reconcile Europe and restore the balance between Becoming and Being, between Heraclitus and Plato. Of course, as Pater pointed out, Plato himself was "incurably . . . a dualist" and had sought to find a compromise between the One and the Many: committed as he was in theory to a lifeless, static One, Plato, in practice, would "suffer [the world] to come to him . . . with the liveliest variety . . ."[12]

What finally seems to have swayed Plato toward compromise was Pythagoras and his doctrine of number. Countering the Parmenidean theory of rest, Pythagoras, wrote Pater, once again "set the frozen waves in motion . . . brought back to Plato's recognition all that multiplicity in men's experience," and did so with the balance of "disciplined sound," the "reasonable soul of music." "Pythagoras planned it"—so begins "The Statues": Pater gives him the same compliment, crediting him with perfecting Parmenides' abstract "unity of Being": "Pythagoras seems to have found that unity of principle . . . in the dominion of number everywhere, the proportion, the harmony, the music, into which number as such expands. Truths of number: the essential laws of measure in time and space. . . ." It is to the work of art that Pater, like Yeats, applies the Pythagorean influence, considering its chief benefit the check it brought against the surging doctrines of the infinite: "those eternities, infinitudes, abysses, Carlyle invokes for us

[10] *Pages from a Diary Written in Nineteen Hundred and Thirty*, pp. 18–19.
[11] *Plato and Platonism*, p. 41.
[12] *Ibid.*, pp. 46–47.

so often" (Hulme was not the first to descry this aspect of Romanticism). In Pythagoras Pater finds no "cultus of the infinite... but in the finite," "art as being itself the finite, ever controlling the infinite, the formless." Even the contraries of One and Many, Odd and Even are "reducible ultimately to terms of *art*...." Finally Pythagoras helped Plato to find "unity-in-variety": the goal of art, like the goal of Plato's "theory of ideas," is the "eternal definition of the finite, upon... the infinite, the indefinite, formless, brute matter, of our experience of the world."[13]

And so Heraclitus taught "progress" and Parmenides "rest": Pythagoras taught the philosophy of "re-action." Plato then executed his dualistic "compromise"; upon it, Yeats seems late in life to have built his own. "The Statues" bears out such a conclusion, and even if the poem owes nothing to Pater—which is doubtful—it owes almost everything to the history of the philosophic progression Pater sets forth in *Plato and Platonism*: Heraclitus, Parmenides, Plato. "The Statues" is Yeats's great parable poem, his final reconciliation between the motion and rest of reality, his vision of a past and his prophecy of a future, and his daring image of an art powerful enough to save a civilization.

As early as the essay on the Japanese Noh plays, in 1916, Yeats spoke of the "traditional measurements" of art as a "philosophic defence" against naturalism: the stylized and the formal he considered —at the time—characteristic of Asia (Japan) and Egypt. Phidias he felt was "naturalistic," supplanted eventually by the "august formality" of Callimachus.[14] But in "The Statues" Phidias becomes the executor of "traditional measurements" in Hellenic sculpture, and Yeats has shifted from Asia back to Europe. For this shift he once again would have found confirmation in Pater's *Greek Studies*, where the Hellenic aesthetic is offered as the turning point in the fortunes of European art, leading to the art of the middle ages and the Renaissance. As we shall presently see, the background for "The Statues" follows a similar lineage: Phidias, William Morris as identified with medieval art, Hamlet and Titian.

What finally attracted Yeats to what he called in his essay "An Indian Monk" (1932) the "European sense of form" was his inclination toward a philosophic and aesthetic position of containment within finite freedom: Man, like the work of art, asserts and strives; but "At stroke of midnight God shall win." This oscillation between self-assertion and self-surrender was illustrated and objectified in the

[13] *Ibid.*, pp. 51–52, 59–60.
[14] "Certain Noble Plays of Japan," *Essays*, p. 278.

tension and struggle between Ionian and Dorian, Asiatic and European tendencies in Greek art and history. The division operates in Pater's interpretation of Greece as it also was to serve Yeats in *A Vision* and elsewhere.

According to Pater, Greek sculpture evolved from its mystical beginnings to the Doric discipline of a "severe and wholly self-conscious intelligence," whose chief contribution was the animation of the human form: "One early carver had opened the eyes, another the lips, a third had given motion to the feet. . . ." Ionian and Dorian "met and struggled and were harmonised in the supreme imagination, of Pheidias. . . ." Like Yeats, Pater discerned relationships between supreme Greek sculpture—"clear and graceful and simple"—and the work of the "Japanese flower-painter," a conjunction that made compatible East and West, delicacy and mass, intricacy and focus, "sense" and "soul," the "*design* in things designed," the "rational control of matter everywhere."[15]

Pater proceeded to compare this Hellenic achievement to Renaissance painting, to Titian in particular, who plays a major role in "The Statues." For both Pater and Yeats European art seemed influenced permanently by Asia, and the best of the Eastern contributions prevented both gross realism and loss of style. One of Yeats's central aesthetic conceptions, as we have seen, was the illusion of motion. In "The Statues" Phidias' sculptured forms "moved or seemed to move," and Pater, too, recognized this illusion as one of the great achievements of high Hellenic sculpture, "the marvellous progress" which made for appearances: open eyes "so that they seemed to look,— the feet separated, so that they seemed to walk." In fact it is this illusion of motion which Pater sees as the line demarcating Greek from ancient Egyptian art, the "energetic striving . . . in organic form" of Greek sculpture as distinguished from the exclusively, and static, "mathematical or mechanical proportions" of the Egyptian representations of the human form: "The Greek apprehends of it, as the main truth, that [sculptured man] is a living organism, with freedom of movement, and hence the infinite possibilities of motion . . . ; while the figures of Egyptian art, graceful as they often are, seem absolutely incapable of any motion or gesture. . . . The work of the Greek sculptor . . . becomes full also of the human soul." Motion, gesture, and soul: they were the ingredients of Pater's (as of Yeats's) aesthetic which animated the opposing qualities of quietude, stillness, silence. Phidias consecrated in marble and in bronze man posssessed

[15]*Greek Studies* (London, 1895), pp. 29–30, 231.

of a "reasonable soul"; and the anonymous art of earlier periods gives way now to the identifying skills of the individual artist, his "subjectivity," though that subjectivity is not so private as to lose the imprint of the culture it is dedicated to display.[16]

Pater makes clear that the Ionian element of Greek culture, freer and more sensuous than the Dorian, is not to be slighted, and that the vestiges of its influence in European art remain desirable as a ballast against the rigidity of Dorian severity. But Pater recognizes the great qualities of the Dorian spirit, its devotion "towards the impression of an order, a sanity, a proportion in all work, which shall reflect the inward order of human reason, now fully conscious of itself. . . ." Clearly such an art—and, in Plato, such a philosophy—had its limitations; yet, for all the freedom, variety, and liveliness of the Asian-Ionian temper, it, too, was severely limiting and, Pater asserts, prevented the unification of Greece by insisting on an unintegrated and isolated individuality which never acceded to the making of a whole design: whether in art or in politics. Against this centrifugal tendency Plato fought his philosophic wars, countering with the One against the "'myriad-minded,'" with calm against flux. Exaggerated as Plato's philosophy sometimes became, it has come to stand—for Pater—for a sanity, a sense of coherence, a view of "things as they really are," a "sense of proportion." To all this Yeats eventually gave his allegiance: the "rational, self-conscious order, in the universal light of the understanding."[17] That is the meaning of Yeats's remark at the end of his life that he was no longer a "mystic" but had measured reality "plummet line," had made his own calculations.

Of course measurement was not incompatible with Yeats's matured "mysticism"—a Pythagorean mysticism in which the soul played a primary role. For Hellenic sculpture brought to Asiatic Greece not merely order and proportion, but "a revelation of the soul and body of man." How highly Pater regarded the culminating Dorian influence may be judged by what he attributed to it, precisely the same feat as Yeats does in "The Statues": the defeat of the Persians at Salamis. Embodied in the marbles of Aegina, Pater found the "full expression of . . . humanism," man with a sense of "inward value":

> In this monument, then, we have a revelation in the sphere of art, of the temper which made the victories of Marathon and Salamis possible, of the true spirit of Greek chivalry as displayed in the Persian war, and in the highly ideal conceptions of its events. . . .[18]

[16]*Ibid.*, pp. 250, 252–253. [17]*Ibid.*, pp. 263–265. [18]*Ibid.*, pp. 269, 273.

These Aegean marbles become for Pater a focal point from which he departs backwards and forwards in history; they remind him of Homer as they do of Chaucer, of the primeval and the medieval world; and, from thence, he moves forward to the Renaissance and his own time. Yeats traverses the same ground. Already in his diary of 1930 he had referred to the "Irish Salamis," and it is clear that he now considered his art an example for his race—responsible for a new Salamis, a restored order with a "reasonable soul," a turn of the Great Wheel. Free of the egotism of a purely subjective and critical attitude, Yeats hoped his own art could, like the statues of Phidias, give his race the Imago they required.

Most discussions of "The Statues" begins with the citation of the two passages most obviously related to the poem.[19] The first is from the *Autobiography*:

A reproduction of his [William Morris's] portrait by Watts hangs over my mantelpiece.... Its grave wide-open eyes, like the eyes of some dreaming beast, remind me of the open eyes of Titian's "Ariosto," while the broad vigorous body suggests a mind that has no need of the intellect to remain sane, though it give itself to every phantasy: the dreamer of the middle ages. It is "the fool of fairy... wide and wild as a hill," the resolute European image that yet half remembers Buddha's motionless meditation,

[19]Existing criticism on "The Statues" is remarkably divergent. In the following pages, I offer no complete reinterpretation of the poem, but rather employ aspects of it to serve my own development of the Yeatsian aesthetic. My use of Pater, Schiller, and Plotinus, and my examination of the prose contexts of the poem, will add, I think, some dimensions of meaning not previously explored; however, I am, of course, indebted to the previous discussions of the poem, particularly to those by Hazard Adams and F. A. C. Wilson (see below). On Pater's theory of history in relation to Yeats's see the two excellent essays by Thomas R. Whitaker: "The Early Yeats and the Pattern of History," *PMLA*, LXXV (June, 1960), 320–328, and "Yeats's 'Dove or Swan,'" *PMLA*, LXXVI (March, 1961), 121–132. The most recent, and the most instructive, essays on Pater's criticism are René Wellek, "Walter Pater's Literary Theory and Criticism," *Victorian Studies*, I (1957), 29–46, and Ian Fletcher, *Walter Pater* (*Writers and Their Work* series; Longmans Green & Co., 1959).

The following critics have attempted extended analyses of "The Statues": Hazard Adams, "Yeatsian Art and Mathematic Form," *Centennial Review*, IV (Winter, 1960), 70–88; Richard Ellmann, *The Identity of Yeats*, pp. 188–190; Vivienne Koch, *W. B. Yeats, The Tragic Phase* (London, 1951), pp. 57–75; John Unterecker, *A Reader's Guide to the Poetry of William Butler Yeats*, pp. 278–281; Peter Ure, "'The Statues': A Note on the Meaning of Yeats's Poem," *RES*, XV (1949), 254–257; F. A. C. Wilson, *Yeats's Iconography*, pp. 290–303. Although my own comments are obviously indebted to all the criticism that came before, I am in essential disagreement on certain points with several critics. Adams and Wilson have done the best work, and some of my conclusions are similar to theirs, although my aim, as already stated, is not to offer an autonomous interpretation. No one has yet, I think, explained satisfactorily the whole of the third stanza.

and has no trait in common with the wavering, lean image of hungry speculation, that cannot but because of certain famous Hamlets of our stage fill the mind's eye. Shakespeare himself foreshadowed a symbolic change . . . in the whole temperament of the world, for though he called his Hamlet "fat" and even "scant of breath," he thrust between his fingers agile rapier and dagger.[20]

The second passage appears in *On the Boiler*:

There are moments when I am certain that art must once again accept those Greek proportions which carry into plastic art the Pythagorean numbers, those faces which are divine because all there is empty and measured. Europe was not born when Greek galleys defeated the Persian hordes at Salamis, but when the Doric studios sent out those broad-backed marble statues against the multiform, vague, expressive Asiatic sea, they gave to the sexual instinct of Europe its goal, its fixed type.[21]

To these two passages may be added a third, also from *On the Boiler*, which—curiously enough—has not been quoted in conjunction with "The Statues," though it appears to belong to the poem as closely as the other two:

. . . thought is not more important than action; masterpieces, whether of the stage or study, excel in their action, their visibility; who can forget Odysseus, Don Quixote, Hamlet, Lear, Faust. . . . Hamlet's hesitations are hesitations of thought . . . ; outside that he is a mediaeval man of action.[22]

These excerpts are, of course, out of context, and examining the context of the first two yields some interesting results. Yeats begins section xii of *Four Years* (*Autobiography*) with an account of his initiation into the William Morris circle at Kelmscott. He goes on to describe the room on whose wall hung Rossetti's *Pomegranate*, "a portrait of Mrs. Morris, and where one wall and part of the ceiling

[20] *Autobiography*, p. 87. I reproduce two paintings, both of which were at one time known as "Titian's 'Ariosto,'" and both of which are likely candidates for the painting Yeats mentions. I am unable to establish with certainty which portrait Yeats had in mind: each reader will no doubt make his own preferential choice. For a full bibliographical account of the history of these two paintings see Cecil Gould, *The Sixteenth-Century Venetian School* (London, 1959), pp. 59–61; 114–116. In 1888 (after Yeats had already been in London) the National Gallery recatalogued the supposed Titian portrait of Ariosto to "Portrait of a Poet, by Palma," but the Titian association may well have lingered on after the "official" change was made. In 1915 the National Gallery was still cataloguing the genuine Titian as "Ariosto(?)" but in 1929 the painting was officially called "Portrait of a Man." Yeats's reference (see above) is from *Four Years: 1887–1891* in *The Trembling of the Veil*, published in 1922 and probably written, in first draft, during 1915–1916.

[21] *On the Boiler*, p. 37.

[22] *Ibid.*, pp. 33–34.

were covered by a great Persian carpet." Yeats felt himself encircled by pattern and design and it made him uncomfortable. He expresses disappointment at the taste of the ageing Morris, who seemed "content ... to gather beautiful things rather than to arrange a beautiful house." Yeats's "sense of decoration" ("founded upon the background of Rossetti's pictures") was satisfied only in the drawing-room "by a big cupboard painted with a scene from Chaucer by Burne-Jones." Yet, despite the heavily designed surroundings, the strongly imposing figure of Morris emerges sharply, and Yeats fixes his attention on the man—on "his spontaneity and joy . . . ," claiming that of all possible lives he would wish to live it is Morris's "rather than my own or any other man's." It is at this point that the passage already quoted begins.

From the sense of design, with its cluttered but no doubt sensuous richness, Yeats has moved to the image of Morris, the single image that crosses the design, the one image that crosses the many-headed, to purloin, for the moment, the language of the poem. The description of the portrait (see Plates VII and VIII) also bears re-examination in the light of the fuller context, for the "wide-open eyes, like the eyes of some dreaming beast," suggest an intensity of contemplation, the guiding physical mark of Morris that must have caught his attention even when he first met him. Similar effects were probably generated by the "broad vigorous body" which "suggests a mind that has no need of the intellect to remain sane, though it give itself to every phantasy: the dreamer of the middle ages." Clearly, Morris is a dreamer *about* the middle ages, and the hulking physique is Yeats's familiar "thinking body" which, coupled with the "expressive" eyes, produces that curious double effect: motion and stillness, passion and wisdom, dance and trance. The image is, we are told, the "*resolute* European image that yet half remembers Buddha's motionless meditation...." Hamlet, "lean image of hungry speculation," rapier and dagger "thrust between his fingers" (Yeats speaks here of "certain famous Hamlets of our stage" but in the poem the distinction between Shakespeare's character and his modern interpreter is *not* made explicit) appears to be the antithesis; and the "hungry" is what makes the speculation parasitic, getting its nourishment from the body it makes "lean." Speculation and Meditation: that is the great antithesis, for the first is full of desire and intellectual arrogance, whereas the second awaits "the crisis," shaping what has been given to the mind, accumulating it to grow "fat," not giving back what has been shaped speculatively and sceptically. The comparison was implicit in the discussion of the portraits by Strozzi and Sargent, but the Venetian gentleman painted by Strozzi is no William Morris, no "fat / Dreamer of the Middle Ages." In fact, he appears to be, physically at least, a lean man, and the description of him better parallels Hamlet's than Morris's: "Whatever thought broods in the dark eyes... has drawn its life from his whole body; it feeds upon it... all was an energy flowing outward...." Although the Venetian gentleman's body too thinks, it thinks with an energy that is released "outward," not stored, as it were, inwardly. (President Wilson's eyes are vacant.) Also, in the third passage, from *On the Boiler*, quoted at the beginning of this discussion, Hamlet is equated with action, and action is given a higher place than thought. Moreover, Hamlet is called a "mediaeval man of action." One cannot have it both ways. If Yeats meant to have the ambiguous association of Morris as a dreamer both of and about the middle ages, and if the middle ages are meant to imply a more quiet and contemplative quality than the energetic Renaissance, then Hamlet cannot be Morris's antithesis in one sense and a medieval man of action in another. Clearly Hamlet and his "wavering, lean image" are not intended to serve as an entirely negative image juxtaposed to an entirely positive image of Morris. The "action," "visibility," "energy" which Yeats praises so often are a part of the speculative man, at least at one point in his development. Morris, as will appear, stands before Hamlet in that development, half-way between Buddha's "emptiness" and President Wilson's, resolute for action but still contemplative, contemplative but not yet wholly speculative.

Yeats now moves forward to examine Morris's personality and the Anti-Self image of his art: the "dream world of Morris" as the "antithesis of [his] daily life," the "joyous" man who "called himself 'the idle singer of an empty day,'" fashioning in his art "new forms of melancholy, and faint persons, like the knights and ladies of Burne-Jones." For Morris, the whole creative act with all its attendant energy was antithetical to the art it produced; and "having all his imagination set upon making and doing he had little self-knowledge."[23] A biographer of Morris, who either did not know or at least made no use of Yeats's remarks, interprets Morris along similar lines: "Morris grew up in prosperous seclusion... so that his chief notion of how to employ his enormous energies was derived from romantic fiction which applauds, alternatively, exploit and altruism." But, for a time, "Contact with the brutality evident in Froissart and implicit in Malory . . . destroyed his romantic Victorian conception of Chivalry and divorced tenderness from exploit, thus associating it with failure." It is

[23] *Autobiography*, pp. 86–88.

only a happy marriage and a flourishing business that again permit him to ally "tenderness with success. The result was quiet narrative poetry on heroic subjects, which began to be disturbed [in time] by Icelandic Saga and the old longing for conspicuous exploit."[24] For Yeats, of course, doing and dreaming were not incompatible: the dream was a fulfilment of the act.[25] But Morris's kind of dreaming —meditative, not speculative—was equivalent to a mode of action different from Hamlet's, action that resembled the "reverie" of Richard II, which yielded the intensity of active mind and passive body, like that of the Buddha.

The image of Morris hovers, in a very real sense, over the whole of "The Statues." First emerges the designer, whose personality created art with "character enough" because of the passion in his real life, which was resolute and dedicated to action. Morris is the sort of man who is singly more powerful than the design he creates, whose design is only "half-anonymous," the vigorous mind which can create the art of repose. This in turn projects the dreamer—and therefore also the giver of dreams ("Gave women dreams and dreams their looking-glass"), whose dreams, though quiet and even melancholy, generate a good deal of energy in being dreamed. In a sense Morris relates to Phidias, for by creating dreams he created audiences for these dreams, who became mirrors for the objects to which they paid homage. That is, after all, the essential intention behind the first stanza:

> ...boys and girls, pale from the imagined love
> Of solitary beds...
>
> . . . .
>
> ...pressed at midnight in some public place
> Live lips upon a plummet-measured face.

The enormous claim for art which the second stanza makes, the defeat of the Persians at Salamis, is no idle claim: culture shapes; force only executes. Ideals are faced by those who eventually absorb them (having sought them in the first place), those who themselves thereby become ideals. Phidias' statues, as I have already suggested, are mirrored back upon themselves by those who "stare" at them. The ideal of art becomes the reality when that reality (that is, the spectators who "stare" at the statues) takes on the nature of the ideal itself and, through it, can effect a victory like that at Salamis.

[24]Gerald H. Crow, *William Morris, Designer* (London, 1934), pp. 15, 54.
[25]This is what Yeats meant when he insisted that all art was "dream."

Such a total integration between art and audience Yeats had himself sought to achieve for the Irish through their mythology. In the final stanza the Irish must "climb" to their "proper dark" to "trace" in this mirror reflection "a plummet-measured face," to become what ideal art is. Although the statue of Cuchulain in the Post Office was of course a later commemoration of the events of 1916, the image that Yeats has in mind when Pearse "summons" the ancient hero is an art-image, an image meant to symbolize a cultural unity. However short-lived the victory on Easter Monday, it was, as at Salamis, Cuchulain who fathered it, and Pearse and his men (the "banks of oars") who carried it out. It is almost certain that Yeats meant to associate the statues of Phidias, as ideal-images, with the "statue" of Cuchulain both before and after it actually was put into mould: the title of the poem is plural for more than one reason. The optimism of this idea is undeniable: it is based on an assumption about human nature, and the Irish, which Yeats did not often support; man seeks to live among the ideals he lives for.

The second passage that belongs to the genesis of "The Statues" (from *On the Boiler*) also has a context worth widening. Again Yeats's general subject is design. The invocation to return to "Greek proportions" begins innocently enough with an account of a designer whom Yeats had hired for his "sister's needle...." Diana Murphy, the designer whom he finally engaged, is praised "with one reservation":

> Of recent years artists, to clear their minds of what Rossetti called "the soulless self-reflections of man's skill" depicted in commercial posters and on the covers of magazines, have exaggerated anatomical details. Miss Murphy's forms are deliberately thick and heavy, and I urge upon her the exclusion of all exaggerations, a return to the elegance of Puvis de Chavannes. There are moments when I am certain that art must once again accept those Greek proportions....

A good share of the attack here is directed against the sheer arrogance of reflected power—" 'soulless self-reflections of man's skill' ": the exaggerated bodies (like those by Augustus John in the drawings at Coole), "thick and heavy." Bulk is to be reduced to elegance, and proportion becomes a limiting factor which, by decreasing distortions, also makes more real. That is perhaps the crucial distinction. Measurement, not recognizable objective form, makes the imitation of reality "real."

In *A Vision* Yeats finds himself in agreement with the archaeologist Josef Strzygowski, for whom "the East... is not India or China, but the East that has affected European civilisation, Asia Minor, Mesapotamia, Egypt." Strzygowski found among

> the nomad Aryans of northern Europe and Asia the source of all geometrical ornament, of all non-representative art. It is only when he comes to describe such art as a subordination of all detail to the decoration of some given surface, and to associate it with domed and arched buildings where nothing interferes with the effect of the building as a whole, and with a theology which so exalts the Deity that every human trait disappears, that I begin to wonder whether the non-representative art of our own time may not be but a first symptom of our return to the *primary tincture*. He does not characterize the West except to describe it as a mirror where all movements are reflected.[26]

Byzantine art had achieved such a non-representational design, though its evolution goes back to Pythagoras and Phidias, both strong influences, through Alexander, on the Near East. Yeats also told Edith Shakleton Heald to remember when reading the third stanza "the influence on modern sculpture and on the great seated Buddha of the sculptors who followed Alexander."[27] So the line between Phidias and modern times is an unbroken development with Alexander serving as a midpoint or intermediary. Byzantium might be considered the first culmination of a Phidian development though there were significant differences in direction. "We and the Greeks," Yeats writes in *A Vision*, "moved towards intellect, but Byzantium and the Western Europe of that day moved from it."[28] Byzantine nonrepresentationalism was far less conceptual than any of its predecessors. In one sense, however, Byzantine art resembled Phidian art closely: both managed to capture and embody culture-ideals in a single image—within and also beyond the geometrical design that ordered their respective arts.

Yeats was fairly clear about the role of the Alexandrian period in the drama of history: "I identify the conquest of Alexander and the breakup of his kingdom, when Greek civilisation, formalised and codified, loses itself in Asia, with the beginning and end of the 22nd Phase, and his [Alexander's] intention . . . to turn his arms westward shows that he is but a part of the impluse that creates Hellenised Rome and Asia." The statues of this influence "represent man with nothing more to achieve," but they are not vaguely abstract immensities—they have been "measured."[29] Indeed, they represent the Hellenic influence on Asia, on the *later* statues of Buddha, the "great seated Buddha" of Japan, who is as measured, as symmetrical, as balanced

[26]*A Vision*, pp. 257–258.
[27]*Letters*, p. 911.
[28]*A Vision*, p. 282.
[29]*Ibid.*, p. 271.

as anything Pythagoras ever planned. Neither "empty eyeballs" nor Buddha is meant as an Asian antithesis (mystical) to the West (practical), for, as Yeats saw it, the lines of history after Alexander merged rather than warred as sharply divided impluses. As for the 22nd phase, Yeats characterizes it as "Balance between ambition and contemplation."[30] And that returns us to Morris and Titian's "Ariosto"—the "resolute European image that yet half-remembers Buddha's motionless meditation ...," resolution and meditation sharing between them "ambition" and "contemplation."

But what of Phidias? It is now necessary to take the poem from the beginning, and to pay close heed to its chronology, for the poem tells the story of civilization from Pythagoras to the present: at least it projects metaphorically the aesthetic revolutions and their influence on culture and history from the Greeks to the present.

Pythagoras was not only a mathematician, but a philosopher and somewhat of a mystic as well; and the theory of numbers, perhaps his chief accomplishment, was to influence, as Yeats suggests, the way man looked at reality. For despite the abstractions of the number theory, it enabled man to think of his universe numerically, in quantitative terms; it permitted him to count off, as it were, the one from the many. Pythagoras, therefore, brought to Europe an essential feature of its subsequent culture: the self-consciousness of the individual, countable object. This was the "impulse" of "common antiquity"—"An impulse towards what is definite and sensuous, and an indifference towards the abstract and the general ... the lineaments ... of common antiquity. ..."[31] The man who can isolate and count the objects outside himself is also acutely conscious of his own singleness. Here he reaches something akin to the Indian ascetic's final insight, "a single timeless act ... all existence brought into the words: 'I am.' It resembles that last Greek number, a multiple of all numbers because there is nothing outside it, nothing to make a new beginning" —it is self-enclosed.[32] Pythagoras' numbers, embodied in the statues, "moved or seemed to move": motion and stillness, dance and trance, energy and meditation, so balanced that immobility suggested motion, art life. Yet, *though* they moved, or seemed to, they "lacked character":

[30]*Ibid.*, p. 157.

[31]*If I were Four-and-Twenty*, p. 36. Throughout "The Statues" Yeats implicitly parallels the Greek and the Irish temper, for which he would have found sanction in Arnold's "On the Study of Celtic Literature": "The Greek has the same perceptive, emotional temperament as the Celt; but he adds to this ... the sense of *measure*; hence his admirable success in the plastic arts. ..." (See *Complete Prose Works*, ed. R. H. Super [Ann Arbor, Michigan, 1960], III, 344.) Yeats was keenly aware that the Irish had to add this "sense of *measure*" to their "emotional temperament."

[32]"The Holy Mountain," *Essays and Introductions*, p. 462.

movement (life) alone suggests individuation in the extreme, which is what Yeats meant by "character." What the statues lacked in character they made up for in passion, the element of the tragic action which breaks the "dykes that separate man from man"; the passion is in the statues, not only in the boys and girls who kiss their lips. Of course, the passion in the statues reflects theirs, just as they reflect the passion in the statues: that is what makes the statues so overwhelmingly real, real enough to permit Yeats the image of them being made love to in a "public place" without appearing absurd or investing sculpture with the ability to arouse purely exhibitionist responses as if it were pornography. For Yeats the conception of reality making love to its embodiment is an earnest one, for in that union reality recaptures the ideal which embodiment always expresses. Art becomes a part of life, becomes—in the Morris sense—even "useful." The lips that press on the "plummet-measured face" are "Live lips," and they bestow a kiss that was intended to animate, miraculously, like the kiss by Eithne Inguba that brings to life the dead Cuchulain, the kiss of passion that meets passion, desire that fulfils desire. Imagined love has made the boys and girls "pale" because phantasy is no substitute for passion; so that they have come to the statues not only to animate them but themselves as well.

The first stanza, then, attributes to Pythagoras' numbers two results: individuation balanced by passion, the "definite and sensuous" in "marble or in bronze." The statues have the power of replenishing the passion-hungry boys and girls not merely with sexual desire but with a sense of life that ensues from the union of man and woman—life, literally and metaphorically. To the family, Yeats agreed, may be attributed the whole "origin of civilization which but exists to preserve it": given this, it seems quite "natural" that "its ecstatic moment, the sexual choice of man and woman, should be the greater part of all poetry." For such choice is crucial, a "single wrong choice may destroy a family, dissipating its tradition . . . and the great sculptors, painters and poets are there that instinct may find its lamp."[33] That, finally, is the function of the statues; that is why the boys and girls come to them.

It is interesting to linger a little on the relation of number to beauty, to rhythm, balance and unity, in short, on the meaning of number as an aesthetic element, particularly as Yeats expresses it in "The Statues." We know for certain that Yeats had read Plotinus as early as the twenties in Stephen Mackenna's fine translation. In the fifth volume, *On the One and the Good* (the Sixth Ennead), Yeats must

[33]*If I were Four-and-Twenty*, p. 14.

have noted with interest the tractate on numbers. Here Plotinus considers the meaning and nature of number in relation to a series of metaphysical problems.

In attempting to search for the Real Being of number, Plotinus arrives, through a sequence of subtle arguments, at a notion that places number almost as the primum mobile of existence: number, or "oneness," he sees as "something prior to man and to all the rest... prior also to even movement, prior to Being, since without unity these could not be each one thing...." And it is through number, prior to all things, that we attain unity of all multiplicity. Unity is, of course, the pattern of multiplicity, the One that is derived from the Many: "You see something which you pronounce to be a unity; that thing possesses also size, form, and a host of other characteristics you might name...." How, then, is such Unity attainable? How do we discern the One in the Many? To begin with, says Plotinus, we must recognize that all multiplicity must initially be bounded, for "limitlessness and number are in contradiction," just as Yeats argued that the "one image" had to defeat the "many-headed," the "Asiatic vague immensities," which he identified with the Persian invasion of Greece. Hence, says Plotinus, number is "definite":

it is we that can conceive the "More than is present"; the infinity lies in our counting: in the Real is no conceiving more than has been conceived; all stands entire.... It [number] might be described as infinite in the sense that it has not been measured—who is there to measure it?—but it is solely its own, a concentrated unit, entire...; what is limited, measured, is what needs measure to prevent it running away into the unbounded. There every being is Measure; and therefore it is that all is beautiful. Because that is a living thing it is beautiful....

It is toward the word beauty that Plotinus has aimed his argument: number is necessary not only to account for rhythm (motion) but for pattern, for the unity of form, for the equipoise between motion and rest, for the principal element in beauty, oneness, which in turn is also complementary to The Good. (Here the resemblance to the moral-aesthetic argument of Schiller examined previously is clear.) The only remaining question is: How do we attain this unity of beauty? Or, since Yeats very nearly adopts Plotinus' language, we should ask: How do we attain Unity of Being?

Generative of all, The Unity is none of all;... not in motion, not at rest, not in place, not in time: it is the self-defined, unique in form or, better, formless, existing before Form was, or Movement or Rest, all of which are attachments of Being and make Being the manifold it is.

But how, if not in movement, can it be otherwise than at rest?

In his essay "Louis Lambert" (1934) Yeats asks a similar question:

> The Word is that which turns number into movement, but number (division, magnitude, enumeration) is described by Séraphita as unreal and as involving in unreality all our science. Two and two cannot be four, for nature has no two things alike. Every part is a separate thing and therefore itself a whole and so on. Is movement reality or does it share the unreality of number, its source?

"The answer is," said Plotinus, "that movement and rest are states pertaining to Being, which necessarily has one or the other or both."[34] Being, then, is itself the ultimate manifold of which rest and motion are "attachments" and these attachments possess Unity by virtue of *number*, the "definite" manifested prior even to Being. Number, Being, Movement, Rest: this is Plotinus' declension, his causal sequence; Unity and Beauty are, finally, attained in what he calls "Ideal-Form," and such "Ideal-Form" is for Plotinus, as for Yeats, the visible triumph of a single unified object that has defeated confusion and discord:

> All shapelessness whose kind admits of pattern and form . . . is ugly . . . ; an ugly thing is something that has not been entirely mastered by pattern. . . .
>
> But where the Ideal-Form has entered, it has grouped and co-ordinated what from a diversity of parts was to become a unity: it has rallied confusion into co-operation: it has made the sum one harmonious coherence. . . .
>
> And on what has thus been compacted to unity, Beauty enthrones itself, giving itself to the parts as to the sum. . . .[35]

Certainly Yeats sees the Phidian statues, fathered by Pythagorean numbers, neither moving nor at rest, as Ideal-Forms of Being, objectified in art, and as a unity of multiplicity, richly endowed, in the Plotinian sense, with Beauty.

The beginning of the second stanza of "The Statues" offers little difficulty: just as the oarsmen at Salamis merely executed the ideals of Phidias, so Pythagoras merely "planned" them—the creators, the sculptors, are the true shapers (though the artist clearly needs both theoreti-

[34]Plotinus, *On the One and the Good, Being the Treatises of the Sixth Ennead*, tr. Stephen Mackenna and B. S. Page (London and Boston, 1930), pp. 142–143, 154–155, 159, 160–161, 241–242. The quotation from Yeats is from *Essays and Introductions*, pp. 442–443.

[35]Plotinus, *The Ethical Treatises*, tr. Stephen Mackenna (London, 1917), p. 80. I am indebted to Professor John Arthos for alerting me to certain of the passages in Plotinus used in the preceding discussion.

cian and sailor or soldier). The "Calculations that look but casual flesh" are described in so off-hand and minimized a manner in order to contrast with the maximal effect they have wrought, the saving of a civilization. It is here that Phidias first enters the poem, following Pythagoras, born, probably, the year Pythagoras died. At this point Yeats is intent on describing the nature of the art-ideal which defeated the Persians; what that ideal was and how it came to be is suggested in the final line of the second stanza, but we must look elsewhere too for clues and directions. Phidias' art Yeats describes in *A Vision*: "...before Phidias, and his westward-moving art, Persia fell...."[36] The sentence is perhaps ambiguous, since it could conceivably imply that the "westward-moving art" came from the East; it did not, of course: its ideal nature was Western and in that sense it moved toward the West. When it moved against the Persians it naturally moved—in terms of the way it faced at least—East; and when it finally moved East with Alexander it had already ceased to be Phidian and was headed toward "Byzantine glory" after the fall of Rome. "Doric vigour" is in the ascendant "after the Persian wars": "One suspects a deliberate turning away from all that is Eastern..." (it is a natural impluse to avoid all resemblance to an enemy who has nearly conquered you), as the athlete replaces the "Parisian-looking young woman of the sculptors...."[37]

Phidias was only about twenty when the battle of Salamis was fought and had not, of course, achieved what Yeats attributes to him in the poem. In *A Vision*, however, the chronology is clear, the height of Phidian art coming *after* that battle, not before it, though it is a culmination not a new beginning. Subsequent to the victory at Salamis, with the conscious rejection of everything Asian, comes a fruition in the confluence of two Greek impulses: "in Phidias Ionic and Doric influence unite—one remembers Titian—and all is transformed by the full moon, and all abounds and flows."[38] Indeed, "one remembers Titian," and his "Ariosto" and Watts's portrait of Morris. The father of them both, Phidias had shown how to combine vigour (ambition, energy) with elegance (contemplation). As one looks at the portraits in question, their meaning becomes clearer: they are European with a lingering Asian influence, just as Phidian art, despite the efforts to shake off Asian influences, had still some trace of them left from the Persian wars.

[36] *A Vision*, pp. 270–271.
[37] *Ibid.*, p. 270.
[38] *Ibid.*

In *A Vision* Phidian art is not yet the great ideal that Byzantine art will become because it spells too much "systematisation": "Phidian art, like the art of Raphael, has for the moment exhausted our attention." In fact, Phidian art represents to some extent an over-balanced Apollonian stabilizer, as contrasted with the more natural pre-Phidian art which resembled, Yeats supposes, the plays "enacted before Aeschylus and Sophocles . . . both Phidian men."[39] But the loss of some primitive spontaneity must have seemed well worth it to Yeats when he came to write the poem: Phidian "systematisation" created a culture that was strong enough to preserve itself against engulfment by its antithesis. (The last two lines of the second stanza have already been commented on at length.)

When Yeats offers the age that follows Alexander as a clue to the reading of the third stanza, he indicates that he has moved at least a century and a half beyond Salamis. But the "one image" need not, of course, "cross" the "many-headed"—in a literal sense—*at* Salamis: clearly Yeats is telescoping history to suit his image of it. "After Phidias [who died *ca.* 432] the life of Greece . . . had moved slowly and richly . . . [and] comes rapidly to an end."[40]

> One image crossed the many-headed, sat
> Under the tropic shade, grew round and slow,
> . . . .
> When gong and conch declare the hour to bless
> Grimalkin crawls to Buddha's emptiness.

With Alexander comes the real fusion of Europe and Asia, West impregnating East: even the Emperor's two wives were Eastern princesses. From the death of Phidias to Alexander the Doric-Ionian balance had been brought to a full flowering—and then to extinction. Phidian art (and its influences) has gone full circle: it had first spread across the West and then across the East, bringing eventually the achievement of Byzantium, until the "westward-moving Renaissance" (Titian here parallels Phidias' "westward-moving art") brings the end to that Justinian empire too: "all things dying each other's life, living each other's death."[41]

The "one image" can by now be viewed as a very rich one: it embodies all that has been suggested in the motion of history from Pythagoras through Alexander, from Byzantium through the Renaissance. That the image crosses does not mean merely that it traverses, but also that it neutralizes, literally covers over, though does not cancel

39*Ibid.*, p. 269. 40*Ibid.*, p. 271. 41*Ibid.*

out, the "many-headed," just as the apexes of Yeats's historical gyres cross when they presumably meet as they penetrate each other. And that the image grows in the tropic shade suggests at the least Alexander's conquest of Asia Minor, the Hellenization of that part of the world; some of the slow and rich development that Yeats attributes to post-Phidian Greek culture surely occurred in Alexander's age.

There remains Hamlet. The Hamlet Yeats alludes to in the poem is not the melancholy Dane, the dreamer, but his antithesis: the frenetic, agile, Renaissance man with a rapier ready to strike. It is not the contemplative or even the speculative side that seems most in Yeats's mind, but rather the cruel Hamlet, the impulsive Hamlet, the active and passionate man. He is "thin" because he feeds on nothing—flies; his energy consumes him away; it is not pessimism or scepticism but the nervous anxiety of freedom which, in the Renaissance spirit, makes Hamlet self-conscious of the awful implications of being free. This burden of freedom he shares with Faustus. In the prose passage from the *Autobiography* Hamlet resembles one of those men in Italian portraits whom Yeats, taking the notion from a German critic, has described as awaiting death from behind—the defensive man whose freedom permits him no rest from motion. But the fear and the freedom both mark him out apart from the design; William Morris, it is worth noting, is painted against a backdrop of design (though it is true he too emerges out of it).

"When Pearse summoned Cuchulain to his side": living man summoned the dead. Throughout the poem, we have been given what Nietzsche called a kind of "monumental history"; and the summoning of Cuchulain by Pearse is like the one image, the "personality," which —against great odds—forges a path along which it leaves its influence and at the end of which stands a new image for a new civilization. As Nietzsche put it: "One giant calls to the other across the waste space of time. . . ."[42] The commemorative statue now in the Dublin Post Office was intended (at least in the poem) to serve the same purpose

[42]Nietzsche, *The Use and Abuse of History* tr. Adrian Collins (Library of Liberal Arts, no. 11; New York and Indianapolis, 1949, 1957), p. 59. Nietzsche has several comments to make in this essay which are relevant to "The Statues." Of the modern deification of knowledge he says: "Knowledge, taken in excess without hunger, even contrary to desire, has no more effect of transforming the external life, and remains hidden in a chaotic inner world that the modern man has a curious pride in calling his 'real personality' " (p. 23); "The culture of a people . . . can be, I think, described with justice as the 'unity of artistic style in every outward expression of the people's life' " (p. 25); "*You can explain the past only by what is most powerful in the present*" (p. 40).

as the statues in the first stanza: to become an ideal that can exercise a creative function by making images of itself in its beholders. And so the Irish, wrecked by formlessness, are envisioned as having to climb to the "proper dark"—the dark of the moon that begins a cycle, so that they too may grow round and slow, developing meanwhile, like Phidian culture, a rich heritage. In that sense too they must "climb" up to the statues to kiss them, to give life to the images that in turn will give life to them.

"The Statues" celebrates the single, conscious, countable and measurable image of art as it climbs out of the vast design of history—the tide of the engulfing flood—which it conquers. It also celebrates the artist and his work as the vital life-blood in the history of a culture. In 1930 Yeats wrote: ". . . I disliked the isolation of the work of art. I wished through the drama, through a commingling of verse and dance, through singing that was also speech, through what I called the applied arts of literature, to plunge it [the work of art] back into social life."[43] The re-integration of art and social life is the major theme of "The Statues," and in this poem Yeats claims for art the highest mission and the noblest purpose since Shelley's *Defence*. Against the isolated, professional artist of modern times, amputated from his culture, Yeats sets once again the possibility of what he once called the great "Artificer" meeting his destiny in the "moment" of his age. Yeats knew—as others still do not—that for society to take the artist seriously, the artist must take seriously the society on which he makes his demands. The test of a great culture lies in its willingness to struggle beyond the instinct of self-survival toward self-realization; and to realize itself, a culture must have an Image worth preserving. The poem may have relevance today far beyond what even Yeats could have guessed: the thought of another Salamis no longer seems so remote.

IV

I began this study by claiming for Yeats an epic imagination in conflict with, but also sustained by, a lyric-dramatic talent. In a letter to Dorothy Wellesley, in 1936, Yeats writes: "the writer of ballads must resemble Homer, not Vergil. His metaphors must be such things as come to mind in the midst of speech. . . ."[44] Homer's epic capaciousness is here not considered incompatible with either song or drama: on this point Yeats had been consistent all his life. Writing of Bridges'

[43]*Diary*, p. 13.
[44]*Letters*, pp. 854–855.

The Return of Ulysses in 1896, he had praised it because "it moulds into dramatic shape . . . those closing books of *The Odyssey* which are perhaps the most perfect poetry of the world, and compels that great tide of song to flow through delicate dramatic verse. . . ."[45] The commingling (to use one of Yeats's favourite words) of epic, lyric, and drama produced that "ancient simplicity and amplitude of imagination" (early phrases) which governed Yeats's aesthetic throughout: the union of the Kabbalistic water and fire learned in his youth—"The water is sensation, peace, night, silence, indolence; the fire is passion, tension, day, music, energy."[46] Always Yeats would work for a union of intensive and extensive wrought to final perfection in the "single image."

Yeats insisted that "a single image, that of Christ, Krishna, or Buddha [cannot] represent God to the exclusion of other images."[47] That is, neither in art nor in history is the single image ever final: there are many such images, and their importance lies less in what they are than in their singleness.

When, at the end of the fifth book of *The Odyssey*, Odysseus makes a desperate, final attempt to emerge from the tumult of the sea by gripping, with both hands, the rough edge of a rock, as the angry waves spill over his exhausted body, the single image—perhaps for the first time in European literature—thwarts the design: the design of the gods and of men. Odysseus' strength and his cunning, the Prometheus in him, are as necessary to his success as are his fear of the gods and his rational mistrust of the divine order. The fearful sceptic and the believing but proud man: this is the Odysseus who sets in motion his own shaping powers against those that shape him. And in the end he survives and triumphs precisely because he chose to fight the design while never for a moment losing sight of its real and potent existence, never underestimating its strength, as did his crews. He accepts the game; he sticks to the rules.

The Odyssey is also a story of leadership and an object lesson on the unreliability of the group; it values the individual more than the whole, because the whole, signified by Odysseus' crews, repeatedly shows itself untrustworthy. In this sense the epic stands against the sentimentalizing of man's interdependent helplessness, which so often serves as the insidious rationalization for the abridgement of personal

[45] "The Return of Ulysses," *Essays*, p. 246.

[46] W. B. Yeats, *The Celtic Twilight*, p. 6. *Letters on Poetry from W. B. Yeats to Dorothy Wellesley*, p. 95.

[47] "An Indian Monk," *Essays and Introductions*, p. 433.

liberty in the name of the Whole. In *The Odyssey* man survives singly—he is, to use Yeats's words, "self-sufficing"—while the crews go down en masse. This is not to say that a man is an island, for the self needs the world for its own fulfilment: "The world is necessary to the Self, must receive 'the excess of its delights'. . . ."[48] But a good leader is only good if he can lead when there is no one left to lead—when he can lead himself. Odysseus is such a man.

He is also the first European hero, and he is the most bourgeois of them, setting for his ideal not a romantic goal of the unknowable (Dante already romanticizes him to point up the Christian objection to the quest of limitless adventure) but the return to the two values which Yeats, too, thinking like an epic poet, recognized as primary and essential: soil and family. "I understand by 'soil,'" Yeats wrote, "all the matter in which the soul works, the walls of our houses, the serving up of our meals . . . and by 'family' all institutions, classes, orders, nations, that arise out of the family and are held together, not by a logical process, but by historical association. . . ."[49] It is only through soil and family that traditions are preserved, and a man can surrender to these two Absolutes for, belonging to them, he merges with what he owns.

With Sophocles and Aeschylus, both "Phidian men," the design is stronger than in Homer ("measurement" and "calculation" rule), and in this sense Yeats's concept of Unity of Being is post-Phidian. First it assumes a disunity of being and second it strives for an order that would, if not solve, at least explain the complexity of the universe. By Unity of Being Yeats suggests a confluence that would again become a single image in the vast design: unity would reduce the design to order and pattern, but it would conquer the design itself, dominate it, so that in a way there would be no design at all. Perhaps Yeats seems caught in an ambiguous position: while he pushed for Unity the process of attaining it seemed to be a blending of all disparate elements, which when accomplished made for another singleness, not the sum of all parts but an entity itself dominant: the single image disappeared into the vast design to re-emerge the single image. The anonymous artificers of Byzantium succeeded in creating a single culture image so strong it made more distinctive and stronger the original single individuations that went to the creation of the design:

The painter, the mosaic worker, the worker in gold and silver, the

[48]"The Mandukya Upanishad," *ibid.*, p. 483.
[49]*If I were Four-and-Twenty*, p. 13.

illuminator of sacred books, were almost impersonal, almost perhaps without the consciousness of individual design, absorbed in their subject-matter and that the vision of a whole people. They could copy out of old Gospel books those pictures that seemed as sacred as the text, and yet weave all into a vast design, the work of many that seemed the work of one, that made building, picture, pattern, metal-work of rail and lamp, seem but a single image. . . .[50]

The word "design" has been used here with deliberate looseness, partly to suggest, by analogy, the central relationship between the aesthetic design and the metaphysical design—man and the universe—that appears throughout Yeats's work. For Yeats worried about the metaphysical design and he never found any single relationship that exactly suited his needs. The Christian design placed man between God and the beasts; the Greeks, by and large, excluded man from the design except in so far as he was a victim of its operation: though excluded by the gods, the Greek could not afford to live without them. Only the East has provided for a union with the divine of which the divine is not jealous, probably because the Eastern ascetic is willing to dissolve his persona, is not jealous of it, a dissolution neither Odysseus nor Faustus could even contemplate. Yeats borrowed freely from all views, including the Greek Necessity and the Christian longing for a unity that would close the gaping chaos that followed the Fall. But he always sought to balance between the self-consciousness of freedom and the consciousness of surrender: "I am always, in all I do, driven to a moment which is the realisation of myself as unique and free, or to a moment which is the surrender to God of all that I am. . . . Could those two impulses, one as much a part of truth as the other, be reconciled, or if one or the other could prevail, all life would cease."[51] Man can neither live outside the design nor lose himself in it; but to survive he must retain both impulses. Although he can never relinquish the image of Self, the only way of ensuring against that Self ultimately alienating itself from the world is to make it serve the design that is its nearest kin. That was the accomplishment of the Byzantine craftsmen and artists when, collectively, they expressed a single image of their culture without violating their individual talents. The design is the shape given it by its artificers.

To create a vast design that would resolve itself into the single image, Yeats had constantly to resist the temptations toward diversity —toward what he himself called "hodos chameliontos." Always the

[50]*A Vision*, pp. 279–280.
[51]*Diary*, p. 19.

grasp of the concrete came to his rescue; the consciousness of the *Comédie Humaine*, his Antaean imagination, would never permit him to sink into dreaded abstraction. "The mystical life is the centre of all that I do and all that I think and all that I write," he wrote to John O'Leary in 1892. Forty-six years later, also in a letter, he wrote differently: "Am I a mystic?—no, I am a practical man. I . . . have made the usual measurements, plummet line, spirit-level and have taken the temperature by pure mathematic."[52] The second letter is ironic as the first is naïve, but both reflect accurately the state of mind at the time they were written. Yeats learned how to make the "usual measurements, plummet line"—and surely we are at once reminded of the "plummet-measured face" in "The Statues," whose lineaments Yeats wished to trace in his own version of re-creating the conscience of his race. The mysticism of 1892 had, by 1938, become "measured": and the calculations yielded something of a synthesis.

The trinity upon which Yeats said he would found a literature is pre-eminently European, and reflects a characteristically Yeatsian reconciliation of Christian secularism (his father's influence was permanent) and orthodox theology:

> I would found literature on the three things which Kant thought we must postulate to make life livable—Freedom, God, Immortality. The fading of these three before 'Bacon, Newton, Locke' has made literature decadent. Because Freedom is gone we have Stendhal's 'mirror dawdling down a lane'; because God has gone we have realism, the accidental, because Immortality is gone we can no longer write those tragedies . . . those that are a joy to the man who dies.[53]

Freedom—that gift of the Renaissance which Yeats equally prized and feared—is the freedom to be and not to be, the man-made metaphysic which gives the soul sanction to be "self-delighting" and "self-affrighting"; but God is the check on that freedom, an equivalent of the old Necessity. God is faith: we must, as Kant said, behave as if the Absolute existed, though its existence be forever beyond any human epistemology. As ways of life and as techniques of art, Realism and Materialism were for Yeats empty of such faith precisely because they expressly refused to acknowledge the God beyond the freedom of man. For a divine Necessity they substituted a social or economic one, and Yeats recognized that such determinism, despite the sometimes "happy ending," deprived man of all freedom. The realist's conception of the

[52]*Letters*, pp. 211, 921.
[53]*Diary*, pp. 49–50.

vast design never paid homage to the single image: his canvas may be large but his humanity is defeated by detail and becomes the very abstraction which the illusion of verisimilitude was meant to prevent.

As I stated at the outset of this study, the East-West dualism remained operative in Yeats's thinking throughout his life. But there can be no doubt that, in the final accounting, he cast his lot with the West, with Europe. Europeans, he felt, could not live Eastern lives merely by changing their clothes, for a heritage resides in the blood, in the bone, in the spirit of a culture. And the Irish were, after all, Europeans:

> By implication the philosophy of Irish faery lore declares that all power is from the body, all intelligence from the spirit. Western civilisation, religion and magic insist on power and therefore on body, and hence these three doctrines—efficient rule—the Incarnation—thaumaturgy. Eastern thoughts answer to these with indifference to rule, scorn of the flesh, contemplation of the formless. Western minds who follow the Eastern way become weak and vapoury. . . .[54]

Such weakness was a danger implicit in "Irish faery lore"; and all his life Yeats was attracted by vapours and shadows: by the Celtic twilight, by French *symbolisme*, by the poetry of Keats and Shelley, by the frailty of aestheticism, and, indeed, by the East itself, whose wisdom and quietude were to teach him much. Yet eventually he would resist all the vapours, assert his power and his intelligence through his body and his spirit, and emerge as the "one image" in triumph over the "formless." We may regard his life, in Plotinian terms, as a work of beauty, for it stands as an example against the ugly, that which has no shape and hence no purpose either.

The aesthetic always has its philosophic analogues. Yeats's attempts to combine, in his conception of art, the virtues of anonymity and personal utterance reflect his belief in man's struggle to participate in the larger scheme and yet to remain a unique and feeling individual, to whom suffering and illumination will come as they have come to no one else:

> Tragedy wrought to its uttermost.
> Though Hamlet rambles and Lear rages,
> And all the drop-scenes drop at once
> Upon a hundred thousand stages,
> It cannot grow by an inch or an ounce.

Wordsworth's ascent of Snowdon in Book Fourteen of *The Prelude*

[54] *Autobiography*, pp. 292–293.

has its parallels to Yeats's climb of his tower stair, or to the flight onto the golden boughs of the Byzantine poems, or to the Chinamen's ascent of their mountain in "Lapis Lazuli." For the highest imagination, said Wordsworth, "the enduring and the transient both / Serve to exalt"; Yeats put it another way: man is "self-sufficing and eternal. . . ."[55] God and man (and his freedom) are both Absolutes of the same antinomy, each created and reflected by the imagination. And that comprehensive imagination, expanding toward God and contracting toward Self, shifting always from the impulse to surrender to the impulse to assert, hovers—like Yeats's golden bird—over the world, "Spread over time, past, present, and to come."

In becoming the single image, the vast design surrenders none of its capaciousness: it merely asserts, through the shape of its image, the identity which accrues to it when the parts have been sacrificed to the whole, when the many merge into the one. That single image in Yeats's aesthetic is an heroic image, one of the "heraldic" images which it was his aim to restore to literature. It embodies the annunciating freedom so characteristic of his temperament—a freedom from the design itself, Odysseus out of the sea. In daring to flaunt such an image before us in times that had nearly forgotten the power of images, Yeats proved himself master over that half of anonymity which, if it were to command, would truly obliterate us. The aesthetic of contraction and expansion is ultimately an emblem of life, the breathing in and the breathing out of existence. To maintain that rhythm Yeats committed himself to the perpetuity of contradiction which besets the human condition. And in undertaking that struggle he engaged in the conflict that has defined the history of Europe: individual against Kronos. Like the Greek tragedians, like Shakespeare, like Goethe, Yeats too could cry "Spude dich, Kronos!" with a love and a reverence that neutralized final bitterness. He was the last to have been able to do so in our time; in that sense, he remains the last of the great European poets.

[55] *Letters*, p. 805.

BIBLIOGRAPHY

A. WORKS OF YEATS

ALLT, PETER and ALSPACH, RUSSELL K., eds. *The Variorum Edition of the Poems of W. B. Yeats.* New York: The Macmillan Company, 1957.

BRIDGE, URSULA, ed. *W. B. Yeats and T. Sturge Moore: Their Correspondence.* London: Routledge & Kegan Paul Ltd., 1953.

EGLINTON, JOHN, W. B. YEATS, A. E., and W. LARMINIE. *Literary Ideals in Ireland.* London: T. Fisher Unwin, 1899.

ELLIS, JOHN EDWIN and WILLIAM BUTLER YEATS. *The Works of William Blake, Poetic, Symbolic, and Critical.* London: Bernard Quaritch, 1893.

HORTON, W. T. *A Book of Images.* Introduction by W. B. Yeats. London: Unicorn Press, 1898.

YEATS, J. B. *Letters to his Son W. B. Yeats and Others, 1869–1922*, ed. Joseph Hone. London: Faber and Faber, 1944.

YEATS, WILLIAM BUTLER. *The Autobiography of William Butler Yeats.* New York: The Macmillan Company, 1953.

——— *The Celtic Twilight.* London: Lawrence and Bullen, 1893.

——— *Collected Poems of W. B. Yeats.* London: Macmillan and Company, Ltd., 1933, 1952.

——— *Collected Works.* Stratford-on-Avon: The Shakespeare Head Press, 1908.

——— *Essays.* London: Macmillan Company, 1924.

——— *Essays and Introductions.* London: Macmillan and Company, Ltd., 1961.

——— *Four Plays for Dancers.* London: Macmillan and Company, Ltd., 1921.

——— *If I Were Four-and-Twenty.* Dublin: The Cuala Press, 1940.

——— *The Letters of W. B. Yeats*, ed. Allan Wade. London: Rupert Hart-Davis, 1954.

——— *Letters on Poetry from W. B. Yeats to Dorothy Wellesley.* London: Oxford University Press, 1940.

——— *Letters to the New Island*, ed. Horace Reynolds. Cambridge, Mass.: Harvard University Press, 1934.

——— *On the Boiler*. Dublin: The Cuala Press, 1939.

———, ed. *The Oxford Book of Modern Verse, 1892–1935*. Oxford: At the Clarendon Press, 1936.

——— *Pages from a Diary Written in Nineteen Hundred and Thirty*. Dublin: The Cuala Press, 1944.

——— *Plays and Controversies*. London: Macmillan Company, 1923.

——— *Plays for an Irish Theatre*. London: Stratford-on-Avon: A. H. Bullen, 1911.

——— *Plays in Prose and Verse*. London: Macmillan Company, 1924.

——— *The Secret Rose*, with illustrations by J. B. Yeats. London: Lawrence and Bullen, Ltd., 1897.

——— "The Theater of Beauty." *Harper's Weekly*, LV (November 11, 1911), 11.

——— *A Vision*. London: T. Werner Laurie, Ltd., 1925 (private publication).

——— *A Vision*. Revised edition; New York: Macmillan and Company, 1956.

——— *Wheels and Butterflies*. London: Macmillan Company, 1934.

B. WORKS ON YEATS

The following items represent a selective list of books and essays about Yeats which have treated my subject. The essays by Adams and Faulkner are the only works which have concerned themselves exclusively with Yeats's theory of art; Faulkner's essay appeared after this book was completed and accepted for publication. (The studies by Melchiori and Reid also appeared after my work was completed; where possible I have tried to take account of them.) Other specific debts are cited in the Notes.

ADAMS, HAZARD. *Blake and Yeats: The Contrary Vision* (Cornell University Press, 1955).

——— "Yeatsian Art and Mathematic Form," *Centennial Review*, IV (Winter, 1960), 70–88.

ELLIS-FERMOR, UNA. *The Irish Dramatic Movement* (London, 1939, 1954).

ELLMANN, RICHARD. *W. B. Yeats: The Man and the Masks* (New York, 1948).

——— *The Identity of Yeats* (New York, 1954).

FAULKNER, PETER. "Yeats as a Critic," *Criticism*, IV (1962), 328–339.

GORDON, D. J., *et al.* *W. B. Yeats, Images of a Poet* (Manchester, 1961).

FRYE, NORTHROP. "Yeats and the Language of Symbolism," *UTQ*, XVII (1947), 1–17.

HALL, J. and STEINMANN, M., eds. *The Permanence of Yeats* (New York, 1950). Essays by various hands.

HÄUSERMANN, H. W. "W. B. Yeats's Criticism of Ezra Pound," originally published in *English Studies* (August, 1948), 97–109.

——— "W. B. Yeats's Idea of Shelley," *The Mint*, ed. Geoffrey Grigson (London, 1946), pp. 179–194.

HENN, T. R. *The Harvest of Tragedy* (London, 1956).

——— *The Lonely Tower: Studies in the Poetry of W. B. Yeats* (London, 1950).

HOUGH, GRAHAM. *The Last Romantics* (London, 1949).

KERMODE, FRANK. *Romantic Image* (London, 1957).

MELCHIORI, GIORGIO. *The Whole Mystery of Art: Pattern into Poetry in the Work of W. B. Yeats* (London, 1960).

LOMBARDO, AGOSTINO. *La poesia inglese, dall'estetismo al simbolismo* (Rome, 1950), pp. 249–288.

PARKINSON, THOMAS. "Intimate and Impersonal: An Aspect of Modern Poetics," *Journal of Aesthetics and Art Criticism*, XVI (1958), 373–383.

——— *W. B. Yeats, Self-Critic* (University of California Press, 1951).

——— "Yeats and Pound: The Illusion of Influence," *Comparative Literature*, VI (1954), 256–264.

REID, B. L. *William Butler Yeats: The Lyric of Tragedy* (University of Oklahoma Press, 1961).

SPITZER, LEO. "On Yeats' Poem 'Leda and the Swan,'" *Modern Philology*, LI (1954), 271–276.

STAUFFER, DONALD A. *The Golden Nightingale* (New York, 1949).

UNTERECKER, JOHN. *A Reader's Guide to William Butler Yeats* (New York, 1959).

WILSON, F. A. C. *W. B. Yeats and Tradition* (London, 1958).

——— *Yeats's Iconography* (London, 1960).

ACKNOWLEDGMENTS

Grateful acknowledgment is due to the following for permission to quote from copyrighted material:

To Mrs. W. B. Yeats, A. P. Watt & Son, Messrs. Macmillan & Company, London, The Macmillan Company of Canada, and the Macmillan Company of New York for permission to quote from the works of W. B. Yeats (these are listed in the Bibliography).

To Routledge & Kegan Paul Ltd. for permission to quote from Schiller's *On the Aesthetic Education of Man*, tr. Reginald Snell (London, 1954).

To Holt, Rinehart and Winston Inc. for permission to quote from *The Divine Comedy*, Rinehart Editions, tr. H. R. Huse (New York, 1959).

To Harvard University Press for permission to quote from *Letters to the New Island*, ed. Horace Reynolds (Cambridge, Mass., 1934).

To Oxford University Press for permission to quote from the Introduction to *The Oxford Book of Modern Verse*, chosen by W. B. Yeats (Oxford: at the Clarendon Press, 1936).

To Rupert Hart-Davis Limited for permission to quote from *The Letters of W. B. Yeats*, ed. Allan Wade (London, 1954).

To Faber & Faber and Christy & Moore, Ltd. for permission to quote from *J. B. Yeats: Letters to his Son and Others*, ed. Joseph Hone (London, 1944).

I should also like to thank the following for permission to reproduce photographs of paintings in their possession:

The National Gallery of Ireland, Dublin

The National Gallery, London

The National Portrait Gallery, London

The Trustees of the Tate Gallery, London

The Freer Galley of Art, Smithsonian Institution, Washington, D.C.

Archives Photographiques, Paris (Louvre)

I am in particular debt to the Director of the National Gallery of Ireland, Mr. Thomas McGreevy, for his informative correspondence regarding the

Strozzi portrait; and to Mr. Cecil Gould, Deputy Keeper of the National Gallery, London, and Mr. Wilbur D. Peat, Director of The John Herron Art Institute, Indianapolis, Indiana, for helping to identify the two "Ariosto" portraits.

Parts of this book were originally published, in somewhat different form, in *Criticism* and the *University of Toronto Quarterly*. Acknowledgment is due to the editors of both journals, and to the Wayne State University Press and the University of Toronto Press, for permission to reprint.

INDEX